An investigation into the Other Side of Irish life

DARA deFAOÍTE

C000174369

First published in Ireland in 2002 by Maverick House,
Unit 115, Ashbourne Industrial Estate,
Ashbourne, Co. Meath
www.maverickhouse.com
email: info@maverickhouse.com

This edition 2004

ISBN 0 9542945 6 4

Copyright for text © Dara deFaoíte 2002, 2004
Copyright for typesetting, editing, layout, design
© Maverick House Ltd

Printed by Mackays of Chatham Ltd

*The paper used in this book comes from wood pulp of managed forests. For every
tree felled, at least one tree is planted, thereby renewing natural resources.*

The moral right of the author has been asserted

All rights reserved.
No part of this book may be reproduced or transmitted in any form
or by any means without written permission from the publisher,
except by a reviewer who wishes to quote brief passages in connection
with a review written for insertion in a newspaper, magazine or
broadcast.

A CIP catalogue record for this book is available from the British
Library.

DEDICATION

For Sue and Jodie, who make it all real

CONTENTS

ACKNOWLEDGEMENTS

In the course of writing this book I came into contact with many strangers, whom I am now indebted to for their insight, kindness, and opinion.

I would particularly like to thank Peter Costello for his time and trust placed in me with a number of his fine books. I would also like to thank Gary Cunningham (a dedicated cryptozoologist), Carolyn Fisher at RTE, Mary Callanan at Thoor Ballylee, Richard T. Cooke, Michael Martin and the people of Cobh.

I'd like to thank Bonnie Vance, Seán Ryan, David and Eamon Dowd, Fergus and Ann White, Olivia Robertson, Cormac Bourke, Colum Stapleton, Padhraic Faherty, John Murphy at Appletree, Dave Walsh at Blather.net and all at Maverick House.

PREFACE TO 2ND EDITION

In the year since the first edition of Paranormal Ireland hit the shelves I have been regularly asked whether researching and writing this book has changed my perception of the phenomena of ghosts, unknown creatures and UFOs.

Fortunately, I can reply that 'nothing has really changed'. I can still approach this amazing area of human experience with the fascination and open-minded respect it deserves. And, as a person with no actual, first-hand experience of paranormal activity, such as those documented within, I maintain that objective viewpoint and keen, unbiased longing to hear and retell the tales, sometimes harrowing, often tragic and at times comical, that drew me towards this strange side of life from a very early age.

If anything has changed it is my resolve not to discount the unexplainable, especially in the light of those people very close to me recalling events, encounters and supernatural run-ins they have had without any earthly means to rationalise.

In the months following the first publication I also received a wealth of mail from across the country and abroad from ordinary, everyday people wishing to share their own mysterious experiences. I have been in the enviable position of receiving letters and e-mails, fantastic in their subject matter but no less credible for that, which kept me enthralled, bewildered and amused during my own work-day life.

But this is all just part and parcel of the fabulous nature of the paranormal; the mystery, the fear, the desire to understand or the resignation that the truth may never be fully comprehended.

This will always remain an area of endless storytelling, of heightened perceptions, of fantastic beliefs, and of terrifying possibilities.

I am delighted to see this book make a second and newly updated outing and I hope you enjoy Paranormal Ireland as much as I do.

DdF 2004

INTRODUCTION

The first strange thing I noticed while researching paranormal experience in Ireland was the huge amount of personal anecdote from reasonable-minded people across all walks of life.

There is hardly a sceptic amongst us, who doesn't know at least one person who has had a run in with some aspect of the supernatural.

This author, being one such sceptic, was wholly surprised to hear close friends and associates recall their own unnerving encounters; be it a Friday the 13th mishap or a face-to-face encounter with ghostly apparitions.

Because of their seemingly unexplainable nature, these events are rarely spoken of for fear of censure or ridicule. Paranormal experience flies in the face of rational thinking and can easily discomfort those who do not wish to accommodate such fantastic notions. But fortunately these experiences are recounted and the range is inexhaustible.

While this book focuses largely on contemporary paranormal experience in Ireland, such encounters are by no means unique to this island.

Lake monsters, UFOs, alien abduction, big cat sightings, poltergeists, ghosts and classic hauntings have been reported from every corner of the world for as long as history can record.

This global experience of the unknown goes partway to demystify the paranormal and allow successive generations to make sense of their own encounters. In an attempt to shed further light on the mystery of ghosts, UFOs and 'unknown animals', the author has travelled the length and breadth of Ireland and talked to individuals who have made understanding the paranormal their vocation.

This book sets down various theories and ideas held by well-known Irish psychics, druids, cryptozoologists (researchers into unknown animals), priests, witches, and UFO contactees. This expert opinion is backed up by the wealth of first-hand experience recalled by lay people across the country.

In order to get a working perspective on this broadest of subjects, it was first important to separate the many different paranormal phenomena at play in Ireland today.

* * *

This was possible in three manageable sections. The first of which focuses on the world of ghosts, poltergeists, death-warnings, and what is generally referred to as the spirit world.

It is a given that there are more dead people in the world than there are those alive. The cessation of these innumerable lives and energies on the instance of death does not ring true for the living who experience very real physical interference from those thought long departed.

Ghosts are an all too real phenomenon for thousands of people in Ireland, and have become part of the furniture in some of the country's more notorious haunted houses.

The explanation behind such interference is manifold. A sudden or violent death with unfinished business left behind and traumatic events being etched onto the very walls and fabric of the landscape are just a couple of theories proffered in this study.

Then there are the psychological factors explaining all things that go bump in the night. Poltergeists, being noise ghosts as opposed to visual manifestations, are believed to occur in houses where high levels of emotional energy have become a dominant force.

Most cases of poltergeist activity are known to centre on houses occupied by individuals whose brain patterns are in constant flux, including teenagers, newborn babies and mentally disabled children.

The first section of this book also focuses on the perceived danger and potential benefits to those who open themselves to the paranormal through séances and other psychic communication.

* * *

The second part of this journey into Irish paranormal experience concentrates on the area of cryptozoology, or the study of hidden animals, not recognised by formal zoology but supported by anecdotal testimony.

Just as Scotland boasts its famous Lough Ness monster, so Irish lakes have resounded with accounts of similar mystery beasts spotted both in, and out, of the water.

There have been so many lake monster sightings over the last century that experts believe they are dealing with as many as three unknown aquatic species in Ireland.

In the same field, Alien Big Cats (ABCs) has become a popular term for the sightings of large and vicious looking wild cats not native to Ireland, but sighted throughout many wooded areas. As the evidence will show, Ireland is home to more creatures than often meet the eye.

* * *

In the third section, Paranormal Ireland looks at the quest for, and the various beliefs in, extraterrestrial (ET) life and the great mystery surrounding UFOs.

The people of this island have long held a fascination with the skies above and those celestial bodies dotted throughout. We have only to look to the prehistoric tomb at Newgrange, Co. Meath, built more than 4,000 years ago, to empathise with an ancient respect for our place in an unfathomable universe. The early construction of Newgrange, a mathematical wonder in which the rising sun's rays penetrate an ancient burial tomb, only on the shortest day of the year, continues to baffle engineers and scientists alike with its primitive, pin point precision.

Over the ensuing millennia, active minds on this relatively dark, northern isle have maintained that sense of intrigue with outer space. In the last fifty years ufology has boomed, and for many, is one of the more credible areas of paranormal investigation.

Science writer, Ian Ridpath, stated that, 'since the lifetime of advanced civilisations is ten million years, there could easily be as many as one million advanced civilisations like ourselves, or more advanced, in our own galaxy.' Because our own galaxy contains over 100 billion stars and is just one of countless galaxies in the universe, the statistics, it is fair to say, are weighted in favour of ET life.

It is the human condition to attempt to make sense of these experiences. It is also this human condition, which allows us to realise how very little we actually understand about our own existence, the power of the mind and the space in which we live when weighted against such a mass of unexplainable phenomena.

As the oft quoted line from Shakespeare's Hamlet runs, 'There are more things in heaven and earth, Horatio, than are dreamt of in your philosophy.'

DdF 2002

CHAPTER ONE

Ghost Boy

There was nobody else in the room. The wooden shutters, which barred the tall windows, were swung open and a slant of brilliant, mid-evening sunlight played across the whitewashed interior.

The man was alone. His family remained on the roof of the old castle, taking in the rugged expanse of the east Galway countryside. He studied the small room for a moment and contemplated the sun's radiance as it engulfed the entire window frame; illuminating the bare space within, sending listless dust motes across silent streams of warm light.

He positioned himself at an angle, diagonally facing the open window and adjusted the focus of his trusted camera lens. Nothing appeared to be out of the ordinary; the very stillness of the place seemed to compliment its time worn endurance. Only the sound of evening bird song accompanied nature's light indoors.

The aperture in the man's camera clicked open and shut, and momentarily broke the peace as the picture was taken. He straightened up and imagined, or at least hoped, he'd taken a fairly atmospheric shot of the sitting room of one of the world's greatest poets, William Butler Yeats.

What David Blinkhorne discovered when he developed his holiday snaps, however, was not to correspond with the image he had expected to see.

In the empty room, where clear evening light filled a sparsely decorated space, there now stood a short, spectral figure in the foreground of the only photograph David Blinkhorne took in the poet's sitting room that day.

The ill-lit and slightly translucent human form is thought to be that of a young boy. The figure is visible from just below the knee to the top of his head. Despite a definite outline, his apparitional form looks almost featureless. He appears partly transparent where the window frame and chair bisect him at the head down his left side.

Who is he, and how did he get into the holiday photographs of an English visitor to Thoor Ballylee, home of W.B. Yeats, near Gort, Co. Galway?

There was nobody in the room with the photographer at the time he took his shot, and there was no way a shadow could have played against the intense rays of light coming through that open window.

'I was alone in that room. The sun was very bright outside and the inside of the building was subdued,' said Blinkhorne who wrote to the curator at Thoor Ballylee on receiving his developed exposures.

'When the film was produced, as you can see, there is the image of a child in the foreground,' he wrote. 'I have taken the film back to the shop, who say it is on the negative and it is not an overlap from another photograph. In fact, there is nothing similar anywhere on the film.

'I note in Yeats's poetry that he refers to, dare I say, ghosts. Who knows, it may be one of many sightings,' wrote Blinkhorne.

This letter, accompanied by a copy of the ghostly exposure, only further convinced management and staff at Thoor Ballylee (now a fabulously restored interpretative centre celebrating Yeats's life and work) that the old Norman Tower was indeed haunted.

Yeats himself believed the tower to be inhabited by the ghost of an Anglo-Norman soldier, who treads the winding stair he so passionately wrote about.

'Before the ruin came, for centuries, rough men-at-arms, cross gathered to the knees or shod in iron, climbed the narrow stairs', wrote Yeats.

Indeed Yeats's strident belief in the spirit world, his vocation towards all aspects of the occult, and his claims that he regularly contacted ghosts through séance work would, for some, make his castle home a most hospitable place for such entities to manifest.

In fact, prior to the arrival of Mr. Blinkhorne's ghostly picture in August 1989, one of the castle's curators talked of a 'presence' in and around the worn stairwell, and refused to enter certain parts of the building after evening had set in. The nervy curator was joined in her anxieties by her dog, which displayed irrational symptoms of fear in many downstairs rooms of the castle.

Thoor Ballylee was built some time between 1275 and 1335 by the Norman de Burgo family as one of 32 such fortified residences across the western region. The lands and towers remained in the name of the Catholic de Burgos, or Burkes, as they had become known, until the Penal laws of the seventeenth and eighteenth centuries saw them pass forcibly to Protestant landowners.

By the mid-nineteenth century the building, known as
Islandmore Castle, was home to the Spellman family, who
were masters of the workhouse at nearby Loughrea. Yeats
first visited the tower in 1896 and when, on the death of
Mrs. Spellman in 1902, the family gave up their residency,
Yeats's interest in the old place was fired. The castle passed
into the hands of his great friend, Lady Gregory of Coole
Park. In 1916, much of the surrounding land was acquired
by the Congested Districts Board and sold off to local
small landholders. Nobody wanted the old ruin, and Yeats
was able to buy it for a mere £35.

The poet renamed his new home Thoor Ballylee stating,
'I think the harsh sound of Thoor amends the softness of
the rest.' He set about a labour of love restoration of the
austere structure and lived there with his wife, Georgina
'George' Hyde Lees, between 1919 and 1928. The Yeatses
had two children, Ann and Michael, during their first years
at the castle.

It was while in residence at Thoor Ballylee that Yeats
wrote much of his most celebrated poetry, won the Nobel
Prize for Literature in 1923, and delved further into the
world of the supernatural with the aid of his wife George,
whose psychic abilities allowed her husband to make the
contact with the spirit world he so readily desired.

Thoor Ballylee today is a place of pilgrimage for Yeats
lovers from all nations. David Blinkhorne, from Stratford-
Upon-Avon in Warwickshire, England, was one such
devotee.

'As a family we had decided to make W.B. Yeats our
theme for our annual holiday and were visiting points of
interest around the west of Ireland. Thoor Ballylee was
one of those places,' recalled Blinkhorne.

The date of this visit was 3 August 1989, fifty years after W.B. Yeats's death. The Blinkhornes arrived at the tower at approximately 5.45 p.m., moments before it was due to close. The last slide show of the day had finished, but they were told they could have a quick look around.

'While we were on the top of the tower one of the curators came up to tell us that they were about to lock up. I asked him if he would mind me taking a photograph of the window in the sitting room. He saw that as no problem, but told me he would have to undo the shutters again, so I left my wife and children on the top and ran down with him to take the photograph. The curator opened the shutters and then left me alone.'

A keen amateur photographer, Blinkhorne used a Pratica camera with Kodak film (300ASA), and did not use any flash.

'I have no idea why the figure should be in the photograph. The film was developed and printed in Boots, the chemist in Stratford-upon-Avon. On first seeing the image, I took the film back to Boots and asked them if this was a fault in the production of the negative. They told me that the image was on the negative,' he said. 'There is no image remotely similar on the rest of the film.'

Yeats's former home also receives many visitors who claim to be psychic and have told staff that they clearly felt the presence of a spirit in the room where the apparitional figure appeared before Mr. Blinkhorne's camera.

'Even one of the coach drivers who brought a tour group out, told us that he'd felt something strange in that room while waiting for his group to finish the tour. He said it was not a "bad entity",' recalled Mary Callanan, curator at the castle. 'This man said he was often made aware of such phenomena, claiming he had certain psychic abilities,' said Callanan.

The author of the photograph, on the other hand, had never had any such encounter. 'I have never had an experience like this before, and no previous paranormal experiences. I had no feelings while visiting the tower that it might be haunted, but I was well aware of Yeats's many references to ghosts and his interest in the world of spirits,' he said.

Some believe it was an energy projection of Yeats's son Michael, who was born and brought up at Ballylee, and lives today in Dalkey, Co. Dublin. Others maintain it is the spirit of an earlier resident of the castle.

But there is also the theory that what David Blinkhorne photographed on that day in 1989, was the image of a young ghost whom W.B. Yeats knew all too well.

It is felt that the Blinkhorne photograph may hold the spectral image of 12-year-old suicide victim, Harold Blake, who Yeats claimed to have regular contact with through séances, while staying at Renvyle House some 30 miles away.

Renvyle House in Connemara was home to fellow man of words Oliver St. John Gogarty. In the early 1920s, the house became a haunt for Gogarty's literary clique, and with them, their lust for experimentation in all matters of the occult. W.B. Yeats and his wife would often spend time there, conducting séances and contacting spirits.

Yeats, who married 25-year-old English woman Georgina Hyde Lees in 1917, discovered that she had the ability to act as a medium for him, and put him in direct contact with the world of spirits. Georgina allowed her husband to write automatically through her summoning of spirits.

Gogarty wrote frequently of his experiences at séances held at the house and, in particular, of Yeats's prowess in the area.

It was at Renvyle that Yeats communicated with a boy of 12 years who according to his wife, Georgina, wore a brown velvet suit during his manifestations before her.

'My wife saw a pale-faced, red-haired boy standing in the middle of the north room. She was by the fireplace when he first took shape. He had the solemn pallor of tragedy beyond the endurance of a child. He resents the presence of strangers in the home of his ancestors. He is Harold Blake.'

The boy told the poet that he had hung himself at the age of 12, and had previously lived on the site where the Gogarty house now stood. Yeats communicated with Blake through a system of 'automatic writing' led by the spirit itself.

Could this boy be the apparition who appeared in the empty sunlit sitting room of Yeats's own home some 30 miles southeast? There is little doubt that the poet and his cohorts carried out the same occult practices at Thoor Ballylee as they did at Renvyle, and may have summoned this Harold Blake to appear there. It is also safe to say that the figure in the Blinkhorne picture is that of a child no more than 12-years-old.

The poet is said to have struck up quite a relationship with the young ghost at Renvyle, and set down strict orders for it not to frighten his children, or the children of the house while they stayed there.

Yeats announced that the boy objected to people being in the house. He subsequently ordered the ghost to walk the house no more and not to move furniture or terrify those who sleep nearby. Could Yeats's young, summoned ghost have been called upon between the two homes at the poet's behest?

There is no evidence to suggest that a ghost bearing this tragic youngster's likeness ever rambled the stairways of Thoor Ballylee during the Yeatses' tenancy, and no tales of Yeats's children ever having come into contact with ghosts in the castle.

In a short interview with *The Irish Times* in 2000, the poet's son, Michael Yeats, said he had 'no interest in spiritualism and the occult' as his parents had. 'I'm very fair-minded,' he commented. 'I'm prepared to believe in ghosts the day I see one.'

In September of 2000, Michael donated a collection of over 100 notebooks, files, and copybooks of material written by his father, relating to matters of the occult to the National Library of Ireland. There were also 3,000 pages of automatic writing put down by Yeats's wife through her contact with spirits.

The mystery of the boy in the Blinkhorne photograph will no doubt remain just that – a mystery. But such mystery will naturally lead to all manner of conjecture. It is thought the figure has his hands inside the pockets of a pair of dungarees and it is often argued whether he is looking at the camera or if he has his face to the window, possibly shocked by the recent illumination of the room?

Those who have examined the picture, including professional photographers, conclude that no shadow could have fallen onto the sunlit window frame, as the only source of light in the entire room was coming in strongly from the outside, forcing any shadow to fall in the opposite direction. Anyway, there was nobody else in the room with the photographer at the time he took the shot.

In the absence of any hard and fast explanation to the Blinkhorne photograph, numerous theories have been proffered regarding 'the boy in the window'. Foremost amongst these, is the former tenant's conjuring of ghosts and spirits with the help of his psychic wife, George.

It is thought that Yeats's fascination with the occult had left his Thoor Ballylee home open to all manner of guests from the other world and that the Blinkhorne photograph is a rare snapshot of the supernatural energies imprinted on the building's thick walls.

At the age of 20, Yeats founded the Dublin Hermetic Society – a group of like-minded individuals devoted to all avenues of the occult. Three years later while in London, he joined the Hermetic Order of the Golden Dawn, an organisation that incorporated traditional European cabalistic magic and astrology.

Séances, black masses, experimentation with telepathy and clairvoyance, astrology, and magic of all kinds enraptured the poet's keen intellect.

Yeats's appetite for tapping into 'magic' was wholly insatiable. 'If I had not made magic my constant study I could not have written a single word of my *Blake* book, nor would *The Countess Kathleen* have ever come to exist. The mystical life is the centre of all that I think, and all that I write,' he once said.

Yeats remained a member of the illustrious Golden Dawn body, an association he never publicly flaunted, for over thirty years, and at one stage had a heated tête-à-tête with its most notorious member, Aleister Crowley, over the issue of leadership.

In Ireland, he also made contact with many groups and individuals practising all kinds of mystical worship. In a biography of the poet by author Stephen Coote, Yeats's link to practitioners of black arts is clearly drawn.

Coote wrote, 'Yeats now discovered in Dublin a "whole colony" of black magicians "of the most iniquitous kind".'

Yeats claimed he was amused by their 'hideous costumes' and worship of Isis. The tone of his letter admirably captures his scepticism. 'The black magicians have invited me to drop in on an incantation now and again as a compliment to my knowledge of the black art. They have not got enough in the way of soul left to cover an old sixpence, but that does not matter much for the present.'

In an essay entitled *Magic*, Yeats wrote, 'I believe in the practice and philosophy of what we have agreed to call magic, and what I must call the evocation of spirits.'

Yeats drew great inspiration from the spirit world and wrote prolifically during this period.

'I have a great sense of abundance, more than I have had for years. George's ghosts have educated me,' he wrote in a letter to a friend.

His one-act play, *The Words Upon the Window Pane*, was also composed around a spiritualist séance at which the spirit of Jonathan Swift communicated through his wife.

However, Yeats knew ghosts of his own and was well regarded as a man in league with such entities. None knew this more so than his old friend at Renvyle House, Oliver St. John Gogarty.

'If you met Yeats, you met enough of faery, as much as I am ever likely to meet,' Gogarty wrote.

Today Renvyle House is a luxury hotel and carries with it the legend of a haunted building. During the 1960s, both staff and customers at Renvyle testified to seeing a 'tall man wearing a dark suit' appear from the mirror in the room, thought to be the chamber where Gogarty's clique carried out their séances. Guests have often talked of a similar figure seen walking through the corridors of the old house.

Just as Yeats's genius left its inimical and indelible mark upon the world of arts and literature, so perhaps his occult dabbling and conjuring of spirits left such an impression on the buildings in which he practised.

CHAPTER TWO

The Ghost Convention

There is scarcely a townland or parish across Ireland that cannot boast its own ghost. Haunted buildings both new and ancient, city streets and back-roads which leave the passer-by chilled, strange lights on the bog, shadows and whispers at the crossroads, and furniture and crockery flying across rooms of their own accord, all support the romantic notion of what we perceive to be the work of the mysterious ghost.

The stories, both legend and contemporary, are endless; their detail enhanced by their fantastic and inexplicable nature. For most, however, the idea of the ghost treads hand-in-hand with the unpleasant emotion of fear.

But why, in a universe which science is only now beginning to figure out, should we cower, discredit and fear what many psychics and parapsychologists believe is just a hidden and very real extension of our own reality?

The level of scepticism in modern Ireland towards the world of interfering spirits and the restless dead runs naturally high, but few deny the potential for such anomalous activity.

In December 2001, a group of ghost experts, psychics, witches and enthusiasts gathered at the first ever All-Ireland Ghost Convention in Cork on a mission to demystify the fears and hype surrounding ghostly experience. The venue for this inaugural event was Cork City Gaol, which is reputed to be one of the most haunted buildings in the southern capital.

During its 100-year reign of incarceration over much of Munster from 1824 to 1923, the old Cork lockup facilitated some of the most appalling instances of misery imaginable during nineteenth and twentieth century Ireland.

Long before its first execution in 1928, a healthy percentage of its unhealthy inmates died where they were thrown, some only infants and some mothers with babies. It came as no surprise to guest speakers from the convention's expert panel, that an 'overbearing, supernatural presence' was evident in the building during proceedings.

The All-Ireland Ghost Convention was contrived by Cork man, Richard T. Cooke, as 'a serious platform', which would give a voice to individuals who have experienced, and are continually haunted by ghostly occurrences.

According to Cooke, the now annual event is designed to 'take a therapeutic approach' towards shedding whatever light it can on the ghost phenomenon for those too scared to lead a normal life after whatever they have encountered.

'The idea behind the convention is to peel away those layers of fear and suspicion, and to get people to understand ghosts better, and not to be afraid of them or of openly recounting their stories. The dead can't harm you. Only the living can do that. The only thing that causes fear is the unknown. The more you talk about these things, the more that fear will disappear,' professed Cooke.

Indeed, the old Cork Gaol proved the ideal location in which to delve into all things otherworldly. Despite a complete refurbishment of the old building during the 1980s, staff at the heritage centre today report regular 'creepy' occurrences beyond their control and without rational explanation.

Just days after the centre opened in 1993, one member of staff said she could distinctly hear the sound of a child's voice crying, 'Daddy, Daddy', over and over from the building's west wing. When she went in search of what she imagined to be a lost child separated from its parent, she encountered something altogether more eerie.

The staff member told colleagues that she came across a mysterious woman dressed in an olive green shawl who, when she approached her, disappeared through a two foot wall. The apparition was of a tall, thin, dark-haired lady dressed in a black skirt and headdress. The ghost figure has since been spotted on a number of occasions and has been given the nickname Olive, because of her defining shawl. The building is also said to reverberate with strange noises, unaccountable footsteps and distant voices.

Another staff member told Pauline Jackson, author and guest speaker at the inaugural Ghost Convention, of another mysterious encounter while closing up one evening. The woman was talking to a visitor about the building's long history. As she began to lock up and as her talk continued, a number of voices were heard in conversation, also in the old gaol's empty west wing. This employee told Jackson that the voices were all male, and struck an authoritative tone, which led them to think of the wardens from the old prison.

Jackson recalls another eerie incident, recorded in her book *Ghosts of Cork*, which occurred during restoration work on the old prison in the 1980s.

The strange event involved two electricians who discovered they had an extra helper one day, who managed to lighten their workload by up to a third. One of the men, while busying himself sending wires to his mate upstairs on the top floor, later discovered that his workmate was in a completely different area of the building, and was, in fact, down on the ground floor. The workers were amazed at the speed in which their jobs were completed and shocked to find that nobody else had been in the building on the day.

Such strange reports coupled with others of a much more haunting and personal nature are all part and parcel of the proceedings at the All-Ireland Ghost Convention.

Cork farmer Jim O'Loughlin captivated and terrified the gathering at the 2003 All-Ireland Ghost Convention, recounting some of the many run-ins he has had with the supernatural.

O'Loughlin was an invited speaker at the third annual convention, officially opened by Lord Mayor of Cork Colm Burke, again at the old City Gaol in October 2003. O'Loughlin told the congregation that, like many people in Ireland, he had grown up hearing all manner of ghost stories and tales of unexplainable interference from outside our realm.

This grounding, however, was of little comfort when he was forced to confront the strange reality of certain paranormal experiences for himself on three different occasions.

'When I was in my twenties I took a job spreading lime on land near Dungarvan, Co. Waterford,' O'Loughlin told the eager gathering.

'There was no one around the fields that day but myself and I didn't expect to see a soul all day during my work.

'It was a lonesome old place, just a big expanse of ploughed land. So I worked away unhindered until suddenly I could see this man standing up at one end of the field. You could see him clear as day against the white of the lime on the ground.

'I thought at first it was someone approaching but the next look I gave in that direction seconds later there was no sign of him at all. "Well," I thought to myself, "he's gone away with himself. He's clever enough," I thought because a lot of stones fly out of the spinner that spreads the lime and he could have been hit.

'I drove the tractor on towards the top of the field and turned around and to my amazement there he was again in the same spot just standing without movement. He cut a stark figure, plain against the earth, slightly stooped with a rope tying his coat in the middle and carrying a stick.

'I was just finishing up at this time and something inside made me not move to approach the fellah, so I turned to drive out the gate. I will never forget the shiver that went up my back as I left that place.

'I had about twenty miles to drive home and I swear I was looking back all the way I was that frightened,' said O'Loughlin.

Two years passed and Jim O'Loughlin had all but put behind him that unnerving experience in the lonesome field when it was brought back to him.

'I was going out with a friend one evening and we met these two girls at a dance. One of them recognised me, "You're the lad who was spreading lime outside Dungarvan a while back aren't you? Did you ever see the man above there in that field?" she asked me.

'In an instant it all came flooding back. I was shocked and immediately asked could they tell me anything about him.

'"He wears an ould gabardine coat with a rope tied around the middle of it, a hat and he has a stick in his hand" they told me.'

According to the girls an old man of about 70 or 75 years had come into the area from about 20 or 30 miles away to view a farmhouse that was for sale many years ago. While he was taking a look around the place he died suddenly in one of the rooms of the house and to this day he has been seen still looking around the land.

'This was all news to me. I was a complete stranger to the area and had never heard of any of this but what I saw that day matched their story dead on,' O'Loughlin said.

Jim O'Loughlin also recalled to the 2003 Ghost Convention what he describes as a 'terrible experience' and one he endured in the company of a number of friends and reliable witnesses.

'A friend of mine was doing a written history of the Nire Valley in Counties Waterford and Tipperary, so myself and another two pals spent four days out with him collecting the correct names of places and picking up anecdotes of things he might want to include. Just as we were coming to the end of the research he took us up to Clonmel for a meal and to have a chat and say thank you for our help,' said O'Loughlin.

'We had a great night and got to know each other quite well, leaving Clonmel for home at about 1.30 a.m. But as we were driving out the Nire Road to all our surprise we met a friar trotting down the middle of the road dressed in traditional garb of sandals, a brown habit, and a white cord around his waist. He was also defined by a beard he wore nearly down to his waist.

'This friar was moving at a fair pace up the middle of the road towards the car. But as soon as he was in front of us he disappeared. We pulled over to the side of the road with a screech. But there was no sign of him. Where had he gone? Did he go through the car or over it? He couldn't have gone over the fence because there was a river running fast on the other side of it,' O'Loughlin recalled.

'There were five of us in the car that night and we all swore to have seen this cleric. We decided to drive back up the road to try and make sense of it all. But we could find neither sight nor sound of him. We drove two miles in either direction but gave up because of the late hour.

'At this stage we could only go on home so we dropped everyone off and I suppose thought no more of it until three weeks later, John, the man who had hired us to do the local research, died suddenly while out of the country.

'We went up to Glasnevin Cemetery for the funeral. To our absolute amazement the priest who was reciting the prayers at the graveyard was dressed and looked the exact same as the friar we saw run towards our car that night. There was no difference at all; he had on the same robe and a beard of equal length over his chest.

'I don't pretend to know how these things happen but I believe it was something like a premonition of death coming to the group traveling in the car that night,' said O'Loughlin.

He also told the 2003 Ghost Convention that on another occasion he was at the Nire lakes making a video for a friend who he explained 'couldn't make their way up there.'

'It was in the early 1990s when I went up with my daughter and a friend of mine and as we were driving down through a lonesome road along the back of a mountain we saw this dog; a massive thing standing at the side of the road.

'He was as big as a donkey and jet black; I'd never seen anything like him in my life before. He was like one of those big wolfhounds and his two eyes were shining bright as if he were a parked car.

'I remember I said to Neddy, the guy beside me, "He's a queer looking yoke. He's not for anything good now."

'My friend just said, "He's probably out killing sheep or something."

'I brought the man to his door and he asked us in for a cup of tea. Well, the minute I put my foot on the ground out of the car I got this awful chill and I went inside and began to fret, for no apparent reason, on how I was ever going to get home,' said O'Loughlin.

'There were three lonesome roads I could take home and in my mind one was worse than the other. I eventually got going anyway and made it onto the main road without incident. We got home and really thought nothing more until the following week when I got a phone call from Neddy's sister telling me he had died during the day.

'I'll always remember how Neddy had taken no real notice of that black dog but had seen him alright. And I always think that when you get a chill up yourself like that there is always something about, something at play on a supernatural level.

'I checked around the locality whether anyone owned a dog like that and there was no one who had even heard of a black dog that size but plenty who know that a black dog appears to foretell a death,' O'Loughlin said.

Despite a citywide buzz of excitement in the build up to the first ever Ghost Convention (organiser Cooke received a barrage of calls asking whether a ghost would actually appear or not) the convention was run in a largely informative manner, rather than as an illustrative one. According to Cooke, 'a profound respect has to be met when dealing with those who find themselves disturbed by the paranormal. It's no theme-park.' He is quick to stress that 'this is a serious convention, if you want a spooky show then you can pick up a comic in the corner shop.'

Cooke's experience in the paranormal took a definite turn towards the strange in the summer of 1997 when, in his professional capacity as a registered psychotherapist and hypnotherapist, he came face to face with his first 'indisputable haunting'.

'I was approached in June 1997 by a man asking for help with something in his old family home, which was way beyond his control and was ruining his life. This man was going through a separation from his wife at the time and took up temporary residence in his mother's house, where he had grown up. His mother had died a number of years previously, and his father was living elsewhere, so he found himself alone, or so he thought, in the big old farm building of his youth.'

Through consultation, Cooke discovered that his new client was so seriously affected by what was going on in his new home, that he had become dependent on prescription sleeping pills to help him get any semblance of rest, and that he had begun to 'seriously abuse alcohol' in an effort to cope. Naturally, when dealing with a mind addled by alcohol and drugs, the Cork therapist took an initial sceptical view of the man's claims that 'a ghost in the house' was plaguing him.

'I had treated cases of over-active imagination down through the years and remained suspicious. I went out to visit him in his house and gradually got to know him better,' said Cooke.

The man in question, who Cooke said he cannot name for professional reasons, holds a directorship on the board of a very prominent company within the county.

'He came to me saying that his professional position was at serious risk from the psychological effects of what was going on in that house,' said Cooke. After four sessions in Cooke's Cork city clinic, the psychotherapist was invited out to his client's home just three miles from the city centre.

'I remember it clearly. It was about 10 p.m. on a beautiful July evening, and we sat down in the old front room of the farmhouse with a cup of tea. We had only been sitting there about 20 minutes, when I distinctly heard footsteps creaking on the floor directly above our heads. I looked him dead centre in the eyes and said, "who's upstairs?"

'The man shrugged his shoulders and looked towards the ceiling as if to show he was no stranger to the noises, which I could now hear above our heads. A moment later I heard a door creaking and then shutting after itself. The footsteps quietened for a short period but then struck up again. Now they carried on across the landing and into another room, where a further door was heard being shut. We looked up first of all to where the noise had come from and when we resumed eye contact he announced that, "this is exactly what I've been talking about; this is what plagues me, Richard."'

The counsellor recalled their four previous sessions in the safety of his city clinic, where his client remarked on the house's creakings and groanings but nothing had prepared Cooke for his initiation into the real thing.

'Hearing tales of hauxntings from a person verbally is a very different thing to actually witnessing a supernatural event.' He remembered his client saying to him, 'Richard, imagine me going into my boardroom and having to explain this type of thing to its members. I would be removed immediately.'

At this stage of events, the ball rested firmly in Cooke's court. It was up to him to decide whether to run for cover or accept the unexplainable.

He decided to proceed with the case, and ventured upstairs into the house on his own that same night, to check out the area where the footsteps and door shutting had come from.

'I looked under carpets for wires or tape recorders. I checked every cubby-hole for any sign of artificial interference but there was nothing, not even a draft from open or poorly insulated windows, but I knew I had heard what I had heard and it had been so very real. I left the house that night at 11.20 p.m. with a very creepy feeling. I remember lying in my own bed later on, wide awake half expecting to hear whatever was in that house to sound up under my own roof. I was extremely spooked.'

The worst thing for Cooke was that he wasn't able to put a label on this thing, as he might do in the case of most of his clients. 'It wasn't a phenomenon caused by a human being, as in it wasn't a real person that you could see and touch, but it was a definite presence and I couldn't deny that.'

His client told him that as a child he remembered experiences around the farm, which could not be explained by either his parents or himself.

Objects would be moved around the yard with no reasonable explanation. This was the bane of his life as a youngster, as he would be blamed for the toppling of huge barrels and the shifting of tools, which he swears he had no part in.

Cooke returned to the house and witnessed similar sounds from the upstairs rooms. He began to conjecture on what course of action was needed. Although he states that he readily believes in ghosts and most aspects of the spirit world, he also freely admits that he 'is no authority on the subject.'

The only way he could think of dealing with this phenomenon was to attempt to 'communicate with whatever was in this house.'

'This man was away from his wife and children for over five months, and now he had to contend with a paranormal encounter on top of everything else. I needed to take a very positive move and attempt to bolster his belief in his own sanity,' said Cooke.

'The second time I visited his family home we heard the footsteps start up again. We also heard the same doors being opened and shut, so I suggested we try to talk to whatever was there.'

Cooke prescribed a list of 'positive affirmations', which he set out on paper. These he would initially incant with his client 'in a bid to bring peace to the house.'

'I'd like to welcome you into this home, if I can do anything for you, let me know,' his client read aloud with him. 'I'd like to know you, I'd like to meet you, could you give us a message and can we help you?' they said. These affirmations were based on a belief system, which, according to Cooke, would restore his client's faith in his own sanity and assure him of his right to live in his own home, no matter what influences were there with him.

These recurring supernatural experiences had become an absolute reality for this man, and as a witness, Cooke was ready to vouch for him. 'He needed to accept what was going on here. I've seen so many people with their lives turned upside down by fear of supernatural experience. They have all needed a reason and an explanation for what's happening to them,' he said.

After seven weeks of repeating these affirmations, with and without his counsellor, whatever was in the house during the summer of 1997 gradually subsided of its own accord.

This first hand introduction to the world of the paranormal would later steer Cooke towards putting on Ireland's inaugural Ghost Convention.

'I don't believe in coincidence any more. I believe that there is a reason for everything, and that supernatural occurrence like this can be dealt with in a therapeutic way.'

'If you live in constant denial about what you've seen and refuse to talk about it, the fear will grow and grow inside of you.'

Cooke believes that ghosts are 'the harmless spirits of people who have done terrible things, or who have had terrible things committed against them in previous lives.' According to the Cork parapsychologist, 'they only want to put right the wrongs they did in the last life and to be sent over to their fellow dead.'

Cooke was one of eleven speakers at the inaugural Ghost Convention. One of his fellow speakers, Waterford-based clairvoyant and member of the Institute of Clinical Hypnotherapy and Psychotherapy, Stan Phillips, talked about his 'Truth of Ghosts'.

'There are, in my opinion, many levels of apparent ghost experience,' said Phillips. 'One of these being the etching onto the fabric of eternity, some occurrence or emotion, which holds such intensity that it echoes and re-echoes down all corridors of time. For example, I believe that if a blind man were to walk through Auschwitz with no knowledge of where he was, then the very walls would call out to him to tell of the pain and anguish that dwells there,' he said. Phillips recalled for the convention his own experience in this regard.

'I have personally had such an experience. A room in an apartment where my family once lived had, unbeknown to us, once been the setting of a particularly brutal murder. Nobody could sleep in that room. No matter how tastefully decorated, there was still the taste and odour of blood painted onto the atmosphere,' he recalled.

According to the Waterford psychic, 'even the relatively insensitive imagination can perceive such essences. It therefore holds, that the more sensitive one will pick up on even relatively mundane events. This is evinced by typical sighting reports of say, the old woman knitting by a long vanished fireplace.'

Phillips told the assembly at the Cork Gaol that of all the ghostly experiences abounding 'there is no one out to get you' and, in fact, the reverse is true.

'The hell and haunting,' he said, 'emanates from this plane. The only pain is to be found in our struggle to absorb the spirituality of these experiences on a human level. We are protected from outside influence by our connection through our souls, with all those who have gone before us. We share forever with our soul and, in consequence, with every other life that soul has utilised down all ages of human experience.'

Another guest, the White Witch of the Isles, Helen Barrett, spoke of her own encounters with ghosts and of the psychological make up of both the trapped spirit and of those most likely to be affected by ghosts.

'Sudden death is a common trait amongst lost souls, particularly children,' she said. Barrett confirmed that the former Cork Gaol was haunted and that there was a ghostly spirit present on the night of the convention. 'Not all hauntings are negative, however,' she said, 'but wherever there is a haunting, it means that the vibration of that place lends itself to all sorts of spirits both negative and positive because it has become an open portal to another realm.'

Barrett advised that all instances of hauntings should be referred to a second party such as a psychic healer or exorcist, because there is no control over these events. 'As an open portal we don't have control over it and once we don't have control over something, we shouldn't be there,' she said.

Also speaking at the first convention was folklorist and author, Stephen Hunter, who recalled some of the county's supernatural oral history. One macabre story in particular, is said to have occurred in the notoriously haunted Majestic Ballroom in Mallow, Co. Cork. According to Hunter, 'some time in the 1960s a girl was asked out to dance by a very handsome young man. As they were dancing, she happened to glance down and what she saw caused her to faint. When she came around, her dancing partner had vanished. She told concerned onlookers that she had just danced with the devil, owing to the fact that he had a cloven foot.' Organiser Cooke, who chaired the event, spoke of one of his early case studies, which involved a bicycle 'with a mind all of its own'.

'I was called to visit a house on the northside of the city, in which a bicycle was creating uproar. The object in question had made a habit of shifting from one side of the hallway, where it had been placed, to the other and took the shins off many of the family members.'

The bicycle, which needed to be left inside the hallway, as there was no side entrance to the house, moved, according to the family, from leaning against the left hand wall to resting against the right hand wall of the same hall over four feet away, by its own means.

Cooke said he 'naturally expected some logical explanation' to the occurrence, particularly as there were four young children in the house. None was to make itself apparent, however.

'I sat in the kitchen of that house with the whole family and made sure that nobody else was in either the hall or anywhere else in the building.'

The group sat in relative silence from about 8 p.m. because that was the time, according to the family, that they noticed the bicycle shift.

'When we came out after 15 minutes, the bike had moved and I couldn't find any earthly reason why this had occurred,' he said.

Since the convention, the Cork counsellor has been inundated with calls from all over the country regarding paranormal disturbances.

The therapeutic theme of the convention has also paid off for Cooke. 'The Saturday after the convention, I got a phone call from a 27-year-old lady, who said that she had got the first proper night's sleep she had in five years after listening to events of the day.

'I have seen people, many of whom are high profile individuals known by the public, crippled by events outside their own comprehension. Ghost sightings are only the tip of the iceberg, as many thousands of people in this country are afraid, ashamed, or embarrassed to come forward for fear of not being taken seriously regarding their paranormal encounters. That is why this convention is so important,' he said.

'It was shown in a recent survey that 80 per cent of people in America believed in life after death, 70 per cent in England and 60 per cent in Ireland,' according to Cooke. 'If most people believe in such a phenomenon, then it transpires that most will believe in the idea of ghosts. We live in a material society in which no one believes anything anymore unless they've seen it with their own eyes. But, there is also a turn towards a more tolerant and spiritual society, which is more likely to be open to the possibility of ghosts.'

The inaugural convention proved a massive success. Further speakers included University College Cork lecturers Mary McCormack and Kevin Power, Titanic Trail author and Cobh Ghost Walk guide Michael Martin and psychic and Cork historian Richard Henchion amongst others.

Cooke's own interest in the paranormal began, he said, as a child when he joined his mother, a nurse in the city's north parish, 'as she went to wash the dead'.

He describes his mother, who died in 1985, as a 'very psychic person' who would walk into a room with a body in it and 'start to converse with that dead person as if she was having an afternoon cup of tea with them.'

'This is how she would deal with the tragedy and sadness of the death placed before her. She taught me not to dismiss the dead or the bereavement process. I learned you must face it in order to be able to deal with it. I believe the same process applies when people are confronted by the supernatural,' he said.

Cooke also talks of two instances from his childhood when he believes supernatural forces came into play to save his life.

'I fell into the River Lee at 10 years of age, where we spent our summers as kids growing up. I had gone under and was drowning. I was being forced out further and deeper under water by currents, when I was suddenly pulled clear out of the water and set on a boat ramp, but there was nobody there. I was pulled out of death's grip, but to this day I can't explain what it was that had saved my life.'

About three years later, he said he was 'with some pals passing a house in the city, which was being demolished. As we were walking, we were laughing and messing and not paying any attention to our surroundings, but I suddenly felt something pull me backwards, and almost in the same movement, a huge old lead slate crashed onto the ground before my feet. If I had kept on walking as I had been, my head would have been split in two. I hadn't seen any danger and was not aware of anything falling but something pulled me back. It was like something physically grabbed hold of me and lifted me out of danger,' said Cooke.

'I am 100 per cent certain there are supernatural forces out there. Call them ghosts, spirits, whatever you want, but they affect us all on many levels.'

CHAPTER THREE

Heart of Darkness

Charleville Castle looms magnificent at the end of a mile-long avenue, winding through some of Ireland's oldest oak forest. Situated on the outskirts of Tullamore, Co. Offaly, Charleville is considered a masterpiece of Gothic Revival Architecture and looks, every spike and turret, the haunted castle it is reputed to be.

However, the macabre air that hangs over Charleville goes far deeper than the superficial splendour of its finely crafted stone and mortar.

Charleville forest was the chosen site for the castle home of Charles William Bury, one of Ireland's leading Freemasons at the end of the eighteenth century. Bury owned vast tracts of land in counties Limerick and Offaly.

This gloriously thick-wooded site is said to have been chosen by Bury because of its history as a place of ancient druidic worship and burial rite, and its documented use as a sixth century monastic university.

The design of Charleville Castle is wholly esoteric and in accordance with Masonic practices. Seven sets of steps lead from the house to seven avenues, reflecting the mason's fascination with number symbolism. The number seven is considered particularly potent within Masonic practice.

The extensive gardens at Charleville Castle, when viewed from an aerial advantage, depict the British Union Jack flag. It is from this symbol of imperialistic brazenness, on top of an ancient Druidic ceremonial ground, according to many parapsychologists and psychics, that much of Charleville's paranormal activity stems.

'Charleville castle is the most haunted castle I have ever stayed at in Ireland,' said Arch Druid Melvyn Lloyd, who carried out a four-hour psychic survey at the Offaly fortress.

'The bulk of the supernatural activity at Charleville has been brought about by a sense of fear and domination, which has emanated from the people who lived there in the past,' he said. With an address in north Co. Laois, the Arch Druid of the Owl Grove immersed himself deep into the world of the paranormal in February 2002, and undertook a 'psychic survey' of two of Ireland's most celebrated, haunted fortresses, Leap and Charleville Castles, which lie at the very heart of the Irish countryside in Co. Offaly. During these psychic assessments, Lloyd came into contact with areas of 'highly charged' ghost activity, some of which would bring about gut wrenching consequences.

Lloyd became aware of his ability to sense ghostly entities, or lost souls, as he often refers to them, at the age of fifteen. His first run in with the paranormal was a noisy poltergeist who moved furniture and opened and closed doors at his mother's house in Devon, England. Fortunately for the frightened teenager, his encounter was backed by similar experiences felt by his mother and others who had lived in the house. From that moment, however, Lloyd's imagination was fired by the supernatural.

In the intervening years, the midlands druid has honed his psychic abilities to tune into ghostly presences and is regularly called upon by house owners around the country to deal with all matters of interference from the other world.

'I've learned that ghosts are aware of who will not be frightened of them, and they will communicate with those people whom they feel they can trust,' said Lloyd. No stranger to such encounters over the last 30 years, Lloyd has also carried out his own brand of exorcism, which he prefers to call 'releasing', in numerous rooms and houses around Ireland.

'You can send ghosts on to their rightful place, or at least, away from where they are trapped with an exorcism, but I've always found that a bit of a strong method to use in this regard. An exorcism ceremony, in the full religious sense, can indeed get rid of the unwanted spirit but I often compare it to using a hammer when, in fact, a more subtle tool such as a spanner is needed,' he said. By 'realigning energy lines', which he claims run around and through the earth, similar to the energies which are proven by acupuncturists to run around the body, Lloyd can send the unwanted ghost on its way and effectively put an end to a haunting.

'These lines of energy can become blocked by houses or roads or railway lines, causing a spirit to become trapped in the one place. A castle like Charleville, which was built on a site known from ancient times for its strong earth energies, is likely to block the flow of that energy and trap spirits.'

Lloyd did not carry out any form of exorcism during his survey at Charleville although he did come across some very heavy 'negative energy and desperate ghosts' in a number of the castle's rooms.

'When I have to do that kind of work I like to call it "a release" for the ghost, which is being sent over. It's a bit like finding a small child who has become lost in a large railway station. What do you do? You take it to a place of safety. If you feel there is a spirit that is lost or who is causing problems to people who are alive, then you direct that soul to a place of safety, and that is precisely what I do by realigning the earth's energies and interacting with the spirit world,' he said. The Arch Druid cites an example of one such 'release' when he was contacted by a friend, who complained of a constantly cold bedroom caused by what he felt was 'a ghostly presence'.

'I asked the spirit to come on to me, to trust me and as I crossed the energy line to where the soul was trapped, I could feel it join with me. I felt it was the presence of a woman in her late 50s, who had not passed over when her body had died. I took her with me, out of the house and down to the crossroads nearby and from there, I released it.'

On completion of his supernatural duties, Lloyd found that he was covered in a grey dust 'caused by static energy from the ghost' he had joined with. However, according to his client, he was also successful in relieving the bedroom of its deathly chill.

Lloyd had stayed in one of Charleville Castle's eerie turret rooms on a previous occasion and was prepared for excessive psychic activity when he embarked on his 2002 survey.

'This castle was built for the most part, as a gentleman's residence by the Anglo Irish. The back garden was designed to represent the Union Jack, which has not leant itself to good energies,' said Lloyd.

The castle's massive, octagonal tower library was also used by the Freemasons for their gatherings and ceremonies during its relatively short time in use. Charleville Castle was built between 1798 and 1812. Its owners, Charles William Bury (the Earl of Charleville) and his heirs, lived lavishly and beyond their means – the house passed down four generations of the Bury family before being sold. So extravagant were the early lifestyles at the castle, that Charleville went all but broke, and had to close up completely between 1844 and 1851. It was occupied intermittently by the Burys until 1931 and was certified a ruin for taxation purposes in 1961. After many years of dereliction, a heritage trust was set up to protect the building and the castle was leased to a number of tenants. The current leaseholder is an American woman, Bridget Vance, whose experience at Charleville has not always been entirely of this realm. Although local lore has long spoken of Charleville as an intensely haunted place, Vance was not aware of any such rumour when she took ownership in 1987. She was living in the castle for about three months with her two children, when she first heard noises 'out of the ordinary' running throughout their new home.

'I was asleep with the children in a big room upstairs one evening, when all of a sudden I heard the running of footsteps above me and the laughing and giggling of children. I thought, "Jesus, somebody's broken in; there are kids up there," so I got the torch and went up to the top floor, which hadn't been developed at the time,' recalled Vance. To her surprise and great relief, she found the vast upstairs area of her new house deathly quiet, dark and abandoned, as she had known it.

'There was nobody up there. It was very strange because what I heard above our heads was the distinct sound of human voices and feet and it was very loud. It happened again and must have happened ten times, the running and the voices, and all the time there was never anybody in those rooms,' she said.

'A short while later, I discovered the sounds had come from what used to be the Bury children's play area, and a room where we later uncovered nursery wallpaper beneath layers of old plaster board.'

Lloyd's psychic survey also revealed the presence of ghostly children at Charleville. After many hours of deep meditation, the Arch Druid entered the building with the aim of psychically tuning himself into whatever supernatural forces lay within.

'There was a little girl of about eight years of age in the upstairs rooms. She walked along with me and I felt as if she almost had her hand placed in mine for much of that time,' said Lloyd.

Bridget Vance also recalled that, at a very early age, her children talked of meeting with a little boy and girl at the castle, and that they held hands together and walked around the house.

'The presence of this girl was felt in the room, which had been the old nursery or the schoolroom,' said Lloyd, speaking of the same area where Vance had her first supernatural awakening at her new Irish home.

The possible reasons behind the child hauntings at Charleville Castle paint a less pleasant picture than the hand-in-hand antics of these supernatural entities. In 1861,

Harriet Hugh Edel, the second child of the third Earl of Charleville, fell to her death from a low banister on the second floor landing. Those who have heard the laughter, footsteps and screams around the old building, are convinced they heard the after life echoes of this girl, Harriet. While Harriet's sudden death provides the most likely cause of a child haunting at the castle, the identity of a second ghost child often heard at Charleville is shrouded in deeper mystery.

In the course of his survey, Lloyd came across the most 'desperate and awful psychic stench', which he said 'was the result of a human being, having been locked up in a room for many years, where they most likely died.

'As we walked along a passageway into one of the turret rooms, I came across, what I can only describe as, a psychic smell. The room was absolutely foul and the psychic energy within was so bad and wrought with fear that it would almost make the stomach churn. There was the presence of a child in there and he'd been kept in there for a very long time,' explained Lloyd.

'We thought he was disabled in some way, possibly both mentally and physically, and he'd been more or less hidden away for all of his short life. His name wasn't on any of the family records of the house. But, it was later discovered that there was a child in the house during the time of the second Earl, who was not recognised as part of the family, and who had died young.' Bridget Vance has also heard the moanings of this second child, and her own research has unearthed the real life existence of a boy by the name of Henry Walter, who died when he was only seven years old, and who was not recorded in the house's history. Despite the apparent secrecy surrounding this child's life, there is a plaque to a child of that name at the Bury family plot in nearby St. Catherine's graveyard.

Lloyd said he was amazed by the intense mix of both good and bad psychic energies during his survey at Charleville, and said it would seem even more haunted than its older neighbour Leap Castle, which has long been regarded as Ireland's most haunted castle. According to the midlands druid, he could feel this energy as soon as he stepped over the threshold of Charleville.

'In the hallway it's not too bad, but I could feel something looking over the banisters at us all the while. It was when we went from there into the long gallery room at the back, that I picked up the presence of an old gentleman who used to be a Colonel or held some rank within the military,' said Lloyd.

'As we came back out of this room and walked along to the foot of the stairs, we felt somebody there with us. When we reached the top of the stairs we felt it again, and realised that we were being followed around by the old military gentleman, who we'd encountered in the first room. He has a bad limp in his left leg, he is very curious and follows you around a bit.

'I then walked around the left hand balcony and picked up the presence of a couple, who might have been children, leaning over the balcony looking down at anyone who was coming in,' said Lloyd. This balcony, according to Vance, has been an area of particularly strong supernatural encounter.

Bridget Vance's occupation of Charleville Castle is coloured with a charming touch of historic irony. According to Vance, her great, great-grandmother had lived in the district of Rhode just ten miles from the Earl of Charleville's estate. Vance's Co. Offaly ancestor was evicted from her Rhode cottage for non-payment of rates by the same ruling Anglo-Irish lords of the land.

'My ancestor ended up in a ditch with five children, before being put into Tullamore jail at the age of 30,' said Vance, who has conducted extensive research into her Irish lineage. In the wake of the Irish Land League movement, Vance's grand relation was eventually reinstated to her cottage, which had to be rebuilt after its demolition at the hands of the landed gentry. The irony of how she has now come into possession of a long-standing lease of Charleville Castle, is not lost on its new resident.

'The people of this castle threw my ancestors out of their homes and sent them to jail, but now the wheel has turned,' she said philosophically. Vance became a long-term leaseholder of Charleville Castle in 1987 and moved into the building with her mother and two children two years later. 'My mother seemed very much in touch with whatever was going on, on a paranormal level, in this house,' said Vance.

'One mid-winter solstice she woke up and thought she saw her husband walking across the room in a red bathrobe, until she realised he was in the bed sleeping beside her still. She told us that a man in a red greatcoat now appeared before her by the window of her room. This apparition was followed by another, of a man in a greyish, green coat wearing stockings and a cravat. The two men were joined in the room by a third figure, who was a lady in a black hooded cowl, who didn't have a very pleasant expression on her face,' explained Vance of her late mother's ghostly encounters.

'In the same instance, a group of hooded figures, who were more faded than the two men and the woman, formed a circle around my mother's bed and made a salute', which Vance believes was a blessing from either ghosts of Masons or from druids, before they vanished. Vance and her mother discovered from looking through literature on the history of the building, that the man in the red greatcoat was, in fact, Francis Johnston, the architect of Charleville Castle, who also designed the GPO on Dublin's O'Connell Street.

'He died an old man but came back in his prime before my mother,' said Vance. The female apparition with the stern face, they believed, was Mrs. Emily Bury who, they also discovered, was the person responsible for putting her great, great-grandparent in jail. The man in the green was identified from photographs as the first Earl of Charleville, Charles William Bury.

Vance believes, as her mother did, that 'Francis Johnston and the Earl were forever concerned about the castle falling into ruin, and maybe they were happy it was now being maintained by us, and she received either a Masonic or druidic blessing to that effect,' she said. Charleville's ghosts have also made themselves evident to visitors and guests of the current residents.

'They seem to like parties and have a habit of interacting with our guests when we have people over,' said Vance. 'When the children were still quite young, a friend of mine went to sleep in one of the upstairs rooms. The kids came down the next morning and said that Jack (an assumed name), was acting very strange and that he had spent the entire night awake with the light on, and had left his door wide open. When Jack came down the next morning, he told us that when he finally got settled into bed at about 2.30 a.m. "two English gentlemen were talking, laughing, drinking and having a wonderful time in the room, but I couldn't see them anywhere."

'This guy was an academic and not prone to such flights of fancy, so we believed him straight off,' she said. There is one particularly frisky male ghost, who likes to touch other male visitors on the back of the neck. According to Vance, he was the son of the second Earl, who had an affair with the poet Lord Byron, who was also a guest at the castle during the early nineteenth century. As far as sharing her space with ghosts, poltergeists and all things that go bump in the night, Vance is resigned yet happy.

'I quite like them, if they want to leave, they can leave, I wouldn't want them to be trapped.'

There are various trains of thought on why we are so regularly confronted with the traditional haunted castle, such as Charleville. As Lloyd said, the construction of a house can often block the earth's energies, so when this blockage is magnified to the size of a castle with five-foot thick walls, such an imposition is bound to create problems. It is also thought that large quantities of stone can act as a device for recording sounds and echoes of the past. There is a theory that sensitive people, such as psychics, could pick up on these interned images and echoes. Lloyd's next port of call was indeed such a weighty mass of stone upon stone, in the shape of Leap Castle.

Leap Castle towers forbiddingly over open Irish countryside from an elevated seat of solid rock just 12 miles north of the busy Tipperary town of Roscrea. This fourteenth century stronghold has long been revered as the country's most haunted castle. Chanting clerics, foul ghostly odours, children's screams, play sounds and laughter, and a female apparition coupled with a dreadful sense of pervading evil, are all said to cling to the battlements of this Co. Offaly fortress. The hauntings at Leap are believed to stem in the main from its barbaric past of family feuds and cold-blooded murder, where brother slew brother, and neighbouring cousins were unwittingly invited to their deaths at the hands of the ruling O'Carroll clan. Destroyed by fire during the civil war of 1922, the central building of Leap Castle has now been masterfully rebuilt as the family home of traditional musician, Seán Ryan. The new occupants, while comfortable at their dream historical residence, are regularly reminded of the building's eerie ways.

Ryan, a celebrated flautist and whistle player, talks of two young girls who are regularly sensed, 'shadow like' playing in the hallway of their home. He remains unperturbed, however, by the presence of the ghostly children and of other supernatural phenomena, which seem to impact regularly upon the many buildings on the ruinous grounds of Leap. Formerly the seat of the O'Bannon clan and known as Leim Uí Bhanain, or Leap of the O'Bannons, Leap Castle passed to the O'Carrolls, the ruling chiefs of King's County, or Offaly as it is known today, soon after it was built. It is the recorded bloody deeds of the O'Carroll clan, which have set a precedent for the chill air, which many say still hangs over the castle today. During the middle ages, Leap provided a strategic fortress for any would-be ruling clan, as it surveyed vast tracts of land and guarded the main passage from the Slieve Bloom Mountains into Munster. According to history, it was a stronghold fiercely protected by the O'Carroll chiefs with an intense, and often barbaric zeal.

At some time during the sixteenth century, the O'Carrolls are said to have invited their neighbouring cousins to a banquet at the castle. It was to be a reception like no other, however, as all invited guests were brutally slain as part of a bitter, inter-clan feud, common at that time. It is also said that Teige O'Carroll cut down his own brother in the castle's chapel as he knelt at prayer. It is from this third floor chapel, known as the 'Bloody Chapel', that Arch Druid Melvyn Lloyd felt much of Leap's paranormal activity.

'Even from the outside of the building, you can sense forms and a presence watching from the upstairs chapel window,' said druid Lloyd after his psychic survey at Leap. The current owner, Seán Ryan, has been told by many elder locals that 'strange lights have been seen' emanating from the single window of the Bloody Chapel down the years, when there would never have been electricity at the castle. This small place of worship on the third floor of the main tower remains undeveloped today, although it is still a consecrated church. Ryan said he became aware of a 'presence' in the chapel a number of years ago.

'I felt I could make out what appeared to be a monk-like figure from the corner of my eye moving around the chapel,' he said.

'We have also heard sounds coming from the upstairs, as if there was a party going on but it always seemed to have a distant air to it. I've heard the noise of the clinking of glasses and the deep murmur of voices,' said Ryan. At one end of the Bloody Chapel sits a small portal set into a wall, leading far downwards to the castle's dungeons with no stairs to descend, or to return by. It is down this tiny and forbidding entrance to Leap's secret 'spiked oubliette' that prisoners were flung to waste away in the castle's dank lower chambers.

Local lore tells of three cartloads of human bones, which were taken from the dungeons when the castle was claimed by the Irish Free State in the 1920s. Leap's most sighted ethereal inhabitants, however, are two young girls who play in the downstairs hall and on the first flight of narrow spiral stairs.

'There are two entities who move about here all the time in the hall, on the stair case and in the upper hall,' said Ryan, 'we come across them almost every couple of weeks or so. They seem to be in their own time frame, just playing around and don't interact or interfere with us at all. We've seen them mostly in shadows. We don't really hear them, but occasionally there's a governess figure with them, who has been known to touch people. This happens a lot to visitors to the castle. She seems to be aware of living people,' said Ryan, whose theory on the ghostly presence of the girls at his home was confirmed for him by a visiting, native American psychic in 2000.

Leap Castle receives regular visits from Cherokee Indians involved in researching their family roots. Thousands of Irish travelled to the Maryland area of the United States during the sixteenth and seventeenth centuries and interrelated with the Cherokee.

'The O'Carroll name married into the Cherokee during the seventeenth century,' said Ryan. A group of Cherokee women who claimed to have psychic abilities, visited the castle in 2000 and immediately picked up on the presence of the girls. 'They were told nothing about what we had sensed. They came in raw to whatever might be here, but the minute they stepped inside, they saw the girls playing there in the main hallway,' he said. One of the women was able to draw a psychic picture of the girls for the castle's new owner.

'I was told their names were Emily and Charlotte and it is believed that Emily haunts the building because her life was cut short after she fell from the east tower,' said Ryan. The link between hauntings and the early deaths of those involved, provides a common thread for parapsychologists trying to make sense of ghostly encounter and disturbance. Druid Lloyd also felt the presence of a 'small being' on the first flight of stairs during his survey.

'I was told there was supposed to have been the ghost of an animal on the stairs and I did find something there alright. I didn't think it was an animal but maybe a dwarf, or small person walking up and down the stairwell.

'A lot of people visiting the castle have seen her fall and heard her screams,' said Ryan. 'The little one, Charlotte, we're not sure how she died. She has a badly deformed right leg which is turned completely backwards and you can sense her hobbling around after the other girl, calling after her all the time.'

Leap Castle passed into the hands of the landed English Derby family some time in the late seventeenth century, when Jonathan Derby married Fionualla O'Carroll and the O'Carroll line of ascendancy came to an end. The Derbys became high-sheriffs of the area and held the family seat until 1922, when it was burnt out in fighting during the civil war. There is a story of Lord Derby, from the late nineteenth century, who became so incensed by talk of bodies left to rot in his cellars and behind the walls of Leap, that he arranged to have a section of his castle examined. When he opened up a wall, however, he was more put out to find three bodies bricked up in standing positions and he is said to have plastered them back in where they were found. Seán Ryan has stylishly rebuilt much of the interior of the main tower. During this ongoing work he is constantly reminded that he is sharing the building with other worldly forces.

'When I'm working here, I get a lot of copycat sounds made exactly the same way as what I've just done, anything like the sound of a saw or even a whistle. We're well used to it now. They don't seem to interfere with us, and anyway, the place is big enough for us all,' he said cordially.

Other ghostly experiences at Leap include a low and rhythmic chanting from the old priest's building, now derelict, to the left of the main tower as you face it. Lloyd's psychic survey took him to the very bowels of this magnificent castle and to the grisly basement area.

'We went down in the cellar at Leap and discovered an ancient guardian from an old stone site that was once there. This was a male guardian, who wasn't particularly threatening or frightening, but was just there and would have been attached to that site from as far back as 5,000 years ago,' said Lloyd. The midlands druid believes that Leap Castle was built 'by people who knew of the energies that went through the land, quite possibly the knights Templar, during the fourteenth century.' On another floor, Lloyd discerned the presence of two entities. 'I came across a serving woman by an old fireplace on the first floor and at the door it felt like there was an old soldier there, who may have been wounded at one time, or it may have been where he eventually died from wounds received in battle. There is also account of a tall woman dressed in red, who is thought to be a descendent of the O'Carroll line, who was murdered as she lay sleeping.'

CHAPTER FOUR

Hush a Bye Baby

The arrival of a first grandchild to any proud parent's home is, by and large, one of the happier events for that extended family. Plans and preparations are meticulously set in motion, rooms are painted, stairs are made child-proof, and an air of excitement settles over the entire house in anticipation of the new arrival.

This was certainly the case at the home of Jackie and Esther Fahey of Corrib Park, outside Galway city when their daughter, Martha, arrived home from hospital with her daughter, Sarah Louise, in November 1996.

The initial joy of sharing such close quarters with their new grandchild was soon marred however, by the arrival to the house of something altogether more odious. The Faheys' lives were to be irrevocably altered within months of their beautiful new relation taking up residence with them. Their home of almost 25 years also took on a reckless, jealous and ultimately destructive poltergeist, seemingly triggered by the arrival of Sarah Louise.

Number 286 Corrib Park was, quite literally, turned upside down by a violent spirit, which drove the living residents out onto the streets on more than one occasion. The early months of 1997 were a 'hell on earth' for Jackie and his family. It wasn't until May of the same year that the entity itself was sent on its way at the hands of a capable parapsychologist and ghost buster.

In the course of her 'healing' the maligned Galway house, psychic and pagan priestess, Sandra Ramdhanie, said she perceived a catalogue of 'religious scandal and infanticide', which had led to the Faheys' haunting. The troublesome poltergeist was alleged to be the restless spirit of another baby who, according to Ramdhanie, was born to a young woman, possibly a nun, and a clergyman who she thought most likely a bishop. In her psychic evaluation of the building, Ramdhanie felt that the child had been murdered at the hands of, or on order of, one or both of its parents, shortly after its birth in the early 1900s and buried in the earth where the Faheys had eventually come to live.

The first sign of any foreign influence at the Fahey house came in the form of a 'putrid smell'. It was a stench so foul, according to Jackie Fahey, that he had difficulty in breathing, and had to resort to using inhalers in order to catch a proper breath. In their harrowing account of the haunting, entitled *The Reawakening*, co-written by Padhraic Faherty, Jackie's son Michael described it as the 'smell of rotting flesh or meat or like urine.'

Foul odours are a common phenomenon in the area of poltergeist activity. A number of documented poltergeist cases have actually reported the daubing of excrement on the walls and onto floors of the afflicted houses. No such smearing occurred at the Galway home, but shortly after the smell first became evident, so too did the appearance of crushed eggshells on the carpet, which nobody could account for.

'I thought the eggshells were just paint and we threw them away as we discovered them, which was on a Friday before going off for the weekend. But they were back on the Monday morning,' said Jackie.

'Eggshells were always the sign of a curse or of a rebirth. If you wanted to curse your neighbour's crop you would go out onto their land and pierce an egg onto a bush and leave it there. By the time the egg would go rotten, your neighbour's crops would also go rotten,' he said.

Grandparents Jackie and Esther did not think anything strange of the smell or the shells, and went off for a weekend break in Waterford, but it was a holiday that would be interrupted by the rest of their family who arrived in the south eastern county terrified out of their minds.

The shells were shortly followed by 'strange' noises from the new, upstairs bedroom of Sarah Louise, usually between the hours of 1 a.m. and 3 a.m. The Fahey household was now suffering all the classic signs of polterkinetic energies at work. Such activity generally includes loud, repetitive noises such as tapping or knocking, the moving and destruction of objects including ornaments, picture frames and furniture, the slamming of doors, and the turning on and off of electrical appliances, and unaccountable flushing of toilets. In short, poltergeist cases are known for their attempts to monopolise the attention of the living.

The Faheys' disturbances also happened to coincide with construction work starting up next door, and for a while, this was thought to be the root of their noise problems. It is also well documented that construction work has been known to bring about or reawaken trapped spirits in a building.

However, the strange noises, foul odour and unexplainable eggshells continued to manifest themselves for many weeks after the building work was completed, well into the New Year.

In her testimony of events, Mary, Michael Fahey's fiancée, described the moment they all felt they were definitely not dealing with something, which was of this world.

On returning from town one evening Michael and Mary found baby Sarah in the care of a babysitter, who told them that Martha had run out of the house screaming with fright. Martha had been watching TV at around 10 p.m. when she heard the sound of thumping from her daughter's room. When she ran upstairs, she found she could not open the door as the noises inside continued. After many failed attempts she ran out and found a neighbour, who brought her back in and opened the unlocked door. Sarah Louise was discovered in a distressed state. Michael and Mary relieved the babysitter and found the house gripped by a deathly chill, particularly baby Sarah's bedroom. They left the house that night, collected Martha and travelled to Waterford, where Jackie and Esther were holidaying during this sinister episode.

On return to Corrib Park, however, they would all be treated again to similar and equally sinister paranormal experiences, which would drive them once more from their own door.

One night the whole family was awakened by the noises in the house. At 3.30 a.m. they gathered downstairs. They heard the baby crying and when they went into her room, found her toys and teddys arranged in a circle around her cot, which was not the work of an eight-month old baby.

The Faheys arranged for a mass to be said in their house the next day, but the poltergeist continued uninhibited by the religious ceremony.

'The masses were no use and, in fact, it only got worse after them,' said Jackie. In the weeks that followed a further mass was said, but this again was followed by the mysterious smashing of a ceramic vase, the upturning and destruction of a picture of baby Sarah and the continuation of loud nocturnal banging and crashing.

'A silver picture frame lifted from its place and hovered in front of me before smashing against the fireplace,' said Mary. Michael said he saw a table upturn and felt a door being slammed shut after him as he fled the house.

'The feeling in the house was just terrible. We got two different priests to say mass there, but it did no good. In fact, whatever was in there didn't like it and went mad altogether,' Jackie said. After many weeks of irrational happenings, Jackie and Esther Fahey were at their wits' end. The home they had lived in for over 25 years had turned against them, and no amount of religious cleansing seemed capable of relieving them of their tormentor.

'Never, ever had I experienced anything like this in my life,' said Jackie. 'I had always believed in ghosts I suppose, because we'd often pass houses where there were stories attached and you'd always pay them a bit of respect but never in my wildest dreams did I ever think I'd be so affected by a ghost in my own house,' he said.

'I wasn't scared until I realised that what we were actually dealing with was spirits and that's when things really began to happen,' Jackie said. 'I remember I started laughing and kind of slagging Michael and Mary when we came back from Waterford especially when I saw Michael saying the rosary in the upstairs bedroom. But then I began to hear stuff. The first odd noise I heard was when I was in bed and I distinctly heard what sounded like somebody hitting an empty plastic bottle off their fist. I thought it was somebody down at the fridge so I went down, but there was nothing there and no noise. It would start up again as soon as I went back to bed though. This kind of thing went on and off for a while. We had an old Cuckoo clock on the wall, which never went but then it started to go off all on its own,' he said.

It was at this time, amidst much media attention on the plight of the Fahey family, that Sandra Ramdhanie paid a visit to Corrib Park.

The meeting was not meant to have happened after the Faheys had been warned against recruiting the aid of Ramdhanie by a Catholic priest, who told them she would only make things worse. However, when she arrived at their door on the good word of a journalist who was covering the story, they were willing to hear her out.

'I didn't believe in these psychic healing people but I thought I'd let her in anyway,' said Jackie. 'I remember she went upstairs and began touching the walls and then asked had any construction work been carried out. I had forgotten about next door and told her "no love, there hasn't" but my young fellah spoke up and told her that next door had just put an extension onto their roof. I don't know how she knew this stuff but it was a good start,' recalled Jackie.

Sandra Ramdhanie had encountered many haunted buildings and trapped spirits previous to visiting the Faheys' home. In 1995 she wrote her experiences as a 'ghost buster' in a book called *Trapped between two Worlds*. She had often dealt with the ghosts of infants since becoming involved in psychic healing during the 1970s.

'I went to Galway with an open mind,' she said. 'I went in as Sandra the person and not the psychic, so it would make a more friendly introduction. I remember I had seen

Esther on TV weeks before and she looked as if she'd really had her fill. She was just sitting outside her home with her head in her hands,' Ramdhanie recalled. 'I went in, and for our first meeting acted only as a sympathetic listener. I told them that I couldn't guarantee anything, but if I could help, I'd do my best.'

According to the Dublin-based psychic and high priestess, she could 'feel and sense and see a spirit' in the house when she entered, but her first approach was to look for a logical explanation.

'A lot of the time the polterkinetic energy in a house is caused solely by the people who live there. Before commencing I have to be able to satisfy myself that what I am approaching is genuine psychic activity, rather than a situation caused by a hysteric reaction.

'I have seen cases of mass hysteria caused in some instances by one individual who hears a noise upstairs, and then the next time something is heard, everybody jumps and, from there, a situation can simply escalate out of control. You have to chip away to get to the root of these phenomena.'

As part of her investigation, Ramdhanie talked to neighbours who verified that lights were seen flashing on and off and that furniture was heard crashing about after the Faheys had fled their house.

'Lights were flashing and we could hear noises as well. We, too, were very frightened and I don't think that any of us slept at all,' said neighbour Valerie Lee. Ramdhanie was less shaken on her encounter with the Galway poltergeist. 'I can truthfully say I have never encountered an evil spirit,' she said. 'I believe that evil is like beauty and is in the eye of the beholder. These spirits usually have a traumatic or violent death. I learned through telepathic communication that the spirit at Corrib Park was a baby born to a young woman, who I felt was most likely a nun and to a clergyman,' said Ramdhanie.

After bringing herself to a 'heightened state of psychic sensitivity' through meditation and breathing techniques, Ramdhanie began to tune into the entity at the Fahey residence. 'I rambled around the house and there were spots where I felt more spirit energy than in others. I could sense it was a baby, but it never appeared to me to tell me things. What I was shown was a series of pictures,' she said.

'The first image I got was of a nun and then a dark smoky room with an earth floor. Then an image of this girl giving birth and a man, who I felt was perhaps her father. I also saw this figure taking hold of the baby and smothering it before it was buried. In the background was another man, who may not have been physically present during these scenes but was perhaps there to identify who the father of the child was, and this man was wearing the red robes of the clergy and most notably those of a bishop,' she said.

Sandra Ramdhanie lives in Shankhill, Co. Dublin. She is Irish born of Hindu and Presbyterian faith, however, she says her 'work transcends religion'.

'I see my work as a healing situation rather than any strict religious dogma,' she said. Having lived in Trinidad during her childhood, where she first came into contact with the supernatural through local voodoo or Obeah men, she returned to Ireland and learned to develop her psychic abilities.

Ramdhanie describes the Faheys as an intuitive family who sensibly realised that all the trouble had started when Martha brought Sarah Louise into the house. 'This spirit baby became very jealous and wanted Martha to become its mother as well. It was almost like a sibling rivalry situation,' said Ramdhanie.

In the course of Ramdhanie's psychic assessment at 286 Corrib Park, the Faheys were paid a visit from a man and woman who told them their family had owned land in the area during the early part of the last century and that the area had long suffered haunting experiences. This man told the Faheys of a farmhouse, which stood where their house and many others stood today.

'Many years ago a relative of his had owned farmland here and the farmhouse was rented to various tenants,' said Jackie. 'One of the families had an only child, a daughter, who became a nun,' Jackie recalled his visitor saying. This information came as a great shock to the Faheys as it had come only days after Ramdhanie went on the record saying she had felt that a nun had given birth to a child in the immediate area.

The visitor also informed Jackie that other inhabitants, prior to these people, had gone through similar terrors, such as blankets being pulled off a person in bed, the sound of a child crying and objects being thrown about.

According to Ramdhanie, 'there has to be a combination of factors for a haunting to occur'.

'The place has to be receptive. You'll always find that there is an underground water system, some kind of energy line and almost inevitably some kind of standing stone or ancient monument near by. A lot of the time spirits are quite young, and this is because the death probably happened instantly through murder or by accident and the spirit does not know it should pass over.

'Very often you have houses that have spirits and the inhabitants don't have the psychic ability to pick up on them. I remember one case where there were 13 people living in the house, and while the majority of them saw cups flying off tables and heard footsteps throughout the house, others never sought an explanation or associated these occurrences with anything other than the living world,' said the psychic.

'There is also usually a connection with the hormonal energies in a house such as teenage energy, which is strongly associated with hauntings or that of a new baby and a postnatal mother as in the Faheys' case,' said Ramdhanie.

The Galway family have always said they 'firmly believe that Sarah saw and played with the ghost baby'. 'When baby Sarah arrived, the spirit may have been energised and have twinned with Sarah in order to seek Martha's love and affection,' said Ramdhanie.

'There tends to be a psychological difference between those who pass on and those who remain in this realm as ghosts. You find that it can be caused by a number of factors such as the occurrence of a violent death or in some instances a suicide, which in haunting cases are really hard to deal with, because they drain your life as you feel this depression coming off the spirit,' she said.

In the Corrib Park case, however, the spirit was only concerned with baby Sarah and in seeking the affections of her mother, Martha.

'This was a poltergeist rather than a ghost. Ghosts are visual images frozen in time. An example of this is the common apparition of the woman in white floating along a landing who doesn't interact with you. A poltergeist is a noise ghost and one that you can only hear and who seeks your attention.'

Ramdhanie had carried out numerous 'healings' on haunted buildings previous to this. In *Trapped between two*

Worlds she said, 'the most common way of dealing with spirit presence in Ireland is by exorcism, which I see as a form of attack, not appropriate in many cases. You could say the exorcist attempts to evict the spirit, while I do my best to re-house them.'

According to the high priestess of the Temple of Isis 'these spirits were once human beings like ourselves and deserve to be treated with the same respect. If I was shouted at and ordered out of a place, I would most likely rebel and that is just human nature.' Ramdhanie said she 'tried to explain to this baby that he could go somewhere else instead.'

'I talk to these entities like I'd talk to anybody. I don't discriminate just because they're in another dimension. I'd ask them, "why are you doing this here? Don't you know you could be somewhere else with your loved ones instead of permanently dragging things around people's houses?"'

Ramdhanie asked the Faheys to join her in a healing ceremony for both the house and the ghost baby, which she believed would release the spirit forever. According to the family, the group held hands in a circle as Ramdhanie set Tibetan incense alight, and placed channelling crystals around the house. She joined the group and tuned into the spirit and set about her healing.

Martha sat in the middle of one of these circles and 'pretended to hold and love the ghost baby' as Ramdhanie coaxed it into the other world through telepathic communication.

'In these cases I am pushing against the spirit presence with what I can only describe as a golden light of love and healing.' The family say they saw the spirit of the ghost baby rise and disappear before their eyes during the ceremony.

'Only for Sandra saw my wife on the RTE news with her head in her hands, we might still be suffering today. We were sleeping in a neighbour's house when she arrived and I don't know if we would ever have been able to move back in to our own house,' said Jackie. Many months and years have passed since peace was restored to 286 Corrib Park, but Jackie and Esther Fahey still remain shaken by their encounter with the spirit world during the early months of 1997.

'It's been quiet here since but it has never been the same. There's never been a day when I go out that front door and come back without the ghost being on my mind,' said Jackie. 'I never stop thinking about it.'

The Fahey grandparents say they remain shaken by every bump in the night. 'I was sitting here on my own one night reading the paper when I heard a bang from upstairs, but not for the life of me would I go up there. I just waited till somebody came back and we turned on all the lights. It was only a picture falling but after what we went through we can never be sure again,' he said.

CHAPTER FIVE

Spirit Forces

The Italian media could only describe as 'spectacular' the grand battle fought out between the 'devil' and the head of the Roman Catholic Church inside the walls of Vatican City in September 2000.

The incident erupted during an audience with the pontiff in St. Peter's Square, when a girl from Monza began shouting in a cavernous voice as if in a fit of rage.

The Pope was compelled to carry out an impromptu exorcism on the seemingly possessed teenager after she began uttering disconnected phrases in unknown tongues, and screaming insults towards him, while displaying a superhuman strength towards Vatican guards who tried to restrain her.

Despite lengthy invocations to the Holy Spirit to come into this girl and an all-round rebuking of the perceived 'evil' within, both the Pope and his chief 'Satan-buster,' Fr. Gabriele Amorth failed in their attempts to 'drive out the devil'.

According to news reports at the time, 'the girl remained possessed. The devil's voice sneeringly laughed from within her at the Pope's failed attempt to drive him out.' The Pope stayed and prayed with the girl for half an hour before leaving her under the care of his clergy, and told her he would pray for her again at length. According to the

Vatican, this was Pope John Paul II's third attempt at an exorcism since he took up the throne more than 22 years earlier.

Despite this very public failure, the event firmly reinstated the medieval and often controversial rite of exorcism to the charter of the Roman Catholic Church. In fact, this ostentatious show of strength took place just months after the Vatican issued its first review on the rite of exorcism since 1614. The 90-page, leather bound *De Exorcismus et Supplicantionibus Quibustam* (On Every Kind of Exorcism in Supplication) was issued in 1999 to dioceses around the globe, to function as an updated manual for those whose duties include driving out evil spirits.

In Ireland, every Catholic diocese is supposed to have an exorcist at its disposal. Church sources state, however, that exorcisms or exorcists have been 'few and far between' in recent decades.

'Cannon law recommends that every diocese should have an exorcist but it doesn't make it mandatory and the fact of the matter is that no diocese in Ireland takes that seriously,' said Fr. Pat Collins, a Vincentian priest who lectures in psychology, religion, and spirituality at All Hallows College, Drumcondra in Dublin.

The Church's move to revive the age-old rite of purging spirits shocked a great number of its members, who no longer regarded their faith as one tied into a supernatural concept of cut-and-dry, good versus evil, perpetually shadowed by all manner of malign spirit.

Although considerably modernised with regard to how the exorcist should deal with the potentiality of the ill mental health of the client during the course of his duties, the new directive has arrived at a time when most modern

Catholics would find it difficult to accept the idea of Satan as a living and thinking being.

In essence, the Vatican successfully managed to redraw the ultra traditional line of Christianity, which states that we live in a world where spirits, possessions, and demonisation are very real phenomena waiting to ensnare the sinner. The Vatican's manual actually informs its dilettantes that 'the devil goes around like a roaring lion looking for souls to devour'.

'To be a Christian is to believe in the supernatural,' said Fr. Collins, who has witnessed a number of attempted exorcisms and dealt with the 'restless dead' in haunted houses. 'The church should be experts in dealing with the spirit world. But, I think the Church lets people down, because it doesn't know how to deal with these things when they actually crop up,' said Collins.

'There is an all-round lack of expertise and dereliction of duty in which the church fails people at these points because it doesn't take the issue seriously enough. When I was ordained, we were all given the rite of exorcism to our great amusement. The bible says that believers will drive out evil spirits in God's name so, in effect, we are mandated to do this work,' he said.

The Dublin priest does not take such a very hard line on the issue, however, and states that 95 per cent of alleged possession cases can be dealt with psychologically.

'If you expect to see the devil, you'll see the devil,' said Collins. 'These people need counselling, encouragement, affirmation, and peace of mind. I have seen priests work people into a lather of emotional frenzy because they had driven home their own belief in an evil presence so strongly when, in fact, the person is no more possessed than I am.'

There are two essential levels of exorcism carried out within the remit of Catholic teachings; the solemn exorcism and the simple exorcism.

'The solemn exorcism is very rare and only carried out on a person whose entire personality, both physically and mentally, has been taken over by an evil spirit,' explained Collins.

'The simple exorcism is performed where a part of a person's personality seems to have come under an evil influence.' The Dublin priest has only once seen the former rite carried out and described it as 'very frightening'.

'It was done by a priest in England and the woman involved roared unnaturally and appeared very strong. She had a large, visible lump in her throat for a long time before that, and when the exorcism was complete the lump was gone. However, I was told later that the woman never bothered with her spiritual life and just reverted back to where she had been. The evil spirit returned and the lump with it. She didn't take any responsibility for her spirituality and the evil came back into her life,' he said.

Within the Vatican's new guidelines on exorcism, published entirely in Latin, are pointers to assist in demonisation recognition. 'Speaking in unknown languages, discerning distant or hidden things and displaying a physical strength that is at odds with the possessed person's age or state of health' are the main telltale signs. It also states that an exorcism should only be tried 'after diligent inquiry and after having consulted experts in spiritual matters and, if felt appropriate, experts in medical and psychiatric science, who have a sense of spiritual reality'. While Collins believes the area of exorcism to be 'a scary kind of ministry', he maintains that the Catholic Church should be more open to investigating the area of supernatural phenomena.

'Most people today have a naturalistic world view where they think there is only this world, that there's no supernatural, no God, no spirits – good or evil – no miracles, and no psychic plane. A lot of priests are not at home with the spirit world. They seem to practise a watered down version of spirituality, which doesn't include these fundamentally important issues. We need people in a diocese who can go out and deal with hauntings, demonisation, and psychic phenomena in a competent manner. Saying mass in the house is not always appropriate,' said Collins.

Having encountered supernatural experience from an early age, Collins is interested in setting up a conference for church people to address 'these strange kinds of paranormal experiences' and to look at what they can offer in exchange.

'Once you believe in God and the Holy Spirit, you are at home with the notion of good and bad spirits, and with the notion that the souls of your ancestors remain in some kind of relationship with you after they depart,' he said.

The Drumcondra cleric is of the opinion that 'besides the normal kinds of sensory knowledge we perceive from day to day, there are many other forms of receptivity impinging on the human psyche.'

'The church would be very wary regarding matters of clairvoyance and ESP and the bible states that you should not engage in divination of any kind, and I would agree with that. But, if a person is psychic there's nothing they can do about it. Things just come to them, which are unbidden. They're not looking for them or thinking about

it, these intuitions are just there in the mind, and I believe
it's genetic and that everybody has an ability in that
regard,' he said.

Collins is keen to stress that he is no 'ghost buster' or
exorcist but, through his work as a minister within the
Catholic Church's Charismatic Renewal movement, he has
come into contact with various aspects of the paranormal.

During the 1990s he was asked to visit the home of a
family living near Omagh in Co. Tyrone, who were
suffering terribly from poltergeist activity for over 20
years.

The family told Fr. Collins that they had continuously
heard the sound of a child crying, witnessed the shaking of
fixtures and distinctly heard the noise of a man's footsteps
treading across the upper floor of their house. The
disturbances had become so bad over the years that the
entire family ended up living in the downstairs area of the
house, which was a considerably large and old building.
'The noises were intensifying and it was having a very
upsetting effect on the family as their children had to be
moved out of their bedrooms,' said Collins.

'I felt very uncomfortable about going there in the first
place because it was all new territory to me. I was just
going on my best instincts regarding what I might do when
I got there and I was very relieved to find that these people
were actually genuine in their fears. When I had
previously talked with them over the phone, I discovered
they had never come up with any explanation or theory
which might help explain the disturbances they had so
long endured. I encouraged them to try and find out what
might have happened in that house, which was over 200-
years old, that could have lead to this haunting. I find it's

just like in medicine, you have to diagnose what the problem is before you can cure the symptom,' he said.

According to Collins, a week before he arrived, the woman of the house, who did a bit of hairdressing on the side, heard an intriguing story about the building. She was cutting the hair of an elderly neighbour who asked her had she known that an awful incident to do with a child, had taken place in that house many years before they'd bought it. 'A child was badly abused in that house at the hands of a man,' the owner heard.

'That was the kind of information we needed in order to diagnostically hone in on whatever was in there.' The Dublin priest said he was not entirely sure how he would proceed with this particular situation, but acted on intuition to 'deliver' the house from whatever haunted it by means of blessed salt, holy water and prayer targeted at specific aspects of the house and its spirits.

'I can only theorise on what caused the haunting at the house in Omagh. Sometimes what you get is a projection from a person or a family, of their psychic feelings outwards onto their surroundings. When certain traumatic events take place in a building which are left unresolved, they possibly leave a strong psychic vibe on that place. This family could then have easily picked up on such a vibe. They had one girl who was very mentally disabled, having been in an accident years before and we know that poltergeists are often associated with the repressed sexuality of a teenage female,' said Collins. 'Poltergeists, or noise ghosts, often occur in homes where there are young women. How that operates I have no idea,' he said.

One theory he shares on the phenomenon he calls the 'restless dead' is that 'somehow or other they can't move on'.

'They become stuck, so to speak, because there are things unresolved from their former life and they don't make the transition fully. It's almost as if they need the human community around them to bring the thing to closure and they will keep making disturbances until they are acknowledged, and in time, their issues are resolved so they can be sent over to the other side,' he said.

In the Omagh incident, Collins prayed with the whole family, 'commended the child to the spirit of the Lord and commended the soul of the man who had done the deed to the forgiveness of God and to the peace of God.' He prayed for the house to clear it of any sort of presence that was there. To the family's amazement and relief after 25 years of chaos, and to Collins' credit, the ghosts at their house ceased being a problem.

'It's up to the people that are here now to use whatever awarenesses they have to help the restless dead on their way. I am confident that the power of God and the power of the Holy Spirit is very great in all of these situations,' he said.

Despite his emphasis on the power of faith and his belief in the existence of the Holy Spirit, Collins is convinced that you also have to be open to the psychic area of the mind to be able to deal adequately with these phenomena.

'When faced with hauntings, the laity resort to the church, which generally means the local priest who, more often than not, hasn't a clue. If he's a man of good will, he will say a prayer and bless the house, but priests have to be more knowing than that to deal with these issues.

'You need to have a sensitivity, almost an empathy to what is going on and to be able to operate on a world view, which is wider than the naturalistic and rational world views held today. You need to be at one with the spiritual and in order to deal with spirits on a serious level, you have to take the psychic very seriously,' he said.

Collins' link to the psychic, he believes, is a genetic one. 'When I was very young I had the impression that my mother was psychic and that the women in her family, including her own mother and her grandmother, also had extraordinary intuition.' He recalls stories of his great-grandmother baking a cake. She would suddenly announce to the room that 'so-and-so would visit today' and it would be somebody who wouldn't have visited for years but, lo and behold, they'd arrive.

'I believe I picked up on whatever was in her side of the family, because I used to get strange awarenesses of things from an early age, which were hard to explain. I'd get weird intuitions of things that I felt were going to happen and then find out they did happen,' said Collins. He cites an example, which occurred shortly after he was ordained in 1971. 'In the 1970s I was teaching in Northern Ireland. I remember coming out of one class to start another and trying to remember what class was I going into when, out of nowhere, came a blinding intuition that Charlie Chaplin would die on Christmas day of that year. This was during the summer.

'I was so certain of this piece of information that I grabbed a colleague and asked him to remember that I had said this thing. He looked at me like I should have been taken away for mental examination, and over the next couple of months nothing else was said on the matter.

'Christmas morning came around and Charlie Chaplin was all but forgotten until I got out of bed and turned on the radio. The first piece of information that reached me was that Sir Charles Chaplin had died. My friend whom I'd told, asked if it frightened me that I'd foreseen this thing, and I said, "no, it would have frightened me if he hadn't died because I was as certain of that as I was of my own existence."'

In another incident, Collins believes he perceived the death of his own mother. 'My mother was telling me about an old friend of hers in England who she had been talking to on the phone. I remember she said to me that it was a pity because she didn't think she'd see him again due to the fact that he was sick and she thought he'd die soon. When she said this to me I got a flash in my mind, which said, "no, you won't see him again because you'll be dead in two weeks." I didn't say this to her, of course, and she was not sick herself, but as it turned out, she did die peacefully exactly two weeks later.'

The Roman Catholic Church sees divination as a sin against religion because, as Collins explained, 'it is an attempt by human powers to know and control the future and is not dependent on God.'

While the Vincentian cleric adheres to church rule on divination, he sees psychic ability as 'a natural power' and states that 'the gift of telepathy or clairvoyance shouldn't be seen as either divination or the occult. It should be seen as a natural ability like music, which some people may have and others may not.

'When it falls into popular usage it does get mixed up in the occult and all kinds of spooky stuff,' said Collins.

'These things should be the object of scientific research, and investigated in a scientific manner to judge if they truly exist or not. These are the new frontiers of the human mind,' he said.

A belief in his own psychic abilities and an initial desire to investigate the 'further reaches of human nature' led Collins to join the Charismatic Renewal in 1974. Founded by a group of US Catholics in 1967, this cross-denominational movement proved an ideal outlet for Collins' work. The Charismatics believe that through the Holy Spirit, they can identify physical ailments in a person from a distance and heal them, sometimes instantly, through prayer.

'It's a prophetic and natural gift where we are able to use psychic sensitivities,' he said. In effect, the Charismatic faith pulls on the supernatural powers to allow its ministry to work. It has returned to a more traditional Christian ethos in that its beliefs are more 'God centred' than 'church centred'. The Charismatic emphasis on heightened emotion and increased lay involvement created an initial rift between it and the Catholic Church during the 1970s and the Vatican has only recently endorsed the movement.

Collins describes a system within the movement known as the 'Word of Knowledge', where he is guided though his own psychic sensitivities by the voice of the Holy Spirit. He said this operates on a number of settings.

'For example, if you were hearing a confession you might get a psychic sense of what a person may have done without them telling you. You wouldn't know how you knew, but you just knew that this person had done X or Y.

'Another way the Word of Knowledge works is during healing services, which we regularly hold, where you would get either knowledge into your mind or a picture in your mind of someone who is going to be healed in the audience. You'd know who and where they were and what was wrong with them in your mind's eye without having physically seen them and it can be quite detailed sometimes,' he said.

He describes one such example from a 'mass for healing' he held in Lurgan. 'I remember I could see this woman in my mind's eye, what she looked like and how she was dressed. I could sense where she was sitting in the congregation and I knew she had a very bad back, and that she was in great pain.

'She had apparently been in great pain for many years and had been recommended to attend this particular mass. I mentioned all of this during the mass and we prayed for her. Afterwards I was approached by the woman I had seen, who told me her back had become better in the course of the ceremony. She got better in just a few minutes.

'Those strange forms of awareness, which are always in the background, are completely natural and can be used by the Holy Spirit for the purposes of healing. It's a combination of natural and supernatural,' he said.

The Charismatic Renewal has produced thousands of lay ministers who act autonomously and without sanction from bishop or bureaucracy. They travel around the country from prayer meeting to prayer meeting, carrying out healing and deliverance ceremonies on request.

One such lay practitioner is Dick Moore, based in Bagenalstown, Co. Carlow. Now in his early 70s, Moore says he has seen it all. 'I've been spat on, puked at and cursed at by people whose lives have been overrun by evil spirits.'

Moore describes himself as a Eucharistic minister and claims to carry out his own brand of exorcism, which he prefers to call 'deliverance'. 'I have the advantage that I'm not going to get a rap of a crozier because I don't represent anybody except Christ and the Holy Spirit,' said Moore. The Carlow Charismatic is less keen on the promotion of psychic ability than his fellow Charismatic Renewal member Fr. Collins, believing it leaves the human soul open to all sorts of evil influence.

'We're dealing with something from another dimension here and, just like the wind which we can't see, we only get to feel the effects of it after it has struck. God created us with free will, but he doesn't unfold our future before us. If it was for our good, he would show us the future and when you sneak out and take a peak at the future behind God's back, you are putting yourself offside, and in most cases you come under the protection of the other side.'

Moore's view of the supernatural is more black and white than that of Fr. Pat Collins'. 'The spirit world is divided into the Holy Spirit and the other side, which is ruled by the devil,' said Moore.

'If we go down a certain road or open ourselves to outside channels through fortune telling or by using tarot cards or the ouija board, we tear a hole in this transparent screen between us and the spirit world, and that portal will not be closed again until the person is delivered,' he said. 'It's not enough to throw away or burn the ouija board because the person has already opened a channel to the other side and so they remain vulnerable.'

Moore is called out to investigate dozens of hauntings, poltergeists and demonic possession every year. 'I've come across the nicest people who would end up spitting, puking and cursing at me because some side of their personality was not under their full control,' he said. 'I've even seen people turn their two eyes towards each other until there is just white. No one should be able to do that. I've seen hands and fingers crooked and locked hard, like you'd imagine a witches' hand to be,' he said.

According to Moore, he receives 'prompts' from the Holy Spirit when he is dealing in healing, or with delivering people from evil. In one instance he cites the story of a teenage girl, who was brought to him by a concerned parent who said she was witnessing apparitions and talking in 'evil sounding tongues'.

'I got an image of something to do with her hair and I told her "the Lord said every hair on your body is sacred". I reached out to bless her and to touch her hair and she made the most awful cat hiss at me over and over again. When I looked up, her hair was standing up as if she had been electrocuted. She straightened her self up and charged straight at me. I caught her and said, "In Jesus' name, I rebuke you" and she fell to the ground. It transpired that she had had a lock of her hair taken during a witchcraft ceremony a number of years earlier,' he said.

Moore's take on the opposing powers of good and evil is fairly clearcut. He follows the line that 'the enemy, the devil, is always trying to trip us up'. 'I'm a nuts and bolts gospel guy, and I know if you do this, according to the Holy Spirit, it will work. I'm no theologian but I've met all kinds of things. I've seen the lame walk,' he said. According to this lay minister, there are many levels on which we can be left open to demonisation besides 'dabbling in the occult' and that it is not always the person who becomes affected by the other side, but sometimes it can be their environment. He talks of a young couple who moved into a house and when they put in a new central heating system, thought they had disturbed some kind of poltergeist energy because strange things began happening around their new home.

'These people had a young son who started having nightmares in the house, and talked about these things he could see in the shadows,' said Moore. 'Then the mother began hearing things around the house every night, and she saw objects move on their own, papers would rise off tables, float around for a small bit and drop suddenly to the floor. But the husband heard nothing. On my word, she went out to collect a priest to have the house blessed and, when she came back, she said she could hardly keep the car on the road. It was as if something didn't want her to get that priest,' Moore said.

'When we looked into her history, we found that she had used the ouija board as a teenager so we delivered her from that and asked God's forgiveness but the noises continued. It later came out that her mother had also dabbled when her daughter was in the womb, so we had to close the door on that one also after which the haunting stopped.' Moore calls this kind of supernatural phenomenon, a 'familiar spirit', which he says will continue down generations until it is delivered. 'I believe that when a channel is opened to the other side it will follow down through that person's genes for their descendents to inherit.'

Although poles apart in their approach to dealing with areas of demonisation and most aspects of the supernatural, Fr. Pat Collins has also formed a theory on the probability of spiritual activity being passed down genetically.

Collins was contacted some years ago by a woman in Dublin who was seeking advice, or a possible cure through prayer, for her teenage daughter who was suffering from anorexia for over six years.

'I had heard of various theories, which revolved around healing the family tree, where the unresolved problems of ancestors were laid to rest,' he said.

These theories suggested that some of the psychological problems which people suffer, have nothing to do with their present life's history, but are interrelated with the spirits of their ancestors and that, if you deal with 'unresolved problems' contained in the family tree, you can break the connection that is leading to the current situation.

'I was sceptical of such theories that said the spirits of the dead could influence the living on a purely psychological plane, because I have great faith in psychology, but I thought there was no harm in holding a mass at this woman's request,' said Collins.

The mother of the anorexic teenager asked that a requiem mass be said for all the deceased members of the family and to commend them to rest in peace so that some form of connection might be broken for her daughter's sake.

'I had a fairly detailed family tree drawn out on a sheet of paper with all the names, particularly on the female line, set down. In doing this we picked up a good deal of information about the problems faced by some of this girl's ancestors, and prayed for their peace and commended their spirits to God.' To Collins' surprise the girl was to overcome her anorexia soon after.

Coming from an academic background and having written numerous books on spirituality, psychology, and religious belief, Collins is certain of the benefits of psychology in helping people overcome a wide range of problems. However, he also recognises an area, which he calls 'spiritual neurosis' that 'may be cured though the power of the Holy Spirit'.

'There are many psychological reasons why somebody would want to commit suicide, but a spiritual person might say that in some cases it's not just psychological and that there is an impingement on their personality, which they need deliverance from. As in the case of demonisation, it's like having a spiritual neurosis.

'There is evil impinging on a part of a person's personality that they need deliverance from. In order for this to work, that person needs to co-operate fully, because you can't go against their will in these cases,' said Collins.

Despite taking a more hands on approach in his deliverance techniques, Moore is aware that he is also 'dealing with two different personalities' and so must adopt a suitable approach.

'You have to be gentle on the person but you won't be gentle on the demon,' he said. 'In the medical field when someone has taken a knock on the head, you try to keep them from slipping into unconsciousness by talking with them; it's the same with demonisation. You try to keep the real person with you all the time. When the demon speaks out you tell it to "be quiet, I'm talking to a child of God." You keep the contact open with the person and stop them from getting submerged under the other thing until you can separate them from the entity they are trapped by.'

Island of Lost Souls

The small port of Cobh on the southern shore of Great Island in Cork harbour has provided a backdrop to scenes of fierce poverty, immense desperation and soul-wrenching tragedy over the course of its short history.

During much of the nineteenth and twentieth centuries, more than three million destitute souls passed through this small island town seeking passage to a better life abroad. Many secured steerage onboard ships and managed to reach the new world. A great number never set foot on dry land again after embarking on ill-fated transatlantic crossings, while those without means found themselves stranded and forced to beg, rob, murder or starve on the streets of Cobh.

Great Island is a place of mass burial. Here, within the walls of the island's old graveyard, lie hundreds of unmarked graves, many piled with corpses of unknown shipwreck victims. Cobh is also famed as the last port of call for the equally ill-fated RMS Titanic. From the 123 passengers who boarded the hulking vessel on its disastrous maiden voyage out of Cork harbour only 44 would survive.

It is little wonder, with such a wretched past of human calamity, that this small port town has one of the highest counts of unconnected hauntings and paranormal experience of any in the country. Eerie reports from varied sources across the island suggest that Cobh's lengthy history of transient human cargo has left a ghostly pall over its streets and houses.

Classic poltergeist hauntings, ghosts of bleeding soldiers and hooded women, black dogs, spirits of destitute mothers and their infants, phantom funerals, spectral corpses piled high and wandering lost souls are just a taste of what Cobh residents have come to fear and, in some instances, take for granted as part of the scenery in this picturesque seaside resort.

Today, Cobh is a vibrant and desirable place to live, just 15 miles from Cork City, where homeowners enjoy strong property prices and the benefit of breathing clean sea air. But beneath the charms of this popular holiday destination lies the greatest concentration of independent ghost sightings from anywhere around the country.

Such is the wealth of Cobh's supernatural activity that it recently prompted the establishment of an organised ghost tour to capture some of the residents' experiences. The Original Ghost Walk of Cobh is run by former Irish naval officer and author of the Titanic Trail, Michael Martin.

His walk takes in the town's more sinister locations where the dead are known to haunt to this day. Martin claims that participants on his trail have 'on more than one occasion witnessed paranormal experience en-route'. Cobh is also home to Helen Barrett, the White Witch of the Isles, who grew up in the town, where she developed her psychic abilities to become one of the country's leading clairvoyants. Barrett remains unfazed by the volume of supernatural phenomena on the island 'due to the amount of suffering and anguish felt there over the last 150 years'.

She has had regular ghost and spirit sightings around the town ever since she was a teenager and said that the island lies on a 'portal to another dimension where the spirits of the dead can easily pass into our own world'.

'The ancients told of 12 gateways in Ireland, which act as portals into another realm and it is known that one of these lies in Cobh,' said Barrett. The first settlers to arrive in Ireland from mainland Europe landed in the south. In ancient times Great Island was named Oileán Ard na Neimhid, deriving its name from Neimhid the leader of the legendary third invasion of Ireland during prehistoric times, who reputedly came from Scythia near modern day Romania.

According to Barrett, the island's settlers 'brought mysticism to Ireland and were very much attuned to great psychic powers, enabling them to utilise such a portal.'

The history of Cobh town, however, is far less ancient. Founded in the mid seventeenth century, Cobh remained a quiet fishing port for over 100 years until it was developed as a strategic fortress during the Napoleonic wars of the early 1800s. On defeat of the French Emperor in 1815, Cobh continued to prosper, styled as a British seaside resort, very much like Brighton in the south of England.

While Cobh grew during peacetime and became a noted health resort for the idle rich, it soon became the country's main emigration port during the Great Famine of 1846/48. A desperate trend in human transience carried on for almost 100 years as Cobh became the country's premier port for transatlantic liners during the first half of the twentieth century.

It was here that the bodies of hundreds of people, killed when the RMS Lusitania was torpedoed by a German U-boat in 1915, were brought.

The World War One bombing killed 1,198 of the 1,959 passengers, 12 miles off the Cork coast. The Cunard shipping company, who ran the Lusitania, had their main office in Cobh so it was ordered that all of the survivors and victims be brought to the town.

Up to 700 passengers were rescued at sea and brought ashore by townspeople as walls of corpses and body parts began to pile up outside the Town Hall, which became a temporary morgue for many weeks.

The legacy of the Lusitania and the trauma it inflicted on the town is said to account for much of the ghostly activity rampant there today. The bodies of 170 victims were carried in procession to Clonmel Cemetery, one mile from Cobh town. They were interred in three mass graves and 24 individual plots, while 45 of the dead remain unidentified.

One of the town's more colourful characters, the White Witch Helen Barrett, has reported seeing, along with other Cobh residents, ghostly re-enactments of the Lusitania's mass funeral procession as it leaves the town for the 'Old Church Cemetery'.

'At certain times such as Halloween, when the realm of the living crosses over with that of the dead, you can nearly take a photograph of the phantom procession which is seen trailing mournfully through Cobh time and again,' said Barrett. 'I have been caught up in that procession with others who also noticed they were surrounded by so much grief and so many dead bodies. I have seen the ghost image of bodies and the body parts of the recovered victims from the Lusitania, stacked high outside the library, which was once the Town Hall,' she said.

The White Witch claims that the Lusitania hauntings are a result of 'the enormous outburst of grief and emotion from that time, which has left a very real impression on the fabric of the town.'

'If a person murders somebody there is an enormous release of energy and that energy is retained in this world in what we know as ghost or spirit form. Now, can you imagine the amount of energy released and the outpouring of emotion that went into the air from the hundreds of people in that funeral procession? Such intense energy does not die, science has proved that energy never dies, it's just like a plastic bag, it will not change for many, many centuries,' said Barrett. She goes on to state that a life cut short by foul means is also more likely to release a stronger energy and so remain as a haunting presence in 'our realm.'

Barrett's view on 'death by foul means' is supported by the chilling theory that the passengers on RMS Lusitania were, in fact, sent to their death by the British authorities.

The sinking of the Lusitania has been shrouded in rumour of political espionage and British government cover-up, unresolved since the First World War. Many, including the present owner of the sunken wreck, American millionaire Greg Bemis, are of the opinion that the Lusitania was not used solely as a luxury liner. Some believe it contained military cargo, including 20 tonnes of mustard gas, highly explosive gun cotton and 12 naval cannons, en-route from New York to Liverpool.

Bemis proffers the theory that the British government secretly provoked the attack on the ship in a deliberate attempt to bring the Americans into the war. There were almost 200 American nationals on board.

Portals to other worlds and political espionage aside, the residents of Cobh have long been scared, thrilled, entertained and physically pushed about by supernatural powers coming to the surface in their town.

In the summer of 1994, Christine Kelleher and her brother-in-law, Dan Noonan, met with a 'terrifying apparition of a lady, hovering above the ground and wearing vintage clothing,' down by the deep-water pier behind Cobh's Heritage Centre, reputed to be one of the town's most haunted buildings. The experience left the pair shaken and 'literally sick with the fear'.

'I had to go down to the pier to collect a key from my husband who was working as a watchman on board a tug tied up behind the Heritage centre,' explained Kelleher, who was driven to the pier in Noonan's work van. 'I was sitting in the passenger seat and was fairly high up so I could clearly see the pier and the tug. We parked right outside the locked gates of the pier. I stayed in the van and Dan undid the gate and walked down to the ship. A short while after he'd gone on board I saw a woman walk straight through the barred gates, which Dan had shut behind him. She was dressed in a red cape with a black band around the hood,' said Kelleher. 'I ducked down in the van I got such a fright. A dog wouldn't get through those gates let alone a human being. What I saw was a girl in her early twenties and she was definitely not of this time judging by the way she was dressed. It was as if she came out of the wall of the heritage centre, passed through the gate and down the pier and then vanished.'

Kelleher described the apparition as being 'so terrifying it seemed to last forever, but I know it was in front of me for a matter of seconds.'

'I'm in no doubt that what I saw was a ghost because it disappeared completely, and there was absolutely nowhere she could have gone. There were no laneways, doors or corners, she just walked through a locked railing and vanished.' It wasn't until Noonan returned to the van with the keys that Christine was satisfied she had not been hallucinating. 'Dan came off the boat and made his way back to the van in a very shaken manner. He looked at me and said, "did you just see that?"'

The brother-in-law's description of a cloaked lady was a perfect match to Kelleher's vision. 'I opened the gate, closed it behind me and walked down the quay to the tug where Michael was working,' said Noonan.

'I first noticed this lady walking along the inside of the wall of the heritage centre as I climbed the ladder out of the tug. I didn't pay too much attention to her until I realised that the figure was floating along, more so than walking. She was moving along in this way for maybe 30 seconds in a red cloak, which reminded me of fashions I'd expect to come from the early 1900s.

'If Christine hadn't said she saw the same thing from a different angle I wouldn't be talking about it today, but having two people see her made it very real for us,' Noonan said.

According to Kelleher, her description of the woman's costume was supported by an elderly woman in the town who told her that 'indeed, years ago they did wear black bands on top of their hoods, which were very often red.'

'It was my only experience of a ghost in the town and I don't want to have another because we were both very shaken and literally sick with fear afterwards,' she said.

It was from this quay, according to Titanic Trail author Michael Martin, that tenders from the White Star Line Company picked up the 123 passengers waiting to board the RMS Titanic lying at anchor less than a mile from the town on 11 April 1912.

The vivid colours used to describe Cobh's Deep Water Pier apparition, tie in with theories put forward by experts in the area of paranormal. 'There are many instances of hauntings by white ladies across the world and particularly in Ireland. This is because the energy released at the time of death will often not sustain its colour over time,' said Helen Barrett. 'A person in the sixteenth century might have seen the ghost of a woman in a red shawl and blue bonnet but if you saw her today she might be a pale spirit, all white perhaps, because the image has faded. A ghost is a mental energy, which can fade just like a photograph can. The spirit, which leaves a body when it dies, is a light and that light is enough to imprint on our consciousness like that of a photograph. This is where the saying "a light went out" comes from when somebody dies, because that is exactly what happens,' said the white witch.

The Heritage Centre features strongly on Martin's Ghost Walk. Originally built in 1862 as the train station to link Cobh with Cork city, the building was also used as a customs hall for passengers travelling abroad and using the Deep-Water quay to board vessels.

In 1994, the year construction of the Heritage Centre was completed, another strange and inexplicable phenomenon occurred. One of the first shops to be housed there was the Irish goods Kilkenny shop. One morning staff came in to find a huge piece of handcut Waterford Crystal taken down from a high shelf and placed in the middle of the floor. It wasn't broken or damaged in any way and it was also noticed that a great many other ornaments and goods would have had to have been moved off the shelves in order to take this large piece down to place it on the ground, but nothing else in the room had been tampered with. No logical explanation was brought forward after everyone in the building had been questioned and the very same thing happened a couple of days later.

Upstairs in the same building at the time of construction, a workman had been given a room as a lock-up for his tools and reported one morning that all his equipment had been strewn about the floor. The only people with a key to this area were the man and his apprentice who got the blame for the mess and had his key confiscated. The youngster professed he knew nothing about it and the following morning when the pair turned in for work the same thing had happened. The man and his helper are said to have made their excuses and left that particular position not long after.

Cobh's reputation as a den of dissolute souls was set down in 1752 by the visiting cleric Rev. John Wesley, founder of the Methodist Church. Wesley is said to have denounced the town as a 'Godless place' and described its denizens as a 'sinful sink of sinners'. Further describing the town he said there was 'nothing to be bought there, neither flesh nor fish, nor butter nor cheese'.

Wesley's puritan dreams for Cobh came to fruition, albeit posthumously, with the building of the striking Wesleyan Methodist Church on Westbourne Place in 1873. Today the façade of the old church bears none of the ecclesiastical hallmarks of nineteenth century puritanism. In stark contrast and undoubtedly to the man's horror, his Cobh ministry is today decorated in beer advertisements with the banner 'Pillars Bar' resting proudly over the old church door.

It is here that staff and customers of the fashionable Pillars Bar are plagued by hauntings and eerie encounters on a continual basis. Bar proprietor Dolores Lyne first became aware of 'a presence' in the building when her assembled team of carpenters, plumbers, and masons embarked on a two-year renovation programme in 1997.

'There came a time after so many unexplained dragging noises, mysterious knocks and bangs on doors and moving tools that we started to joke about it even though we'd lost a lot of help because many people refused to work in the place,' said Lyne.

However, not all the bar's unexplainable occurrences were of such a light or jovial nature, as the new owner was about to find out. 'There was one time I remember when we were having a laugh at one guy's nervousness of the place that the creepiest thing happened to me,' she said.

'I was about to walk up a small flight of stairs when I suddenly ended up on the first landing having only just stepped onto the bottom step. I had been physically pushed from the first step right up to where I fell on my face eight steps higher. It was a definite physical, upward push; there is no way I could have ended up where I did by just tripping. That really rattled me.'

It soon dawned on Lyne that when she talked, joked or alluded to the hauntings in the bar in any form, 'seven times out of ten something would happen directly afterwards.'

The most striking example of this for Lyne occurred during a conversation with the town's Titanic guide Michael Martin.

Martin had just returned from England where he had been researching material from other ghost walks with a view to establishing the Cobh trail. His research took him to churches in York where he learned there was regularly a small door, only three or four feet high, known as the Devil's Door built into the side of a church.

'These doors were included in the structure out of a belief that the devil came in and played about in the church when there was no blessed congregation inside,' said Martin. 'So in order for the congregation to avoid any direct confrontation with the devil on their arrival, church authorities ordered that a small door be built to the side to allow the devil to pass out when anyone entered.'

On his return from York, Martin brought up the concept of the 'Devil's Door' with Lyne and asked had she noticed any such portals, blocked or not, during the renovation process. Lyne told Martin that she wasn't aware of any such door, but during their conversation a glass mysteriously smashed on the table before the two.

'There was nothing extraordinary in this accident, however, when we looked at the table top and began to clean up the glass, we both noticed a very distinctive five shards of glass pointing like five arrow heads in a row towards the eastern wall of the bar,' said Martin.

It transpired two days later, that workmen who were carrying out repair work on that side of the building discovered a small arched door bricked up and under layers of plaster on the outside. 'That for me was very weird,' said Lyne.

'It left me with such a huge sense that something was always listening, always watching us in the bar. The spirit might as well have been having the conversation with us at the time and put in its spoke by way of breaking the glass.'

'I was only then saying to Michael that, "No, there's no arched doorway. Sure I know every stick and stone in the place." I remember he asked again was I sure and just as I told him I was positive, the glass I was about to reach for broke. It wasn't knocked over, it just broke inwards as if there was a force put on it from outside. As I went to put my hand out to pick it up, the top of the glass cracked and smashed inwards and these five shards of glass were left on the table pointing towards one of the walls,' said Lyne. 'I still can't believe that 48 hours later I was outside looking at a blocked up door in that wall.'

According to Martin, the newly discovered door wasn't of the same design as the medieval Devil's Doors described at churches in York but it was a door that neither himself nor Lyne had ever known about.

The incident with the glass immediately came back to both of their minds when workmen uncovered the frame. 'We both believe it was a very strange occurrence or else highly coincidental. We even thought about getting a photograph of the glass at the time but I don't think anyone would credit it, but these are the very things that happen in Pillars Bar all the time,' said Martin.

It remains uncertain as to what exactly haunts Pillars Bar. Some of the locals speculate it is the wrath of the reverend John Wesley coming down on the building because it is now a place of drink and much revelry. However, there has been talk of the building being haunted long before it was ever a bar.

According to Cobh's white witch, a young girl was reported to have been raped at the side of the church in the latter part of the nineteenth century and subsequently ran down to the waterfront and drowned herself at sea.

Martin maintains that the bar is probably the most haunted pub in Ireland. 'Different people feel different things. I myself felt the presence of a very sad woman and always as if something very tragic had occurred in that place. When I have stood upstairs on my own, even in the middle of the day, I'd get a very strong sense of something being present there,' he said.

Lyne is more comfortable with the supernatural inhabitants of her relatively new business premises. 'I do sense a presence – like shadows – in here, but to me it's like they're watching over me so it doesn't bother me. There're no bad vibes even though I think whoever is here gets ticked-off from time to time. Locals say the spirit of John Wesley is freaked out because we're selling pints in here but I don't think so. It's more likely echoes from the 125 years that the building was a church. Owing to the amount of bodies that must have been brought in here, spirits have remained inside for whatever reason but I don't think they're unhappy,' she said.

Unhappy or not, there has been an unwarranted amount of mischief and, at times, damage caused by whatever is haunting Pillars Bar. One of the more clear cut examples of the bar's poltergeist activity was the repeated and identical cracking of one of the mirrors in the ladies toilets. The problem of the cracking mirror was getting out of hand and proving expensive for the new owners after the third looking-glass smashed.

Just days after workers had initially installed the mirrors in the ladies washroom, a large crack appeared in one. The workers thought it was most likely a defective mirror, brought it back and got a replacement. Two or three days later there was an identical crack in the new glass. The contours of the wall were checked, the screws used were changed and the third mirror was more carefully put in place but it too smashed only minutes after being put up.

'I took a spiritlevel down there myself to check the walls and they were dead straight,' said Lyne. 'I supervised the putting up of the third mirror and went back up to the bar area with the carpenter. My husband went down the back stairs thinking we were still down there and when he eventually came up he said to us, "I thought you were going to change the mirror."

'We could only look at him and say that we just had. He naturally thought we were having him on and he brought us down and showed us the new mirror cracked in the exact same way as the first two.' Next time around, they changed the shape of the mirror from a square to oval and it has remained uncracked.

Other activity in the bar includes falling stools, flashing lights, creaking rope noises, mysterious door knocking, footsteps and the sound of rolling bottles. 'The number of nights that my security have had to run up both flights of stairs after hours because of footsteps overhead is colossal,' said Lyne. 'They were convinced we'd locked somebody in upstairs. In truth, we should never have been able to hear those footsteps, even if there was somebody upstairs because the floors and ceiling were soundproofed when the renovation work was carried out.'

Out on the streets of Cobh the hauntings arise in equal measure. In 1942 a man named Bernie Dahl was walking home one evening along Harbour Row towards the eastern end of the town. He is said to have arrived home to his wife in a fretful condition. Mr. Dahl told his wife he had had the most terrifying experience. As he was walking, he'd met another man, but as they approached each other the stranger walked straight through him. Unfortunately for Mr. Dahl, who was obviously lacking in hard and fast evidence of his encounter, he was faced with a certain amount of disbelief from his wife and sons, but he persisted with his story even though the Dahl family pleaded with him to give it up as he would only become a laughing stock.

To Mr. Dahl's credit, however, it transpired that ten years after the reported incident, repair work being carried out on the pavement where Bernie had walked, unearthed a skeleton in a very shallow grave.

It was said to be the body of a man who had met a violent end and was by all accounts not a resident of the town. There was a garda investigation but no identity was discovered. The remains were thought to belong to one of the millions of individuals who entered the port town looking for passage abroad in the late nineteenth century but met with a foul end. Mr. Dahl felt completely vindicated afterwards and passed away some years later convinced that he had met with the ghost of this cut down man buried under the Harbour Row pavement.

Beneath Cobh's St. Colman's Cathedral, famed for its carillon consisting of 42 bells, the largest in Ireland, lies a set of steps known locally as 'The Rock' where a phantom 'Black Dog' is said to lurk.

Black dogs have their roots in Irish folklore but have also been reported all over Ireland and are feared as an omen of death or violent times. 'I have seen the Black Dog on a number of occasions at the Rock. Black dogs are common in Ireland and although they haven't been investigated properly, they are always evil,' said Barrett. 'They are huge ghostly creatures and are to be found in areas where violence has been perpetrated in the past or in a place where it will soon erupt.'

A black dog was reported in Ballaghadereen, Co. Roscommon, in the early part of the twentieth century. It was said to be as high as the witnesses shoulder and was reported to have walked straight through a closed gate.

'When they are seen you can tell things are going to turn particularly bad usually in a violent way. Somebody will get hit or attacked. Usually when a murderer is present there will be a black dog around because they are negative entities.' According to the white witch, there has been a glut of violent acts carried out at the steps of the cathedral and beneath the arch at Casement Square. The roughest period in the town's history, according to Barrett was soon after Cobh was renamed Queenstown. The name remained on the town for over 70 years, from 1849 following Queen Victoria's visit until the war of independence in 1921.

'There were an awful lot of suicides and violent robberies, which left individuals and families destitute on the street between the two centuries,' she said. 'You can always get a bad vibe around the archway. I have seen tortured spirits there to this day. At the turn of the twentieth century, it is recorded that two soldiers fought over a girl down where the arch is now.

'One of the men got stabbed, he was only 20 and died on that spot from his wounds. I have seen his ghost while walking down there. He was cut and bleeding badly. I was with somebody who also saw him but I was able to tell my companion not to worry about him, he was alright,' said the Cobh psychic.

Just below Harbour Row in his flat on East Beach, Dublin man Ray Allen encountered some nerve rattling experiences over a nine-year period. 'There was always an eerie feeling in the upstairs of 10 East Beach. There was just something not quite right about the place,' said Allen.

'Not quite right' might sound a bit mild for a house where the tenants regularly saw and passed through an old woman walking up and down the stairs and where the furniture and music come to life by themselves, but in Cobh perhaps the residents don't expect any less.

'I was only in there two years and this cab driver in town said to me, "do you know that place is haunted?" I asked him how he knew and he told me he had lived there in the mid 60s.' According to the cab driver, his father-in-law who had slept in the bedroom rented by Allen 'often felt the sheets being tugged off him at night' with nobody else in the room.

'It was weird because I had already felt some creepy things in that room,' said Allen. 'There were one or two occasions that I actually sat up in bed and thought there was somebody in the room looking at me. The light was on, because I'd been reading, but I literally jumped out of the bed and ran out of the room. I couldn't sleep in that room on those nights so I went into the couch and slept there.'

Allen's upstairs neighbour in the two flat house also felt the presence of supernatural beings at 10 East Beach. 'Joe upstairs told me that he'd often seen the figure of an elderly, pale woman walking through the house. I thought he'd be joking but he was deadly serious and said that when he'd be walking down the stairs there'd regularly be somebody walking in front of him who wasn't really there.'

Allen said he just accepted the fact that the building was haunted and he said the whole area around Harbour Row gave him a creepy feeling. 'There was one evening after work when I could hear all this furniture being shifted around up in Joe's flat and I thought, "what is he at up there" but when I asked him about it the next day, he said he hadn't been near the place until after 10 p.m.'

On passing Allen's old East Beach abode with a Ghost Walk tour one evening, Michael Martin was stopped in his tracks by one of his entourage. 'The woman told me, before I even mentioned anything about the house, that "somebody has just come out of that building, but they're very nice." I suppose that's just part of it down here,' said Martin.

CHAPTER SEVEN

Many Lives

Where were you in 1619, or for that matter who will you be in the year 6090? Such cosmic conundrums will not interest too many, but they are the serious questions being posed by clairvoyants and hypnotherapists today.

The phenomena of Past Lives, in which a person vividly recalls having lived at least once before, attests, like the world of ghosts and poltergeists, to the shared paranormal and religious belief that the soul survives the body's death.

Reincarnation is not a philosophy endorsed by Ireland's predominant Christian faiths but, on a world-scale and particularly within eastern cultures, the continuation of the soul to another body after death is one of the most ancient and widespread systems of spiritual adherence.

The nineteenth century German philosopher, Arthur Schopenhauer, adequately described the western condition as follows; 'Were an Asiatic to ask me my definition of Europe, I should be forced to answer him: It is that part of the world, which is haunted by the incredible delusion that man was created out of nothing and that his present birth is his first entrance into life.'

Despite this theological differing of opinions, two of the western world's most famous cases of past life existence have revolved around Ireland and, in particular, around the alleged reincarnation of two long-deceased Irish women.

The claimants of these unrelated past life experiences successfully disclosed historical information far beyond their remit and produced details on their alleged past lives, which were too accurate to be considered mere flights of the imagination.

'Past life regression has become a popular form of hypnotic therapy with a view to unearthing traumas rooted in previous lives,' explained Waterford based hypnotist and clairvoyant, Stan Phillips.

'I've never had anybody famous come back. Never had anyone who claimed they were Cleopatra, Joan of Arc or Jesus Christ; it's the plainness of the lives that come to the surface in past life regression, which makes it so credible,' he said.

Past life regression pulls on the conventional Freudian idea, that our adult behaviour is unconsciously determined by early life trauma. It then goes one cosmic step further and applies itself to reincarnation. While practitioners like Phillips claim that 'we all have the potential to visit previous lives', many are born with distinct memories of those lost times.

In January 1989, an English woman, married with two children and with no family connection to Ireland, arrived in Dublin. She had never set foot in the city or even been in Ireland before. She came to find the children, whom she believed she had given birth to, more that 20 years before she herself was born.

Jenny Cockell, then in her mid thirties, arrived in Dublin with only memory snapshots and recurring dreams of a family and of a place somewhere in time and somewhere in Ireland, which she felt she knew almost as well as her own family at home in Northhamptonshire.

Ever since Cockell had reached the age where she could formulate and recall thoughts, dreams and memories, she was convinced she had already lived a full adult life.

In this past life, she was an Irish woman named Mary, who lived somewhere north of a large city, and who died young, shortly after giving birth to her eighth child. As a child, Cockell was plagued by dreams of reliving this woman's death. In these dreams, she would pass through 'Mary's death experience', staring out hospital windows, which she would later identify as an isolation room in Dublin's Rotunda Hospital. While the death experience was 'terrifying' for her as a youngster, Cockell's constant and overriding memory at these times was always one of immense guilt.

'It was a guilt at having left the children alone in the world without a mother after I died,' said Cockell. 'I was only a child but my mind was dominated by a confusion of emotions that would have been difficult even for an adult to cope with. I knew that through death I had escaped from a bad situation of sickness, but in doing so had left the children on their own,' she said.

This, according to Cockell, was 'an impossibly heavy burden for any small child to bear', especially when they had no way to rationalise such dreams. From these early dreams and waking memories of Mary and the children, Cockell drew a link between her other life and Ireland. Through her own 'psychic intuition' she also pinpointed Malahide in north Co. Dublin sometime in the early twentieth century as the most likely time and place for this shared existence.

One of the most striking pieces of evidence to support Cockell's past life theory was a series of maps she repeatedly drew as a child. These were drawn out of memory of where she felt Mary had lived. In 1980 she ordered an ordinance survey map of north Co. Dublin from a local shop in her hometown in England. She told the owner why she wanted it and when the map arrived, she brought her drawings in and found that all the roads marked appeared on the official map. The direction of the train station, her pointer to 'the city of Dublin' and the distance between roads were truly well to scale.

Cockell now realised she had been drawing a reasonably accurate map of Malahide and she became filled with determination to find the children she felt she'd left behind.

Jenny Cockell began to make notes of her past life memories from an early age, and would later publish a compelling account of her successful search for her past life family in her book *Yesterday's Children*. It wasn't until she reached adulthood, with children of her own and Mary still a huge part of her life, that Cockell decided to put meat to the bones of these dreams and set out to look for her past family.

'I knew that I had to try and find Mary's children or my life would always be shadowed by the memories of the past, of grief, anger and loss,' she said. 'The most frightening time of all was when I was very small. I remember thinking "alright this is a dream, so naturally I can change it to make them all stand around me smiling",' she said.

'But I just couldn't do that because it would have been a lie and not what had happened. Inside I couldn't alter what was in my past life,' she said.

It is a widely held belief that the stereotypical child's 'imaginary friend' is, in fact, that youngster's contact with memories of a previous life. This contact tends to be broken as adulthood approaches but, in many cases, confused memories of another existence continue to recur and in the case of someone like Cockell, who claims to have psychic abilities, would remain much to the fore.

The constant sense of guilt at leaving her children drove Cockell to partake in a series of regression therapy hypnosis sessions as an adult.

These sessions would further fuel her conviction that Mary and her children were real people and that she was a part of their lives and of that family who had lived in Dublin sometime between 1898 and 1930.

Cockell began a course of hypnotic regression in 1988. During the hypnosis, a cottage in Malahide was always the 'most consistent feature'. She was now able to see Mary more clearly and could account for at least five children, but felt there might have been as many as eight.

In one session, Cockell had a very vivid recollection of a snare being set behind the cottage to trap wild animals. The trap was set, she felt, by some of the older children. The eldest boy was about 11. The snare was checked daily and she recalled the boy running in telling the others that they had caught something. Cockell remembers coming out of the cottage looking over the heads of the children at a hare in the trap and saying, 'it's still alive'.

During the regression therapy she also pieced together a more concrete geography of the town where Mary had lived. Armed with fresh memories from the hypnosis sessions, she travelled to Ireland and to Malahide where, after much searching and return trips, she eventually came face to face with many of her 'lost children', now decades older than her.

The beginning of this arduous search took Cockell to the ruin of a cottage in Malahide, located as she had drawn it as a child, as 'the first on the left of a quiet, westward lane outside a small village'.

She also found the church she had seen through Mary's eyes and had drawn as a child. It was a Church of Ireland church and was recalled, not because Mary attended it, but because she passed it every day to visit her sister at the other end of town.

'The regression therapy brought everything to the front of my mind in a very three-dimensional form,' said Cockell. 'As I had gone through my teens, I had managed, more or less, to subdue the memories of this family and slot them into a certain place in my life. After the regression the memories were so much to the front of my mind again, that I didn't really have much choice but to go ahead and try and trace my other family.

'If I hadn't done the hypnosis I may have been able to chug along and piece the clues together. It still would have been something I had to do, because at this stage I cannot imagine not having gone ahead with it,' she said.

Cockell's search took her to a place she knew belonged to Mary's life, but the Malahide of 1989 was a very different place to Dublin in 1920. The cottage in her dreams was now an abandoned ruin and the children all gone. With the help of local historians, Mary was identified as a Mary Sutton, who had indeed lived in a house in the lane described in Cockell's visions and had died at an early age after giving birth to her eighth child.

Unfortunately for the past life researcher, Mary's children were scattered after their mother's death to various orphanages and industrial schools around the country.

After a lengthy campaign of placing advertisements in national newspapers, Cockell began to get results as to the whereabouts of Mary's children. Her greatest triumph was finding Mary's eldest son Sonny, then in his 70s, who had been adopted and come to live in Leeds, England.

Sonny was able to confirm as true most of the memories held by Cockell of her life as his mother. She recalls telling him of the stonewall outside the family cottage, which was 'uncomfortable to lean on' because of small, protruding rocks along the top. She talked at length about the characteristics of his brothers and sisters, whom she had never met and could not have possibly known about. She then described a moment in Sonny's life when he was about 11, which sealed their rather tenuous relationship forever.

She recalled the snare, which the children had set to catch rabbits at the back of the cottage. Cockell accurately described the position of the snare and the fact that it was early morning and that the trapped creature was still alive when they came upon it.

'I talked for a few minutes about that morning and then he just looked at me blankly and said, "How did you know that?"'

In hindsight, Cockell believes she has put a lot of demons to rest by tracing her past life. But, she also admits that she was not always so sure it was the right thing to do.

'I had serious doubts about whether I should approach these people, as a complete stranger, with the fantastic notion of being their parent. What I knew, after all, were highly personal memories to them,' she said.

In the long run, however, she does believe it did a lot of good to contact the children. 'I managed to bring all the surviving children together and Sonny, who died at the start of 2002, opened up to some of the things he hadn't faced in his childhood and which I knew he was glad to get off his chest. I was very cautious and didn't push myself towards them. I knew them like children and the main obstacle I had to get over, was the fact that I wasn't the same to them as they were to me.

'I was a complete stranger to them. Even though I was not their mother, I had always felt that way,' she said. Cockell's visionary intuition was tested further in 1994, three years after she first met her 'past life family' when an American film crew wanted to know what room in the Rotunda Mary Sutton had died in.

'I thought this was a bit of a tall order but I was ready to have a go, and drew a diagram of where I thought I remembered dying as Mary. I felt it was one floor up because I remembered being able to see the tops of the trees from the bed.'

From the diagram, the matron of the Rotunda was able to identify where the room was. It was an isolation room in the old part of the building.

'When I first went in with the crew, I saw two windows and thought, "no, that's wrong" because I could only remember one window as Mary. But when I went over to where the bed would have been, there was a pier on the wall, which stuck out far enough to block out the view of the other window.'

Revisiting that room in 1994 helped her to realise how silly she was to harbour any guilt for leaving her children in death.

'I eventually realised that there was no way of avoiding death for Mary and I should never have felt bad about dying, but as a child I could never understand this,' she said. Mary Sutton died in the Rotunda Hospital on 24 October 1932 of gas gangrene, septic pneumonia, and toxaemia.

'There was no way she could have pulled back from that. There were no antibiotics for such illnesses at that time, so death would have had to be accepted,' said Cockell. 'Up until that point, however, I hadn't emotionally accepted death as the only possibility. It was a big turning moment for me,' she said.

While vivid in its detail, Cockell's testimony of her past life is by no means unique, nor is her passing through Mary's 'death experience' an uncommon theme for those who experience past lives.

'The death experience is one of the most common and outstanding aspects of past life phenomena,' said Waterford hypnotist Stan Phillips.

'When I take clients back into past lives, the moment of death is never a problem for them. They can approach the death of their past life and often say, "oh I died there and now I'm floating, I'm free again". They know that this part of us, which can revisit past lives is never ending and that it continues down all time, so death is not the end,' he said.

Through hypnosis Phillips takes clients back into their previous lives. Some embark on lives lost in the mists of prehistory, while others find themselves entering the mind of a person who may have lived only up to a short time before their own birth. 'Under hypnosis my clients go to places shrouded in déja vû, a place where they unearth memories that are so alien to their normal lives, but so natural to themselves in their hypnotic state.'

Regression clients allow themselves to be hypnotised and according to Phillips, are then taken 'back and back until they have reached a particular place of security and safety where they are able to float.'

'I ask them to land on the earth in fullness of strength and to look around them and tell me where they think they are,' he said. It is at this stage that the regression process generally tends to bear fruit. The practitioner will ask his client 'what they see, what are they wearing' and according to Phillips, nine out of ten times they will begin to talk of distant times. Phillips has applied this method of past life regression to himself and discovered up to 'seven previous lives' he is directly a part of.

'I know that there are many, many past lives that impact upon my soul,' he said. 'There are two lives in particular, which stand out for me. They hold the same psychological profile, in that they are both highly frustrated individuals,' he said.

Under his own method of self-taught hypnosis, Phillips brought himself back to a time where he was 'a hunchback in a medieval German court'.

'I was just an anonymous face in the crowd, a real nobody,' he said. 'I remember people queuing up to get an audience with the monarch of the time in order to get favours granted but, because I was always ugly and hunchbacked, I was forever at the tail end of the queue. Here I was, this frustrated person being constantly told in life that I could never get what I wanted.'

Phillips revealed that this regression occurred at a time when frustration was an overriding factor in his life. 'I also took myself back to the life of a minor British politician in the late eighteenth century, who I believe held the name of Charles Fox. He also felt a great deal of frustration throughout most of his lengthy career in the House of Commons. This was caused on the whole by the fact that he could never get to the station he wanted, due to Prime Minister William Pitt constantly getting in his way. In my regression as this man, I drank and did anything to relieve this sense of frustration,' said Phillips.

It's through regression therapy that practitioners like Phillips attempt to address the psychological problems affecting their clients. 'It doesn't really matter who you were in a past life, what does matter is that you can learn from the mistakes or take something from the deeds of the life you shared. It's the lessons you take from your past life that impact on the current one.'

Since a child, Cockell also claims to have visited other past lives but these were 'largely untraceable'.

'Long before the regression therapy to find Mary's children, I have always visited other lives. There were three in particular. One of which was very pleasant but also prehistoric so I didn't dwell on it or entertain any thought of pursuing it.

'I was also an illiterate servant in France prior to the Revolution. It was horrible because I was dirty and ugly and not worth anything to anybody. I hated that one because I couldn't push it out of my mind; it was a horrible thing to remember.

'There was also a woman in Japan who I know I was linked with, but there was no point in pursuing that one because there were no children or tangible ties,' said Cockell. After years of talking with researchers on the phenomena of past life existence, Cockell feels certain that 'this can happen to anybody'.

She states that it is most easily detected in children under the age of six. 'Most children have scattered fragments of subconscious memory up to the age of six, which they begin to forget not long after,' she said.

'I don't think we're supposed to keep on remembering these things from our soul's previous incarnations and at around the age of six our brainwave patterns change slightly. At a young age we produce certain brainwaves, which help induce a state of deep meditation, which allows for past life memories to easily filter in, but adults have to work hard to produce the brain activity to bring about such a meditative state and that's where hypnosis comes to our aid.'

Cockell has found, through her own research, that all of the children who remember past lives share similar traits. 'One is that the death of their past life came early and suddenly, and that there is more than likely unfinished business, such as bringing up children.'

'I was a fairly withdrawn child. My home life wasn't any great shakes really because my father was quite aggressive. I'd rather do anything than face what was going on around me, so I naturally focused most of my energies on these other life memories, which were always there with me. The reason I tended not to forget them as I grew up was because I depended on engrossing myself in them, partly as a form of escape. I became extremely belligerent not to let them go. It seemed the more that people told me they weren't real, the more determined I became not to forget them, because they were so vivid throughout my early life,' she said.

'I always felt puzzled that others seemed unable to remember any of their other lives and, at times, I found it difficult to believe that they could not,' she said. Although a daydreamer and under achiever at school, Cockell later became a member of MENSA, the organisation for people with IQs in the top two per cent of the population. This enabled her to contact Irish Mensa members, who would later assist her in her search for Mary's children.

Cockell puts her past life experience down to reincarnation and is of the opinion that she 'actually was Mary Sutton, because the memories are so personal. I see it as the same soul, which could go on eternally. Obviously the physical form changes but mentally I am part of that soul that made up Mary and countless others, no doubt,' she said.

The most popular theory held, but rarely embraced by western cultures on past life regression, attests to the ancient belief in the reincarnation of the soul. Reincarnation, as espoused by the ancient Egyptians and Greeks, and held as religious dogma within Buddhism and Hinduism, in principle denotes that after death, the human soul or spirit of a plant or animal may live again in another human or animal.

The survival of this soul demands that the human form possess an eternal, non-physical element, or energy, which will not die when the body dies. Despite an outright denial of reincarnation by most facets of Christian teaching, it is a theory which allies itself to the Christian ideal of the immortality of the soul. Yet conventional western culture and religion has largely sidestepped the concept of reincarnation.

Neither Cockell nor Phillips consider themselves religious in the conventional sense, but do share a belief in the continuation of the soul as an energy that cannot die. 'I am connected to my soul, which is taking me down this particular path of my current life and the only one I can live at this time,' said Phillips.

'However, this soul is equally connected to that guy who rode a horse in America 100-years ago. It is also connected to this person who lived in Medieval Germany. All these things are part of my soul's experience but are not necessarily me.'

So, without prescribing to popular religious dogma, how do proponents of past life regression, such as Phillips, account for the phenomena?

'Right back at the beginning of time there was the big bang, a scientifically endorsed theory. Something exploded outwards to create the universe in which we live. The big bang exploded out to fill and create the space, which still grows and grows. Within that moment, that beginning, all the souls and the energy of life including that of humanity existed and were sundered from that one outpouring of energy. Ultimately these souls are lonely, which is why we so desperately seek out comfort and companionship as humans. They are somehow searching for a return to that singularity. These souls have to grow and learn and develop and travel though lives as the universe explodes outwards or contracts. Eventually, I believe, it all comes back together again into a major reunion to mirror the initial bang, but it is an endless cycle,' he said.

'Through hypnosis and my connection with my soul, I can tap into memories and visit past lives. Equally I can tap into memories of the future, where my soul is going to be,' claimed the Waterford clairvoyant. A client attending Phillips' practice displayed signs of entering a future life. Joan (an assumed name), was involved in an unhappy marriage, which according to the 35-year-old Wicklow woman, was coming to an end.

'For two years this woman had been on the receiving end of memories and images, which didn't have any bearing on her present life,' said Phillips.

Joan's dream visions, both during the day and while asleep, were populated by four faces and names. 'The new faces were friendly and she told me she was more comfortable in her daydreams than in the "grim" reality of her unhappy home life.' During a hypnotherapy session with Phillips, Joan embarked on a journey at least 10 years into her future. 'Under hypnosis she had a vision of herself getting married in the year 2010 for a second time, to a man she couldn't identify. In the trance state she mentioned three names to me, which she said meant nothing to her.'

It wasn't until 14 months had passed that Joan returned to Phillips with startling news. 'She was ecstatic. She was still in her first marriage, although separation proceedings had begun,' he said. Joan had been on the Isle of Man for a weekend break with her sister and had met a man with whom she corresponded after returning to Ireland. She met this man again and was knocked back to hear that three of his closest friends, one being his brother, matched the names and descriptions of those people in her visions of three years previous,' recalled Phillips. He admits that, 'time will tell on this one, but she foresaw knowing these people long before she met them and she also saw a second marriage.'

As in all cases of paranormal occurrence, there is much scepticism surrounding the phenomena of past life experience and regression. The jury has been out for quite some time on the subject, and will probably remain so due to the abstract nature of the theories on past lives. In his 1957 book, *Fads and Fallacies in the Name of Science*, Martin Gardner gives his view on the issue. 'Almost any hypnotic subject capable of going into a deep trance will babble about a previous incarnation if the hypnotist asks him to. He will babble just as freely about his future incarnations. In every case of this sort where there has been adequate checking on the subject's past, it has been found that the subject was weaving together long forgotten bits of information acquired during his early years.'

Gardner's dismissive statement came long before Jenny Cockell's successful search for her past life in a country she had no connection with. Gardner's debunking did, however, come on the back of what is probably the most celebrated case of past life regression in the second half of the twentieth century; that of alleged Cork woman Bridey Murphy, documented in 1952 by amateur hypnotist Morey Bernstein.

In a number of hypnosis sessions carried out between November 1952 and October 1953, American housewife Virginia Tighe, then 29-years-old, discovered through hypnotic regression that she shared a life with a nineteenth century woman from Co. Cork named Bridey Murphy. Unlike Cockell's first hand account in *Yesterday's Children*, the story of Bridey Murphy is related through Tighe's hypnotist, Bernstein.

Tighe, a native of Maddison, Wisconsin, had never visited Ireland nor had she ever had much to do with Irish people throughout her life. Under hypnosis, however, she began to speak with an Irish brogue and told her hypnotist that she was Bridget (Bridey) Murphy, daughter of Duncan and Kathleen Murphy, Protestants living at the Meadows,

Cork. Her brother, Duncan, born in 1796, she said, married Aimee, daughter of Mrs. Strayne, who was mistress of a day school attended by Bridey when she was 15. According to Tighe, Bridey married a Catholic man, Brian McCarthy in 1818 in Belfast. She travelled to Belfast by carriage for the wedding ceremony.

The story of Bridey Murphy became legend in 1953 when the American magazine *Empire* commissioned a reporter to spend three weeks in Ireland verifying the account, which was fast becoming a best seller for Colorado hypnotist, Bernstein.

Bernstein's interest in hypnosis began with a chance encounter while entertaining the cousin of a business associate. The cousin, whom Bernstein put up for a night, was a hypnotist and demonstrated his skills on a party guest at his host's house. So impressed was Bernstein that he recalls thinking in his book, *The Search for Bridey Murphy*, why science, doctors, surgeons, and dentists didn't use hypnotism.

Bernstein commenced reading everything he could on the subject of hypnotism. His first client was his wife, who suffered migraines and had attended many doctors and clinics. Bernstein hypnotised her and after a number of sessions she was, to all accounts, cured. He couldn't believe how easy it had been. Word soon got around and he began treating insomniacs, smokers and then began to delve deeper into psychology and eventually 'age regression'. During one session with a subject, Bernstein was alerted to the phenomena of Extra Sensory Perception (ESP) when the subject, with closed eyes, suddenly announced that Bernstein was holding a book and named the title. The hypnotist then held several other objects and his subject described them. Bernstein began to see a distinct link between hypnosis, telepathy and clairvoyance.

It was a short while after this that Bernstein met a man called Val Weston, who introduced him to the concept of reincarnation. Bernstein asked Virginia Tighe to be a hypnotic subject without making her aware of his recent research into reincarnation.

On Saturday, 29 November 1952, he put her in a deep trance and sent her back through several childhood memories and then asked her to go further back to other scenes in her memory.

She began to speak about being four-years-old and being in trouble for picking paint off her iron bedstead. When asked for her name she called herself 'Bridey Murphy'.

Tighe said her mother's name was Kathleen and her father was Duncan Murphy. She also said she had a brother called Duncan and another brother who died very young of 'some kind of black something . . . I don't know'.

When asked when and where she lived she replied 'in the town and the village. In Cork'. She also reported that the year was 1806. Bernstein made tapes of the session in which Tighe said her past life father was a barrister and further on that her husband's name was Brian and she had married him in Belfast. On one tape, Tighe talked of a shop with the name John Carrigan over it where Brian had once bought food. She was also recorded saying they had bought 'foodstuffs' at 'Farr's', another grocers. Under regression therapy, Tighe recalled waiting in a hall and dancing a jig. She said she was a good dancer and liked *The Morning Jig* in particular.

When later approached, Tighe was stunned to hear the tapes and the information she had come out with. She had no memories of the taped hypnotic sessions and simply accepted that she had a previous incarnation as Bridey and got on with her present life.

Tighe's husband pointed out that they had no reference books or encyclopedias in the house where his wife could have picked up all the information. Bernstein decided to see if Bridey had any talents that could be brought out in his subject by 'post hypnotic suggestion' after she had left the trance.

In her third session she talked of *The Morning Jig* and Bernstein told her that when she came out of the trance she would remember that dance.

Tighe was brought back gradually to wakefulness and Bernstein gave his posthypnotic suggestion that she should do a jig for the assembled crowd. According to Bernstein, she walked to the rug in the middle of the room and her 'body became vibrantly alive; her feet were flying in a cute little dance'. Her description of another dance was also confirmed in detail by a lady whose parents had danced the step. After compiling six extensive tape recordings of Bridey Murphy talking through Tighe, Bernstein decided to write his book.

However, his editor decided that the *Search for Bridey Murphy* should also be conducted by independent investigators in Ireland. Noting that neither Bernstein or his subject had ever been abroad, they decided to keep it that way until the book was published.

An Irish legal firm, various librarians and other investigators were hired to search without any contact with Bernstein or Tighe. The search was confounded by the fact that few registrars of births, deaths and marriages were kept in Ireland before 1864. It would prove next to impossible to trace the lineage of a person born before this time. On this news, Bernstein believed he would have to make a trip to Ireland to carry out his own research, which would delay his book considerably. Then information began to filter back from the investigators in Ireland.

A Belfast librarian discovered that there had been a John Carrigan who owned a grocery shop at 90 Northhumberland Street in Belfast.

Further research showed that there was a grocer, William Farr, between Donegal Street and North Street in the city. There was no trace of either shop in 1952 during the regression sessions, however, both are listed in the city directory for 1865-66.

Bernstein also received confirmation of a place called Mourne where Bridey said she stopped enroute to her wedding in Belfast.

As in most reported instances of past life regression, Tighe remembers living through the death of her past incarnation, Bridey Murphy. She recalled on one of Bernstein's tapes how she was 'ditched' intimating that they buried her body in a particular way. According to Bernstein's subject, Bridey died at the age of 66 in the year 1864 after a fall down some stairs.

'I watched them ditch my body,' reported Tighe. 'I watched and there was no night or day like Brian had it,' she said. The term ditched meant very little to those gathered with Bernstein, but he was later contacted by 'an old man in Ireland whose grandfather used the term ditched all the time for burial.'

Bernstein's work is by no means conclusive, and an entire industry has grown around debunking the Bridey Murphy story, but as he said himself the sessions were just a 'personal experiment'. He describes his dabbling in hypnosis as 'the trail of a sceptic, a path first glimpsed when I looked away from business and the latest stock quotations long enough to learn that the wonders of hypnosis are realities, not nonsense.'

– CHAPTER EIGHT –

Cry of Death

A blood-curdling wail on the night air across the Irish countryside carries a spine-chilling note of finality to those within earshot. The source of the wailing is all too apparent, and those who choose to ignore its terrible message block their ears and avoid their darkest thoughts in vain.

This torturous lament is the cry of the banshee and ultimately, the cry of death. There remains a profound reverence and inherent fear of any such unsolicited shrieking across much of Ireland today.

The banshee is one of the most enduring folk legends of Ireland. It is a female spirit said to presage death in certain families by keening and wailing within earshot of neighbours, friends and relatives of the doomed. Sometimes her wailing is heard days, but more often only hours or moments, before the marked person's final breath.

The name *Banshee* comes from the Irish for woman and other world (bean and sídhe). Her roots are lost in prehistory and embedded in lore of early blooddrenched battles between our Celtic ancestors and invading armies.

However ancient the banshee might be, she is still heard today, not generally by those whose death is imminent as has often been reported, but as a forewarning that death

will soon touch their lives. The forlorn, earpiercing wail of
this female harbinger of doom remains a consistent feature
from testimony of those who claim to have heard her over
the ages. Yet descriptions of the banshee's 'physical'
attributes often differ.

She has been seen as beautiful and young and haggard
and old. She is most romantically portrayed as boasting
wonderfully long white locks, which she combs out as she
wails mournfully over and over again.

Despite the name 'sídhe', a term commonly used to
describe characters of the Celtic fairy tradition, the
banshee is not as a rule linked to the fairy faith. In contrast
to the various interactions, which fairy folk are alleged to
have had with humans, animals and their own kind, the
banshee is a steadfastly solitary being. Her only object is to
keen, and she has no interaction with humans other than
announcing to them the imminence of a death.

She has on occasion been reported as a hooded woman
who appears unannounced outside homes, or at the
entrance to a laneway leading to a house where she will
start up her deathly caterwauls.

The banshee has also been described as a lively entity
seen perched on a wall, a gatepost, or a stile clapping her
hands vigorously or wringing them as she repeats her shrill
lament. The most terrifying apparition of this dreaded
spectre, however, is one of the banshee washing the heads
and severed limbs of humans in the streams and rivers of
towns until the waters glow red. It is believed that this
gruesome sight was common before a particularly bloody
battle.

Some believe that her presence is the result of unknown
vibrations picked up by sensitive souls around the time of
death. These vibrations are then translated into sombre

imagery, such as the apparition of a mourning old woman, who wails and moans.

In certain parts of the country, the banshee is also believed to shed her human form and appear at the doors or windows of an appointed house in the shape of a crow, who knocks loudly three times on the wood or glass with its beak to announce its dreaded portent of doom. Of all the spirits in Celtic tradition, the banshee is probably the most frequently authenticated through rational accounts from a variety of witnesses.

Banshee sightings and hearings may differ in the telling, but her message of death is accepted and feared by all, even today in twenty-first century Ireland. She has appeared to families of all class and creed, and does not seem to confine herself to families of Irish lineage, however, there are some Irish clans who claim the banshee comes to them at every death. Whatever her grisly modus operandi, the banshee remains the grim prophetess for individuals of all faiths and social standing in Celtic countries.

In August 1953, a young man by the name of David Dowd living at Rockfield, Claremorris in Co. Mayo, was carrying out repair work to his family home while on two weeks holiday from his factory job. Dowd was 27-years-old that summer, full of life and keen to help out on his father's farm during his break. He was just days into his labours, however, when his chores were cut short by the piercing wail of what he believed to be his own death knell. Dowd was to survive this encounter with the banshee, but tragedy was to strike his family before that week was out. Dowd is now 78-years-old and a well-balanced, widely respected, retired farmer. His many experiences with supernatural phenomena in east Mayo are readily bolstered by peers, siblings, and neighbours alike. He relates his brush with what he now jovially calls 'my friend' the banshee.

'It was the summer holidays and the factory had shut for two weeks so I was doing some plastering work on the walls of one of the rooms to the front of the house,' said Dowd. 'I was there late enough into the night because I was waiting for some of the new plaster to dry before I could carry on. It must have been about 1 a.m. or so when I heard the most terrifying noise coming from outside the window of the room I'd been working in. It was a screaming, which turned my blood cold, and I knew straight away that it was the wail of the banshee,' said Dowd.

His quick deduction on the source of that 'terrifying' sound was largely based on previous encounters with paranormal phenomena close to the family home. The banshee had been heard in the Claremorris area on many previous occasions, often keening through the town itself before a death occurred. Many people in the locality including Dowd, have reported sightings of strange 'lights on the bog' believed to be spirits or fairies. Dowd himself came face to face with various apparitions and 'fairy activity' while growing up and knew from stories handed down, that what he heard now was the banshee's wail.

'A lot of people might think it was just cats, but it wasn't like that at all. I'd heard plenty of cats before and this was much different, much more eerie. It was a long, piercing wail with a slight air to it, but a terrible sound none the less,' he said.

'There was a holly bush out on our lawn at that time and I knew that she was out there under that spiky thing. I was scared out of my wits, but I wasn't going to stand there in the room frozen.'

Dowd got it into his head that he would go and see for once and for all what this banshee was; he would go out into the garden and face it. 'I couldn't leave the house by the front door because it was blocked by dressers and chairs and other stuff cleared out from the room I was working in, so I went to the back of the house. I grabbed a blackthorn stick, which was used by my father on the farm and was leaning against the doorframe. I pulled the door open and got ready to charge around the front of the house, but I couldn't get through the door. I couldn't leave the room. I had the door wide open, but I wasn't able to move my body through it. It wasn't that I was too scared, although I was very frightened by the noise that was still going on, it was as if something wouldn't let me out, I just couldn't move,' he said.

'It was as if there was something pushing me backwards as I attempted to leave the house. It might have been something trying to protect me; I don't know. As I was being held back, I was aware that the wail was going on and on. It's a strange thing, but it was so loud and the force pushing me back so strong that I couldn't tell how long that moment lasted for me,' he said. Dowd was brought back to reality by a call from his mother who was in bed in one of the rooms. 'I remember my mother shouting out, "It's time to stop working now and get to bed David, you're up too late." She never let on she heard the banshee that night, but she knew all about that sort of thing, and had her own personal stories to tell of fairies and strange happenings in the area. I turned back into the house, shut the back door and found myself in the greatest cold sweat I've ever felt. As soon as I was called back to my senses, I noticed that I was wet through. You could have wrung the sweat out of my clothes, it was that bad.'

Dowd's worries weren't to end there, however. The next day he found himself caught in a trance of what he believed was the banshee's making. 'The following morning I got out of bed late, and dressed to come down to breakfast. I found that I'd absolutely no interest in doing anything; it was the most I could do to get a cup of tea into me. I'd lost all interest in the room I'd spent so long plastering the day before and couldn't be bothered in any other area of work on the farm.

'I'd always assisted with farm work when I was on holidays but nothing could persuade me now to get up and do anything for anybody, or even for myself. I can still remember wandering aimlessly up and down the fields for many days after that night. I was in a trance,' he said.

The Dowd family also felt, as they watched their brother and son slip into a 'zombie state', that the banshee had indeed come for him.

'He was like a zombie, just wandering around with no life in him at all. He wasn't doing any work or talking to anybody, it was completely out of character for him,' said David's sister, May Jennings, who still lives in the area. It was David's mother who took the initiative to get her son back from whatever supernatural power was holding him captive. May and her other brother Frank, a carpenter working in Belfast at the time, but also down in Mayo for his holidays, were sent to nearby Ballyhaunis to talk to an Augustinian priest who was alleged to have curative powers.

'There was a Friary in Ballyhaunis and one of the clerics, Fr. Mansfield, was renowned for curing. My mother told Frank and May to see this priest and explain what had happened to me and to ask for his help,' explained Dowd.

They went along with a donation and according to May, 'prayed and prayed with him for many hours to have David restored to the real world'.

'Over the next couple of days I did snap out of my zombie state and managed to recover. Whether it was from prayer or from my family's belief in me, I can't say but I came back to normal, which I never thought I would,' he said. While delighted to see their son and sibling return to the realm of the living, trouble for the Dowd household had only begun. The August holiday was coming to an end and David was able to get back into a routine on time to return to his regular job.

'It was very unlike me to leave a job unfinished, but I had been marked; that's all there was to it, the banshee had come for me. I'd succeeded in shaking the curse, but she had unfinished business now with my family,' said Dowd.

David's brother, Frank, went back to Belfast when the August holidays were over. He was driving his motorcycle towards Cushindal, north of Belfast, where he was supervising the building of a school.

'Frank turned a corner on the way into Cushindal and there was a big rock in the middle of the road,' said Dowd. 'He hit this rock and careered out of control into an oncoming truck and was killed instantly.' Frank Dowd died on 1 September 1953, less than a week after the banshee's wail had been heard at his family home.

'I knew it was the banshee that had a hold of me, but I was brought back and that is why my brother had to go,' he said.

It was common practice amongst large Irish families, whose members emigrated for reasons of employment during the 1950s, to regroup at the parent's home during the summer for two weeks holidays. David's other brother, John and his wife Jane, were also over at the time he fell under the spell of the banshee. They were amongst the last to see Frank alive before returning to their home in Leister, England, days before his death.

'John told us soon after Frank's death that both he and his wife were woken from their sleep by the sound of a powerful motorcycle driving straight through their bedroom the night before the terrible accident,' said David.

The Mayo family's run in with the banshee in 1953 reminded Dowd of a previous experience he had with a mysterious woman near the family home some years earlier. 'I was coming from work in Claremorris sometime in the late 1940s on my bike and, just as I turned off the main road towards home, I met a woman I didn't recognise standing on the corner,' he said.

'I passed her by and maybe 200 yards further along I met the same woman again. I said, "good night", but there was no reply. I continued on the road and about 150 yards up the road, almost at the gate of our house, she was standing at the entrance to our neighbour's, which was known to be haunted back then and still is today. She was dressed in black with an old head shawl. She never looked at me and no reply came from her when I said goodnight for a second time. I knew all the women in the area, and this wasn't one of them, nor would they be out at night in the first place. I can't say for sure if this woman was connected to any banshee, but I put her down as just one more weird experience for me in the area at the time,' said Dowd.

The story of the Claremorris banshee corresponds with other experiences of shrieking, Irish wraiths documented through the years. In lecturer Patricia Lysaght's book, *A Pocket Book of the Banshee*, the sound of this terrible spirit is 'thinner than a human voice and more lonesome than human lamenting.' Lysaght's research has shown comparisons with animal sounds 'especially mating cats and the cry of a vixen.'

All reports of banshee activity talk of the 'extreme volume' and 'extraordinary duration' of her lament. The banshee's wail is an interminable shrill noise, which defies the breathing patterns of any living being. According to Lysaght, the general belief is that the dying person does not see or hear the banshee. This would be true in the case of David Dowd's experience, as his late brother Frank had yet to arrive from Belfast when David heard her cry that night. The idea according to Lysaght's studies is that 'hearing the banshee guarantees your safety.' It is also felt that she does not keen at the precise moment of death, but often days beforehand. Experiences have shown that she is more likely to cry closer to the time of death, when the death of a relative living abroad has occurred. Lysaght relates the following story told by a woman in Dowd's neighbouring Co. Roscommon.

'I remember one night years ago – my father and mother were still alive. It was a Sunday night, a cow had calved and I was up. When I fed the calf I came in and sat by the fire, and had a smoke and a shot of tea. "Well," I said to myself, "before I go to bed I will go out, and have another look at the cow and her calf."

'Well, the very minute I got up off the chair the cry started right outside the window. Well, it put the hair standing on my head. There were a lot of us, big and small in the house at the time, and the cry woke the lot. "What is that?" said my father, down out of the room.

"It is outside the window," said I.

"Put out that light," he said "and go to bed."

"Why?" said I.

"That's it," he said.

"Well," said I, "I thought I would have another look at the cow."

"Now," he said, "don't mind the cow, go to bed."

'I took him at his word, and went to bed. Next morning, I asked him about the cry. "Ah, what was it," he said, "but the banshee." A week later, word came from America that a first cousin of his had died.'

In certain areas of the country, however, the banshee is believed to be an integral part of the fairy faith; a world shaped through centuries of storytelling, witness accounts and encounters with supernatural visions. As an ancient belief system, fairy faith, according to W.Y. Evans-Wentz, author of *The Fairy Faith in Celtic Countries*, 'belongs to a doctrine of souls.' It is a faith 'very much like that wherein civilised and uncivilised men alike place the souls of the dead, in company with other invisible beings such as gods, demons and all sorts of good and bad spirits.'

In essence, supernatural entities purporting to be of the fairy world act in the same way as ghosts or visible and audible spirits.

Regardless of her supernatural lineage, the banshee has long been the spirit of doom, death and bloody warfare. The most famous account of banshee activity in Irish history is recorded in the story of the Battle of Clontarf on 23 April 1014, at which Irish King Brian Boru fell with many of his generals, while successfully holding off Danish invaders.

It is said that the fairy woman, Aoibheall, came to Brian Boru the night before the battle to tell him of his imminent departure from this world. She also appeared to Boru's warrior, Dunlang O'Hartigan, offering him 200 years of peace and happiness if he did not enter battle.

The battle did commence, however, and account tells of the goddess of war, Badb, a manifestation of the banshee, rising triumphant over the bloody scenes. In *The Ancient Irish Goddess of War*, W.M. Hennessy wrote of the battle: 'There arose a wild, impetuous, precipitate, mad, inexorable, furious, dark, lacerating, merciless, combative, contentious Badh, which was shrieking and fluttering over their heads.' While deeply shrouded in mythology and ancient warfare, the Irish goddess of war, Badh, holds as her emblem the well-known 'scald crow' or 'Royston crow'.

Badh has been linked through the crow to the banshee. The crow, it is said, will rap three times on a pane or door to declare its odious intention. Other studies also show that the keening of the banshee will generally be repeated three times before it comes to a halt.

Cork author, Pauline Jackson, tells of a friend of hers, May O'Flynn from Cork city, who received the most 'tragic news' after such a combination of sounds were heard at her house. O'Flynn's experience is told in Jackson's *Ghosts of Cork* book. O'Flynn was in her own bathroom, when suddenly she 'heard three sharp knocks on the front door.' She was alone in the house at the time, and because she was in the middle of washing her hair, had to put a towel over her head before answering the door. However, she was surprised to find nobody there. In the days that followed, O'Flynn was to hear tragic news that 'both her brother and cousin had died in separate circumstances'. An earlier tale of death, as announced by the banshee, was documented by nineteenth century historian, Thomas Crofton Croker.

Croker's report on the demise of Buttevant rector Charles Bunworth marries classic folklore with chilling eyewitness account of the banshee. In the mid-eighteenth century Bunworth, and his two daughters, Elizabeth and Mary, came to live at Buttevant near Mallow in Co. Cork. They were well thought of by both Catholic and Protestant members of the community, and the rector was held in high regard for his benevolent nature towards the poor.

Not long after taking his Buttevant commission, Bunworth fell ill and sent his help, a man named Kavanagh, to Mallow for some medicines. Kavanagh complied, but on his outward journey was assailed by a wailing banshee who told him of his master's ensuing departure. On returning with the medicine from Mallow, Kavanagh met one of the rector's daughters and pronounced in an agitated state, that the 'master is going from us'. His rantings were taken as those from a drunken man, and the daughter chose to ignore such ill words. Kavanagh, however, protested that he was not in anyway inebriated and stated that 'the banshee has come for him . . . and 'tis not I alone who have heard her.'

The notion of a banshee was a preposterous one to the enlightened daughter of a rector, and she dismissed her father's helper out of hand. He insisted on his word, however, and related how he had come to his conclusions.

'As I came through the glen of Ballybeg, she was along with me keening and screeching and clapping her hands by my side every step of the way, with her long white hair falling about her shoulders, and I could hear her repeat the master's name every now and then as plain as ever I heard it.

'When I came to the old abbey, she parted from me there and turned into the pigeonfield next the berrin' ground, and folding her cloak about her down, she sat under the tree that was struck by the lightning, and began keening so bitterly that it went through one's heart to hear it,' came Croker's report of the helper's testimony.

Over the next few days, the rector's health was to deteriorate to a state where it became evident he would not recover. The night before his death, the entire house was shaken by the most ghastly cries of misery running throughout the whole grounds. A number of people had gathered to console and give company to the two daughters as their father lay dying. As they sat, their talk was silenced by a terrible noise coming from the window by the dying man's bed. The sound was the awful wail of a woman's voice and the repeated clapping of hands. The noise appeared to be directed solely at the window by the deathbed. Two gentlemen in the room adjoining the rector's chamber decided to leave the house and discern for themselves where the noise had come from. The men searched the grounds and covered every corner and out building attached to the rectory but found nothing, which would prove likely to make such a racket.

While all was quiet on the outside, the noise had kept up to those sitting indoors and not long after re-entering the house, the two men became aware of the terrible wailing once more. The noise became more pronounced to the group, and was soon joined by a miserable clapping from the window. In the course of events, the rector passed away that night and the supernatural soundings were not heard around the building again.

CHAPTER NINE

Lights on the Bog

They are known by many names. To some they are the 'little people' or the 'shining ones'; others know them as the 'gentry', the 'people of the mounds' or 'the good folk'; but more often in modern Ireland, they are referred to simply as the fairies.

Fairy faith has always had a place in the hearts and imaginations of Celtic people. It is an ancient belief in the presence of mysterious spirits, and of supernatural interference from a hidden realm. They are mischievous, indifferent, vengeful, helpful, and dangerous. They have kept the doors of humans tightly locked at night, and have been seen glowing in the dark, conducting ancient battles with each other or filing in sombre procession to a forgotten fairy funeral.

Fairies are said to be direct descendents of the ancient gods of Celtic faith, the Tuatha de Danann. They are the spirits of warriors and people of this ancient tribe, who battled in Celtic mythology for good against the gods of darkness, the evil Formorians.

Just as ghosts and poltergeists are known to inhabit a world, which occasionally brushes against ours, the spirits of the Tuatha De Danann, the fairy folk, occasionally offer visions to men and women of their world.

According to legend, the Tuatha de Danann were finally defeated at the hands of the Milesians, believed to be half Egyptian and from whom the latter day Irish are said to be descended. The Tuatha de Danann were banished and took sanctuary under the hills from where they are said to rule to this day.

The fairy folk may indeed be the ancient ghosts of pre-Christian cultures, whose echoes have lasted to impact on our present. Their survival today, their character and colourful descriptions, have depended largely upon the handing down of ancient lore. Today's eyewitness accounts, and descriptions of fairy apparition and other fairy related experience hold true to the environment they have long been known to haunt.

It is unsurprising that so many fairy experiences have occurred in similar locations, albeit well scattered throughout the country. The ancient Rath or ring fort, ancient burial mounds, and stone circles are supposed to be the favourite haunts of these mysterious entities.

There are more than 45,000 of these forts in Ireland. Gorse covered and fallen, many of these historic ring forts date back over 4,000 years, while others were built in the early part of the last millennium.

Fairy forts, as they are often called today, are revered as sacred places chosen by fairy people to carry out their mysterious work. Superstition, along with legal heritage preservation orders, have kept many of these ancient forts from the destructive claws of intense agriculture and other construction developments.

It is known that anyone who destroyed or built on one of these forts, or in any way blocked the paths leading to the fort, left themselves open to the full extent of mischief and ill luck, which the fairy spirits residing in that region could conjure up.

Folklorist Lady Gregory, who chronicled much Irish fairy lore towards the close of the nineteenth century wrote, 'The old ring-shaped raths or fairy forts are always fairy haunted. I remember one day searching in vain for one we had been told of. We asked a countryman riding by if he knew of it, but he could not recognise it by any description till my husband said, on chance, "a place the fairies come to".

"Oh the place where the fairies do be; I know that well enough," he said and pointed out the way.'

As in pre-Christian Ireland, the fairy folk are still said to hold influence over our world from their own invisible realm. Even the early Christian settlers recognised their eerie presence, and thought them to be fallen angels destined to haunt our world.

In more recent times, the belief in fairies has remained strong, supported by many eyewitness accounts across the country. They have made themselves visible to numerous soundminded men and women. They have taken away sons and daughters and have caused terrible harm to those who interfere with their lairs.

Fairy size, shape and colouring tend to differ from one encounter to the next, but their identity as the 'shining ones' provides a common description complementing many witnesses reports.

Ard Ban Draoí, or high druidess of the Rose Grove, Eileen Lawrence, had such an encounter with what she believed were the shining ones at the ancient burial ground of Dowth in Co. Meath.

'It happened on a sightseeing trip as I was showing a couple of visiting Welsh druids some of our ancient tombs and druidic sites. We were standing chatting at the grounds of Dowth, when suddenly I could see this amazing bright light shining out of nowhere to the side of one of the mounds. I turned to Mark and said, "can you see it?" and he said, "yeah." We were almost too afraid to speak,' she said.

'It was how I had heard the shining ones, or the Tuatha de Danann, are said to appear. It was a very tall figure of light about eight metres away from us. It was basically a humanoid figure. We could make out its head, arms, shoulders and the upper half of the body. I can't actually remember the lower half of the body, but it appeared quite large,' said Lawrence. 'It was a beautiful experience and one, which I believe was in line with what is commonly referred to as the fairy world,' she said.

Retired Clairemorris farmer, David Dowd, who had his own run-in with the banshee (see previous chapter), lives in his father's home situated just 30 metres from one such ancient ring fort, or 'fairy fort' as the Dowd family call it. Their house is separated from this fort by a narrow road, but one house, now derelict, lies on the same plot of land, and is said locally to be a regular haunt and sighting ground of 'the fairies'.

'We have seen strange fairy lights in this area for years. People would never approach them, or make any effort to investigate,' said Dowd. 'They never really talked about them too much other than to say they had seen "the lights on the bog". I suppose we were scared because so much had been heard about the good and bad dealings with fairies in the past.'

Dowd describes these supernatural fairy lights as 'a soft, warm light as you'd get from the dynamo off a bicycle. It would be nothing like the glare off a car headlight,' he said. 'There'd be a number of bright circles about a foot in diameter, hovering about 10 feet above the ground moving together over and back across the land. We always knew them as the lights on the bog,' he said.

The derelict house across the road, 50 metres to the right of Dowd's own home, shares a field with the fairy fort and has long been the subject of supernatural encounter. 'I was heading out at 5 a.m. for work one dark, winter morning, and the place was awash with incredible light,' said Dowd. This was in a time before rural electrification, so Dowd was naturally shocked by such a vision. 'When you see a streetlight or a torch you can generally tell the source behind it. In this light, the whole house, and for a radius of about 10 yards around the top and sides, was brilliantly lit up. I could see the slates, chimney and out buildings lit up bright as daylight but I couldn't see where it was coming from. I remember I just stood at the gateway and looked up to try and see where the light was coming from, but there was no movement.'

May Jennings also saw the mysterious lights up at the old house. 'It was just a thing we knew happened now and again. We saw it, but never really discussed it; it was felt that the fairies were there and that we shouldn't interfere,' said May.

In recent years, the present owner, also a local farmer, has also seen mysterious illuminations at the house. 'The last time I saw them was sometime in the summer of 2000. It was pitch dark and these lights were dotted throughout the ruin. I know others have seen them many times before me; it's something we don't interfere with,' he said.

Respect for fairy houses, mounds, forts, trees and bushes has always been taken very seriously across much of Ireland. The fairy faith is crammed with stories of paranormal wonder stretching over thousands of years. It is natural that, even in contemporary Ireland, an immense reverence is paid out to what many believe to be mere superstition. However, those affected by the ill work of the fairy people, will readily attest to the need for caution when tampering with the old mounds and fairy thorn trees dotted across the countryside.

Irish druid, Robert Finch, talks of a prominent farmer in Co. Westmeath, who bulldozed a stone circle out of one of his fields because the stones were breaking his machinery. This stone ring, however, was said to be long inhabited by a lively host of ancient spirits who some people believed were those of the Tuatha de Danann.

If the farmer had known the outcome of his impulsive landscaping, he may have thought twice before tampering with the mound. Before the year was out, the farmer noticed that his newly sown crop was far from thriving as it had previously done.

On closer inspection he found that the trace elements and essential soil nutrients had stopped forming in his earth. Over the course of the same year, he also lost £20,000 worth of cattle through fetal abortions. In essence, his land appeared cursed. He tried all methods of agricultural enhancement and took all strands of farming advice, but his land and livestock continuously failed him. At the end of his tether, he approached an open-minded clergyman who knew of Finch's work with healing cursed land.

'This farmer had pushed a load of stones from an ancient circle into the corner of a field, and the ones he couldn't pull out of the ground, he buried deep,' said Finch.

'I found the tops of three stones pointing through the ground in the field and after further searching we unearthed more. From here we substantiated the centre of the circle, and where we knew there should have been stones, which he had removed or destroyed. So, in their place we put crystals into the ground to recharge the earth as it had previously lain for thousands of years,' he said.

When contacted, the farmer was reluctant to talk of his experience due to what he called the 'recurring nature' of these things. 'I would never wish to see that kind of power at work on any level ever again and I'd be afraid that mentioning it might only unearth the worst,' he said.

In Mayo, May Jennings recalls a terrible sickness, which fell on her mother's side of the family after a fairy bush or lone tree was dug up on their land.

'There was a fairy tree in my mother's uncle's field, which was pulled out of the ground and thrown to one side. These trees were said to hold bad luck to anyone who destroyed them, as the fairies met underneath them,' said Jennings.

'I have seen such trees with lights beneath them on many occasions as have many people around.' Lone, or fairy, trees are usually solitary hawthorns, or a ring of hawthorns believed to mark the entrance to a hollow hill in which the fairies dwell.

According to tradition, any human who fell asleep or ate the fruit of these trees, or attempted to destroy them would fall to the reckless mercies of the fairies. 'My mother's uncle fell very ill soon after digging up this tree. He visited a local woman named Betty Muldoon, who people went to for advice on herbal cures and other mental and physical problems. She told him he was to replant the tree, which he promptly did and soon after he regained his health,' said Jennings.

In a 1999 article from the *Irish Times*, distinguished folklorist, Eddie Lenihan, delights in securing the survival of a 'fairy bush' from a multi-million pound roadworks project near Ennis, Co. Clare. Lenihan warned developers that the destruction of the bush would place a curse on the new stretch of road and bring about an increase in motoring fatalities.

The bush, according to Lenihan, was a marker in a fairy path and a rendezvous point for Kerry fairies on their way to do battle with the Connacht fairies. It was under this bush, according to Lenihan, that the Kerry fairies would regroup and discuss tactics. He claims that their blood has been seen on the grass around the tree on a number of occasions.

According to Jennings, a similar tree was also saved from destruction by roadworks in the Knock area of Co. Mayo in 1997. 'They wouldn't cut it down, too much is known about what could happen if fairy trees are destroyed,' she said.

In Belfast, Queen's University plans to further extend the campus, had to be radically redefined after architects accepted advice from folklorists and concerned academics alike, who declared it might be unwise to remove one particularly ominous hawthorn, sited in the middle of the proposed development, due to rumour and legend that it was the stomping ground of the fairy folk.

In *The Fairy Faith of Ireland*, John Boylan from Kilmessan, Co. Meath recalled a man named Caffney who 'cut as fuel to boil his pot of potatoes some of these undisturbed bushes round which the fairies pass. When he put the wood under the pot, though it spat fire, and firesparkles would come out of it, it would not burn. The man pined away gradually and in six months after cutting the fairy bushes he was dead.'

Today, many of these revered fairy trees are seen around the country adorned in rags used as offerings to the fairy spirits. While the fairy faith of Ireland is riddled with tales of ill fortune, falling to those who inadvertently find their actions overlapping with the realm of the gentry, there are also numerous eyewitness accounts of fairy sightings and encounters with mysterious fairy processions.

A retired Donegal truck driver contacted *Paranormal Ireland* to recall his experience with what he could only describe as a 'run in with the fairies.' The man, who did not want his name used because he has never publicly mentioned the incident, is convinced he saw a 'fairy funeral' while returning home in his truck from Limerick approaching Gort in Co. Galway.

'We would regularly go as far as Limerick with deliveries,' he said. 'We had two trucks, which often went out and returned together. When we were coming home one night, about a mile and a half before reaching Gort, I met with this huge funeral procession, so I pulled over to allow it to pass by. I thought it strange at the time, because the funeral seemed to be coming from Gort instead of going into the town where the church was,' he said. 'I also noticed it was a very long procession with hundreds of darkly lit people moving slowly behind a horse drawn hearse.'

The witness said that himself and his fellow driver always stopped for tea in Gort, and when he eventually arrived at their regular watering hole, the driver of the other truck asked him, 'what in the name of God has kept you? I'm here this last 35 minutes.'

'I told him I'd stopped for the funeral; "did you not see it?" He said he hadn't seen any funeral even though he was only 100 yards at most ahead of me all the way.'

Fairy processions are a common theme running throughout eyewitness accounts. In W.Y. Evans-Wentz's study of fairy faith published in 1911, he talked to Sligo man Pat Ruddy, a 'prosperous and intelligent farmer' living beside Benbulben, an area steeped in fairy lore.

'Old people used to say the gentry were in the mountains,' Ruddy told Evans-Wentz. 'That is certain, but I could never be sure myself. One night, however, near midnight, I did have a sight. I set out from Bantrillick to come home and near Benbulben there was the greatest army you ever saw, five or six thousand of them in armour shining in the moonlight. A strange man rose out of the hedge and stopped me for a minute in the middle of the road. He looked into my face and then let me go on my way,' said Ruddy.

According to many, Ruddy should have considered himself lucky, not only for his fantastic vision into the hidden world of the fairy that evening, but for the one reason that not everyone who comes across the gentry live to tell the tale.

Fairies, according to legend, are particularly interested in stealing new-born babies and nursing mothers who, it is said, are made to feed fairy children. They also steal beautiful young women and men who are gifted in music and song.

When a child or adult is taken by the fairies, they are often replaced with a 'changeling', who is put in its place to convince the parents or loved ones that their child, brother, sister or mother is alright. It is said that some people are invited to go with the fairies, while others are taken because they have broken a fairy law or caused damage to fairy ground. In 1948, a young Roscommon man is said to have been replaced by a fairy changeling at his mother's house. The teenager was taken for the sole reason that he was a 'fantastic fiddle player' and according to report, had taken up work building a house on 'cursed land'.

'My aunt's eldest son Joe is known to have been stolen by the fairies, and they left a terrible changeling in his place,' reported Mayo woman May Jennings. 'He went to do some work in a neighbour's house, which was to involve him staying overnight. However, at about 2 a.m. his mother heard a knock on the door and opened it to see what she thought was her son standing before her. "What are you doing back, are you not meant to be starting work first thing tomorrow morning?" she asked. My aunt said he made some sort of a noise as an excuse and shuffled off to his bed. She said that the minute she caught sight of him crossing the threshold, she knew it wasn't her son and she claims to this day that it was a changeling put in his place by the fairies. "They took Joe because he was such a fine fiddle player," she said.'

The next morning, according to Jennings, the lad was too ill to rise and his mother nursed him for a number of days. She swears that wherever she walked in the small house, his eyes would be on her all the time. She came to feel more and more that there was a supernatural presence in the house, and that she could not feel the company of her own flesh and blood.

Joe was to die in Swinford hospital less than three months later after long bouts of fever diagnosed as diphtheria. It later became known that the house Joe was due to begin work on, was marked by spirits and fairies because it was built upon a path that leads to an ancient burial site.

There are numerous tales of how people have retrieved their loved ones from the fairies. It is said that on the evening of 'Bealtaine', 1 May, when the fairy hills open, you can lay a trap and get your stolen relations back. Jenning's nephew was to die young, however, and the family were left with the haunting feeling that he had been taken by the 'gentry' to live his life as an entertainer in their hidden world for all time.

One of the more stereotyped inhabitants of the fairy world is the enigmatic Irish entity, known everywhere as the leprechaun. A virtual emblem of all things Irish, the leprechaun has been regularly sighted, but rarely spoken of for fear of what witnesses euphemistically refer to as the very real 'men in white coats'.

A picture story in the *Irish Press* on 7 June 1967, however, centred on a mysterious little shoe believed to be that of a leprechauns, found in the bog in Co. Donegal. 'But why the belief that it is a leprechaun's shoe?' asked the sceptical reporter.

As an answer, their attention was quickly drawn to the thick heel of the tiny brogue, which was worn down slightly on one side.

When the paper's photographer approached the shoe, which was held tight in a specially built glass box, he discovered that taking a picture of a fairy shoe wasn't going to be as easy as he thought. As the box was held up for snapping, its glass sides suddenly fogged up. 'It doesn't want to be photographed,' said its guardian. The camera was put away and the condensation lifted, but appeared again when the photographer slyly reached for his camera again.

According to the paper, the shoe was not a tourist attraction and it was very rare for it to be shown off in such a way. The reporter concluded that 'condensation or not, he was glad to leave the thing in its case.'

Over the following weeks, the paper received and printed many intriguing letters recounting leprechaun encounters from all over the country.

CHAPTER TEN

Ghost Watch

Pure Flax House in the heart of Belfast held a chilling welcome for the printing company who set up business there in 1991. The ink had hardly set on the first pull off the new presses, when staff became aware they were not alone in their new premises.

Dramatic temperature changes, moving objects and missing files, deathly cries from out of nowhere, soft singing voices and chilling bodily contact with invisible entities greeted workers when they entered the former mill at the centre of Belfast's old linen district. Today the ghostly encounters continue and, in many recurring instances, have left the current inhabitants with an eerie chill.

Built in 1912 as a linen mill to supply an international market, Pure Flax House fast became a place of drudgery, despair and often death for its mainly female workforce, who toiled at looms and spinners for up to 70 hours a week. After 50 years in operation, kept busy through two world wars, the mill shut for good in 1966.

The five storey Edwardian structure had intermittent tenants over the next 20 years, but remained vacant throughout the recession period of the late 1980s. When it reopened as part of an urban renewal programme in the early 1990s, however, the forlorn looking edifice soon threw up the horrors of its not too distant past.

Within weeks of setting up business, staff at the print shop began to report 'eerie encounters'. At first these strange occurrences were thought of as the normal creakings and groanings of an old building. Such innocent theories soon fell short of explaining the sheer volume of paranormal experience, which the building appeared capable of churning up.

Reports of phantom footsteps, a disembodied female voice singing, doors opening and closing of their own accord, swift changes of temperature, and various other unexplained movements all began to filter through staff quarters at Pure Flax House. These claims of poltergeist and ghostly activity were soon offered a healthy dose of credibility when management of the Print Shop called for outside help to identify the source of their troubles.

In 1998, a series of closed circuit cameras were set up around the factory floor designed to feed into a live 24-hour internet website, with a view to capturing some of the ghostly activity for a world wide audience. The 'Ghost Watch', installed by publishing group irelandseye.com, was set up initially as a short term pilot project, but has since captured the imagination of online ghost spotters everywhere.

'We were alerted to eerie encounters with a number of ghostly entities experienced by all levels of staff at the printing works, and discussed setting up our ghost watch project with management,' said John Murphy, editor at irelandseye.com. 'The online response to the webcam system has been enormous. Many thousands of visitors responded in the early months of the scheme with accounts of truly incredible sightings. The ghost watch was meant to be a one week experiment into the paranormal, but interest has seen it last over three years at this stage,' he said.

The ghost watch cameras have also allowed staff at Pure Flax House to maintain their reputation as sane and reasonably minded folk, who came into direct contact with something otherworldly. It wasn't long before management acceded that 'something strange' was at work beside them. 'Many's a time I've got the weirdest sensation that there's someone else here with us,' said Paul McAvoy, production controller at the Print Shop, who was one of the first employees to be 'sincerely shaken' by a seemingly physical presence, which he said reached out and touched him.

'One Saturday morning I was in the warehouse running the press. I was worried that the machine was going to trip so I remained very occupied. I was expecting a colleague in soon after I'd started up. In time I heard him enter, and sensed him coming up beside me. I didn't take my eyes off the press to greet him, but I knew he was there. I felt him tap me four times on the right shoulder and I looked around to greet him,' said McAvoy.

'There was no one beside me. I jumped in fright and did my level best to get back into my work. When he eventually came in, I asked him if he'd been in earlier, but he said he only got in two minutes ago,' recalled McAvoy.

For a short while afterwards, Paul McAvoy's colleagues chided him over his alleged experiences, but the joking soon came to an end. Today, there is hardly a member of staff who has not at some time been affected by an unearthly presence felt while working in Pure Flax House. Most disturbing of all has been a repeated, blood curdling 'cry of anguish', frequently heard ringing throughout the entire structure. Today printers, management, and part-time staff stand resolute in their belief that the listed Belfast building is 'severely haunted and inhabited by at least one supernatural entity.' The most common experience at the plant over the last ten years, has been extreme fluctuations in temperature; a common phenomenon in haunted buildings everywhere. The following testimony comes from the company's accountant, Ali, and editor, Caitlín.

'It was quite a warm morning. We'd been very busy organising stock in the storeroom. We stopped to drink hot chocolate at about 11.a.m. When we returned to the studio, we suddenly felt chilled and remarked on the dramatic change in temperature. The room was ice cold. It felt as if a very cold wind was blowing straight through it, but there was no window open and it was a bright, warm day outside,' said Ali.

'The temperature went so low, I thought I'd need to put my coat on and I remember I shivered for the rest of the day. No amount of work could make us feel warm again,' she said.

This account falls in stark contrast to a separate experience felt in an unlit corridor, which according to Caitlín, 'is always cold'.

On the day in question, however, the temperature rose to a stifling heat, and Caitlín identified this heat as containing the 'warmth of a gas fire, burning candles, melted wax, and sweet incense of an old chapel.'

Far from the haunted confines of Pure Flax House, web watchers also write in to describe eerie visions they have witnessed through the building's web cams. One viewer reported seeing a young woman in old fashioned clothes, 'certainly not an employee in today's workplace.'

'I was casually looking at your webcam in the linen mill site when I saw something that scared me,' said the viewer. 'It was in the corridor. I saw a woman's face and an outline of her body. She seemed to be floating there with her head turned to one side.' Other reports mention patterns of light falling mysteriously on a wall or floor. Some notice objects, such as boxes and paper, moving by themselves in the warehouse.

'It would be easy to discount these reports as the overactive imaginings of people who want to believe in ghosts, but too many visitors have been in touch to tell us similar things,' said Murphy. By popular demand, the webcams were kept in position to carry out further research. During the first two years in operation, the ghost watch site received in excess of two million visits with a whole new wealth of reports of inexplicable sightings online.

'My name is Eric and I am a paranormal investigator living in the United States,' began one report. 'The live video feed I just saw on your web page is haunted. I saw in one frame, a ghostly apparition in the corner by the desk and in the other, a book was in mid air going across the room with no help,' wrote Eric.

While web browsers across the planet watch the mill's macabre goings on from the security of their own homes, workers continue to endure the supernatural air within. However, the ghost watch observation team now believes they have unearthed clues to the reason behind the hauntings at Pure Flax House. According to researchers, the building's most likely unearthly occupant is that of a

16-year-old girl and former linen worker, who died tragically at the mill during its first year of operation.

The story of Helena Cecilia Blunden is both tragic and beautiful. Hers was a life filled by romantic dreams and burning ambition dashed short by dint of her social standing and the atrocious working conditions she was forced to endure. Helena Blunden belonged to a family of Irish immigrant workers who returned from London in 1911 to let Helena take up her final working position. At 16, Helena began work in the spinning room of the Pure Flax House linen mill, in what is now the old markets area of Belfast city. The company's first order was for a batch of double damask linen tablecloths to be laid in the first-class dining room of the ill fated RMS Titanic, which sank on the same day Helena died. The life of a young factory worker in newly industrialised Ireland at the turn of the twentieth century was bleak, to say the very least.

The working class, which had recently emerged in Dublin and Belfast, lived and worked in some of the worst slums and factory conditions seen anywhere in Europe. Work was infrequent and when found, usually involved torturously long hours for a mere pittance in return.

Many of the old mills, like Pure Flax House, still stand but the linen equipment has long been removed and is now exhibited in museums for visitors and history students to admire. Through detailed accounts from surviving workers, the memories and harsh experiences suffered by linen mill labourers like Helena Blunden and her mother are recorded.

The Blundens arrived in Belfast from London after a relation had organised employment for the family. They settled in a small terraced house on Raphael Street close to the mill. According to reports, Helena was a diligent and popular worker. Her head was always full of song and clouded with the romance of the music halls of London. Helena's grand-uncle had been a wandering Irish dancing master in Kilkenny. She, however, was more renowned for her singing abilities. She had danced at the *Feiseana* in Dublin and sung in choirs during her time in London. Helena's love of song and music would offer the teenager the illusion and hope of escape from her daily toil at the mill. Indeed, later evidence unearthed by ghost watch researchers revealed that Helena did actually take part in a public performance and was recorded.

At the time of her employment, Belfast was the biggest linen producing centre in the world. Work was intensive and it was necessary to keep a damp, humid atmosphere in the mills to stop the linen yarn from breaking. The sultry conditions severely effected the lungs of spinning room women, particularly when they finished and went out into the cold streets.

Helena, like most of her fellow employees, would have worked barefoot at the mill so her feet would have been constantly wet on the steel stairways and concrete floors.

On 14 April 1912, Helena was working on an order for shipment to Argentina. She worked from morning to 7 p.m. that day, possibly the seventh day in a row, when a terrible accident occurred. Exhausted by work and weakened by lack of food, Helena slipped on wet steel and plummeted more than 20 feet over a banister, head first onto the cold factory floor beneath. Her young life, her hopes for music hall glory were all cut short in that instant. She died within the damp environs where she had already given over so many of her young hours.

Today, bare footsteps pattering across a landing, followed by a haunting scream of anguish are just a sample of the eerie reports from the building's current occupants. 'Recent encounters have so disturbed staff that no one will stay alone in the building day or night, and everyone is reluctant to work late,' said the ghost watch researchers. Three women have heard a voice yelling in distress, while another member of staff has heard a woman's voice gently humming. On one occasion, the warehouse staff were inexplicably locked into the fourth floor and only managed to get out of the building by using an unlit stairway. The most compelling piece of evidence linking the sudden death of 16-year-old Helena Blunden to the print shop hauntings was uncovered in 1999.

The prosperous Ireland of the late twentieth century could not be further removed from the world in which Helena had lived some 85 years earlier. However, something very precious belonging to her remained at her place of death before being accidentally discovered by print workers.

In the run up to further renovation work in the basement of Pure Flax House, its sole occupiers – the living ones at least – came across some hidden treasures. A series of first edition books, and boxes of photographs depicting early twentieth century Ireland, greatly excited local historians and ghost watch researchers. But more lay in store. For many years employees had been walking past one very remarkable hidden treasure every single day, belonging to none other than Helena Blunden.

In August 1999, the print manager on duty at the mill discovered a cloth bundle buried in an old disused fire bucket still half full with sand, which he grabbed to

GHOST BOY OF THOOR BALLYLEE

The transparent image of a small boy appeared in a photograph taken at Thoor Ballylee, Co. Galway, by an English tourist named David Blinkhorne.

Thoor Ballylee was the former home of writer W.B. Yeats. There was nobody else in the room when Blinkhorne took the photograph. Photographic experts say the ghostly image could not have been a shadow as the only light was coming in through the facing window.

© David Blinkhorne

CHARLEVILLE CASTLE (ABOVE) AND LEAP CASTLE (BELOW)

Charleville Castle and Leap Castle in Co. Offaly are the most haunted castles in Ireland.

Arch Druid Melvyn Llyod carried out a four hour psychic survey at the above castle and said, 'Charleville castle is the most haunted castle I have ever stayed at in Ireland.'

The chanting of monks has been heard from the ruin of the old church building at Leap, left.

© Dara deFaoite

THE DOBHAR-CHÚ (MASTER-OTTER)

- endemic at one time to the west of Ireland (and midlands)
- extinct circa 1970.
- stuffed specimen may exist in Hynes pub Crossmolina Co. Mayo
- length 6 - 8 ft (possibly as long as 12ft!)
- preference for coastal areas
- strictly carnivorous
- strongholds near Achill Island Co Mayo and counties Sligo and Leitrim.
- THE ABOVE IS MY OWN ARTISTIC RENDITION OF THE DOBHAR-CHÚ BASED UPON THE ASSUMPTION THAT IT WAS / IS A GIANT SPECIMEN / SPECIES

DRAWING AND DESCRIPTION OF THE DOBHAR CHÚ
© *Gary Cunningham*

DOBHAR CHÚ GRAVESTONE
The gravestone of Grace Connolly bearing the effigy of the beast, which allegedly savaged her at the shore of Glenade Lake, Co. Leitrim, while she was washing her clothes in September 1722.
© *Dara deFaoíte*

SONNY SUTTON AND JENNY COCKELL (ABOVE) AND MARY SUTTON

Mary Sutton (right) of Malahide Co. Dublin, who died in the Rotunda Hospital Dublin on 24 October 1932. English woman Jenny Cockell has relived Mary's death and life through reincarnation.
© *Jenny Cockell*

RICHARD T. COOKE

Parapsychologist Richard T. Cooke, organiser of the inaugural All-Ireland Ghost Convention held in Cork, October 2001.
© *Dara deFaoíte*

EPSEN SAMUELSEN (ABOVE) AND MEMBERS OF THE GUST TEAM(LEFT)

GUST have led over 15 major monster hunt expeditions around the world, including one celebrated search of Scotland's Loch Ness for the world's most famous lake monster.

© *Epsen Samuelsen*

BETTY MEYLER

Betty Meyler using her crystals to predict the arrival of UFOs. From the reaction of the pendent to a series of questions, she can ascertain whether or not we should expect to see any UFO activity over the skies in the coming month.

© *Dara deFaoite*

ABC CAUGHT ON CAMERA IN FINTONA, CO. ANTRIM

The cat pictured above is suspected to be a puma and left several five-inch footprints in the area (as seen on the right).

Many local livestock were mauled during this time. This sheep was likely to be the puma's first kill.

© *Alan Lewis*

EAMONN ANSBRO
Astronomer Eamonn Ansbro on the roof of his observatory at Kingsland, Roscommon. His camera equipment has been designed to lock onto UFO activity in the skies above Roscommon.
© Dara deFaoíte

UNIDENTIFIED FLYING OBJECT
Jim Flora captured what appeared to be a 'snowball type' spacecraft on camera. He claims that through meditation he can open himself up as a contactee for visiting extraterrestrials.
© Jim Flora

DESMOND LESLIE AND JIM FLORA
Desmond Leslie began cataloguing stories of UFO sightings around Ireland, and joined forces with some high profile, mostly Anglo-Irish characters like himself, who shared the same penchant for extraterrestrial life forms.
© Jim Flora

extinguish a small fire. Inside the oily rags lay what was surely the secret of Helena Blunden's hopes and dreams.

'In 1912, the fire buckets were filled with sand and hung on the wall by the direction of the first owners. With the introduction of fire extinguishers, the buckets became redundant but remained, at the top of each flight of stairs. During recent renovations, a fire began on the third floor. The print manager grabbed two of the fire buckets and emptied sand onto the flames, where he discovered a cloth bundle in one of the containers,' said Murphy.

Unfolding the package, the printer discovered a key, a strange tube and a collection of newspaper cuttings. The tube turned out to be an 87-year-old recording on a brown wax cylinder of Helena singing *Pie Jesu*. The cuttings consisted of a selection of newspaper reviews describing Helena's only performances in Belfast, Dublin, and London in the years up to her arrival at Pure Flax House.

'As an ordinary worker, Helena Blunden probably had no place to call her own and so she used the bucket as a hiding place for her property, thinking it would never be used. After her death nobody knew of the cylinder, so it remained hidden,' said Murphy.

'At first it was not obvious what the tube was. The cylinder was enclosed in presentation paper, but part of the inscription was indistinct,' he said. A forensic examination revealed that the recording was made on 24 January 1912 by Barra MacNasge from The Capricorn and Cornucopia Music Publishing Company.

The newspaper articles all referred to solo singing performances by Helena Cecilia Blunden. One of the reviews was taken from *Saint Malachy's Parish News* and described Helena's rendition of *Pie Jesu,* which was performed at the Confirmation Mass in Saint Malachy's Chapel on 24 January 1912.

'We are certain that the recording and newspaper pages belonged to this girl. The newspaper extracts were published during 1910-1912 and have been verified through archive,' said Murphy. The recording, made three months before her death, lasts only two minutes. If she had lived, Helena may never have found a way out of the mill to play the bigger stages of London and beyond, but her contribution to song and vocal talents have since received much praise.

After confirming the authenticity of the cylinder recording, Ghost Watch consulted Charlie Dawson, emeritus professor and musicologist, who lectured at music schools in Belfast, Dublin, and New York.

'The singer displays an outstanding octave range. There is a maturity and depth of voice, which indicates that the singer has taken lessons and has benefited from a classical voice training,' he said.

According to Murphy, 'this recording was made by the girl who we believe is the ghost who now haunts the corridors and floors of the printworks.' The haunting of Pure Flax House appears to hold no malice towards its present occupants. It is, according to many reasonable minded sources at the plant, merely the echoes of a lost soul who still walks, works and above all else sings her way through the old building.'

CHAPTER ELEVEN

The Monster Hunters

During the summer of 2001 an international exploration team took off in a small motorboat across the depths of Lough Ree from Killinure Point, Co. Westmeath. The three-member crew had travelled to Ireland from Sweden, Norway, and Hawaii on a fact finding mission. Their task was to put meat on the bones of years of anecdote, rumour, and confusion surrounding the alleged existence of a fearful, serpent-like creature supposedly dwelling in the murk of Ireland's third largest lake.

The Swedish-led Global Underwater Search Team (GUST) had come to Ireland to hunt down the Lough Ree monster. Armed with sonar equipment designed to track submarines during the Cold War, the team knew exactly what they were after.

'We came here to find an "unidentified creature" known by many people who live by Irish lakes as the "Horse Eel",' said Jan Sundberg, the GUST expedition leader. The monster hunt trio were acting on word of numerous eye witness reports of mysterious sightings of unexplainable beasts spotted along the 19 mile stretch of lake over the years.

Lough Ree, like its Scottish sister Loch Ness, is reputed to play host to a large, serpent-like beast and has been the subject of numerous sightings for many hundreds of years.

The Lough Ree monster, or monsters (the GUST team are keen to stress there is most likely a family of such creatures if there is one), is the most famous 'unidentified creature' living in an Irish lake. Evidence of this monster was first noted in the eighth-century biography of local cleric St. Mochua of Balla. Mochua refers to a hunt in which a stag takes refuge from his pursuers on an island in the lough.

The hunters, according to the monk, were too frightened to follow their prey for fear of being devoured by a fierce monster said to live therein. The GUST hunters know stories like this and more recent anecdotal evidence from locals and fishermen, hold more value to their research than meets the eye.

'We are looking for signs of a giant eel or snake-like animal, too long for comfort,' said Sundberg. 'It has a nasty-looking head and a number of qualities that you don't see in other animals in the same environment. It moves undulating, up-and-down, and yet it doesn't seem to be a mammal. It is very, very fast, and it can sustain itself in lakes with little or no food,' he said.

Sundberg's description of this aquatic anomaly falls in line with the most compelling account of a monstrous creature on Lough Ree, also documented, strangely enough, by members of the cloth.

On 18 May 1960, over 40 years before the GUST expedition set out, a group of three Catholic priests from Dublin had a most unsettling experience during a fishing trip to the midland's lake. Fathers Richard Quigly, Matthew Burke, and Daniel Murray had just cast off on a pleasant evening's fishing at the height of the mayfly season, when one of them spotted a large, black animal swimming up the lough.

According to news reports at the time, the creature sank below the surface when it was a mere 100 yards away from the priests, then rose again in the form of a loop.

The three clerics made a modest estimate that the beast they saw was no shorter than six feet (1.8m) long from its head to the end of its coil.

'It went down under the water and came up again in the form of a loop. The length from the end of the coil to the head was six feet,' the priests told the press. 'There was about 18 inches (45cm) of head and neck over the water. The head and neck were narrow in comparison to the thickness of a good-sized salmon. It was getting its propulsion from underneath the water, and we did not see all of it,' they said.

'The creature's head was flat like a python's,' one of the priests revealed in Peter Costello's book, *In Search of Lake Monsters*. The GUST explorers were determined, on such bona fide testimony as three priests, that they should delve further into the midlands lake.

'The priest's description was of particular interest to us, because the creature seen on Lough Ree very much resembles those witnessed in Norway, which we have previously monitored,' said Sundberg.

These 'unknown animals' are said to have a horse-like head and an eel-like body and measure anywhere from three meters to 12 meters. GUST called their 2001 exploration of Lough Ree, 'Operation Horse Eel.' Sundberg and his two companions were prompted towards Ireland and its association with lake monsters through Costello's book.

In separate interviews with the three clerics, Costello recorded some fascinating oral evidence from what was seen at the time as three infallible witnesses.

'We looked and there was this object on the top of the water, a couple of humps and a head coming out of the water,' Fr. Matthew Burke told Costello. 'I remember saying to myself, "what the hell is it?" Now, I have been on plenty of loughs and rivers and lakes and I've seen all the usual things in Ireland, but this was nothing I could place at all, at all,' said Fr. Burke. Fr. Daniel Murray also verified his colleague's account. 'There we saw this extraordinary vision of what seemed to me to be a great serpent,' Fr. Murray told Costello. 'We saw the head and the neck extending for about 18 inches above the surface. Then perhaps two feet back from the neck and head was this great big hump – perhaps again 18 inches, it might have been two feet above the surface of the water. The creature, as we described it afterwards, was moving very slowly, perhaps not much more than a human walking pace,' he said. The three priests visited life long lake dweller, Colonel Harry Rice, who tipped off local newspaper, the *Westmeath Independent*, and put up a reward for further information leading to the identity and whereabouts of the Lough Ree monster.

From here, tales of the monster started pouring in. Retired post man, the late Paddy 'Potch' Hanley spoke of his encounter with a strange beast many years previously. Thirty years before the priest's sighting, Hanley and a companion hooked some 'huge creature', which dragged their boat around the lake. It never surfaced and eventually broke the line, which was the strongest pike line made at the time and, according to Hanley, 'the nearest thing possible to a rope.'

In an interview with the *Westmeath Independent*, Hanley said they 'were glad when the line broke', as neither of them believed that they could ever have landed a monster that could drag them about in such a manner. Hanley reported that he heard of other similar incidents down through the years, and claimed that he would not be surprised if there was some unknown kind of monster in the lake.

On the 2001 mission, Sundberg was convinced that what they were after was indeed the often documented, long-necked monster referred to as the Horse Eel. The term Horse Eel stems from sightings in the early twentieth century mostly by farmers who saw creatures, the size of a horse, but low and lizard-like leave the water to graze on land.

Tales from Lough Ramor in Co. Cavan, tell of 'en-chanted water horses' who would come onto land at night to graze on local crops. One story tells of a boy who managed to catch what he thought was a foal and went about training it to work on the farm. This foal was not to be tempered, however, and it soon returned to the depths it belonged to carrying the unwitting boy with it to his death.

The shores of Irish lakes echo with similar tales of mysterious half-horse, half-eel shaped creatures appearing in and out of water and often taking lives back to the deep with them. Further account of the Lough Ree monster concerns an incident, which occurred just months before the priest's encounter. In February 1960, two fishermen were out netting pike just half a mile from the point the priests had their experience. The men's boat was suddenly jolted by something large in their net. As the two attempted to haul the net in, whatever they had caught broke free, through the net itself. 'It must have been as strong as a horse,' said one of the men in Costello's book.

Another account tells of a Mr. F.J. Waters who hooked
something huge and powerful while fishing off Beam
Island. Whatever took Waters' line 'dived rapidly to the
bottom, snapping the line after 70 feet had run off the reel.'
The speed of the dive was, according to Waters,
'impossible for any fish to attain.' Former journalist Jan
Sundberg was not surprised when he heard such stories
come from the shores of Irish loughs, as similar fables
resound around the lochs of Scotland and throughout
Scandinavia.

GUST have led over 15 major monster hunt expeditions around the world, including one celebrated
search of Scotland's Loch Ness for the world's most
famous lake monster. The team won critical acclaim for
their approach of lowering listening devices into the 690
foot deep waters of Loch Ness. Their findings featured on
a *Discovery Channel* special in which Sundberg enthused
about one special sequence, which he says sounded
precisely like large bodies propelled by large flippers,
moving through the water. GUST analysis suggested the
movements resembled a plesiosaur – a prehistoric aquatic
creature – thought to have been extinct since the Jurassic
period during the time of the dinosaurs, but often referred
to as the form the Loch Ness monster has appeared in. The
Loch Ness sequences correlated well with repeated claims
of similar sightings from around the world including those
from Ireland's Lough Ree.

Operation Horse Eel is Jan Sundberg's second Irish
monster hunt. He went to Sraheens Lough on Achill
Island, Co. Mayo in 1975, where tales of a vile looking
monster leaving the water were rife. Sraheens Lough is a
relatively small water way, only 1,200 feet (365 meters) in

circumference yet it has been the location of numerous monster sightings since the early 1930s.

The 'Monster of Sraheens Lough' was most recently spotted in 1968 by two local men whose testimony prompted Sundberg's maiden voyage. The two men, John Cooney and Michael McNulty, came face to face with a 10 foot (3m) long creature crawling from the lake.

Their claims were subsequently backed up in the months and years following, by further independent sightings of a creature matching the same appearance. Sundberg started his underwater expeditions under the GUST banner in 1997. In June 2001, the GUST search for the monster of Lough Ree made some definite progress.

'We recorded a noise that sounded somewhat like what we heard in 1999 in Seljordsvatnet, Norway,' said GUST team member Espen Samuelsen. These recordings were later identified by several scientists as 'a biological sound, and a sound not made by any known animal.'

'There was an estimation that a creature making such a loud sound would have to be around 15 meters long,' said Samuelsen.

After years of research and, according to Sundberg, 'many close encounters with unknown animals' particularly in Norway, the GUST explorers have a good idea of what they are now faced with. 'From experience I believe we are tracing a creature that undergoes a metamorphosis, from a two to three meter lizard-like creature to the 10 to 12 meter eel, or snake-like animal. This unknown animal will almost definitely have fins or paws. It could swim easily by using these appendages in the water or manage to travel over land by the same means,' said Samuelsen.

Like the creature spotted on Achill Island, it is largely believed that these so-called lake monsters have the ability to move about on land, although they obviously prefer the cover of water. It is likely, according to the GUST members, that their existence in Irish lakes depends upon such creatures travelling over land many thousands of years ago. According to the GUST captain, they 'probably came to Ireland over land', most likely after the last great ice age. 'How they feed is a riddle to this day, and for all we know they could eat sediment,' he said. 'Before you can say how an unknown animal could sustain itself, you need to know a lot more about that animal. You also need to consult scientists to have them evaluate your findings and none of them are as yet too keen to help because these creatures are still not accepted as a possible new species. It's a Catch 22, if you will.'

Unfortunately for an organisation like GUST, all the diagrams, drawings, and soundings have not yet convinced the science world to take the issue of lake monsters seriously. The lack of scientific clout behind their chosen career paths does not shake the resolve of the world's leading underwater monster hunting team, however.

'History is full of stories where science dismissed local people's reports of unknown animals, probably because they were too colourfully told, and with some features added,' explained Samuelsen. 'It's like the reports of the hairy man, told by African natives, that came down from the mountains and kidnapped children and women. This was dismissed as native folklore and nothing but fantasy, but turned out to be a true story when the gorilla was discovered soon after by westerners,' he said. 'The panda was also considered a mythical animal, until it was discovered, and catalogued by science,' concluded Samuelsen.

The sounds recorded on Lough Ree during Operation Horse Eel were taken in close proximity to where the three priests had their run-in with the alleged monster. 'We found out after a few days that this was an area where several sightings had occurred, notably the ones of the three priests in 1960,' said Samuelsen. Despite being a shallow lake, only 30 meters deep, Lough Ree is a relatively large waterway measuring nine miles across and 19 miles in length and bordering the three counties; Westmeath, Longford and Roscommon.

The GUST findings, while important to the team, were far from conclusive and a second voyage was soon mooted. 'We got some interesting sounds on the hydrophone but the lake needs to be searched again with proper underwater equipment such as underwater cameras, sonar and Remote Operated Vehicles, the works really,' said Sundberg.

The listening device used by GUST to trace the movements or whereabouts of any possible 'unknown animal' is known as a hydrophone. 'We only managed to search a small part of the area but the hydrophone is so good that it can pick up movements and sound waves from most of the lake. One of the problems with that was that we also caught noise from radio and TV-stations, military installations, mobile phones,' said Sundberg.

The 54-year-old Swede's belief in the existence of these 'unknown animals' remains resolute, however. 'We have had several encounters in lakes in Scandinavia, which convinced me 100 per cent that these creatures really exist. They are very shy, cunningly smart and have developed an ability to hide from man, who they don't trust; no animal does,' he said.

So should these unknown creatures be taken as a fact of life in Ireland? 'Why not, they are everywhere else – lake monsters and sea serpents, however, we prefer "unknown animals". They are lost in the fairy tales only because they haven't been found yet and the reason they haven't been found yet is that no one has looked hard enough for them,' said Sundberg.

CHAPTER TWELVE

Connemara Monsters

Connemara boasts the largest number of documented lake monster sightings of any one region in Ireland. This wild and beautiful expanse of Irish countryside, dotted with peat black lakes and impassable bogs just 30 miles west of Galway city, provides a habitat for a more diverse cross-section of aquatic wildlife than could possibly be imagined.

The area's unspoiled craggy coastline, stunning mountain scenery, and pervading sense of tranquillity, lures thousands of visitors from Irish cities and from abroad every year. These same holiday makers take up temporary residence in picture-postcard cottages, fish on glassy lakes and generally soak up the beauty of the west. But few who travel Connemara's twisty backroads to reach its desolate lakeshores, experience all that lurks beneath.

The secluded waterways of Lough Dubh, Lough Auna, Ballynahinch Lake, Lough Fadda and Shanakeever Lough hold deep and dark secrets for many of Connemara's local population.

For generations, farmers, children, and fishermen have fled in panic at the sight of 'monsters' referred to locally as the 'Water Horse' (Éach Uisge), 'Horse Eel' and 'Water Bull' (Tarbh Uisge). These unknown creatures, who reportedly dwell in the depths of many Irish lakes, are believed to be of similar size, stature and behaviour to their more famous Scottish counterpart in Loch Ness.

They have been hunted, observed, feared, and revered in Connemara and elsewhere long before the first modern day encounters were put on record during the last half of the twentieth century.

Connemara today has become a favourite location for cryptozoologists who make it their life's mission to track down creatures, not formally recognised by science, but supported in some way by anecdotal testimony and eye witness account. The term Horse Eel has become an international byword and common description for lake monsters around the globe. Descriptions of these unknown creatures show a monstrous snake-like animal, up to 10 metres long and over 18 inches in diameter, with an ability to move over land. The Horse Eel is noted by cryptozoologists as an 'elusive and frightfully large creature', which has put the heart across many native Connemara people over the last 50 years.

'I remember as a child I would see strong men come running into the houses because a Horse Eel had come out of the lake and onto their land,' recalled Tom Joyce, who has encountered the creature twice on Connemara's Lough Shanakeever and once on Lough Auna. Joyce and many of his Connemara neighbours speak of this outsized beast as if it were just another, run-of-the-mill part of the area's diverse eco-system.

While local interest in lake monster activity remains largely complacent, the creatures have managed to attract the attention of internationally renowned monster hunters down the years.

Despite a large and varied catalogue of sightings, all similarly described as 'creepy, terrifying beasts', both in and out of the water, the monsters of Ireland's western lakes have remained steadfastly elusive to nets and harpoons. However, experts have deduced that what we are dealing with in Connemara is more than one 'unknown species.'

Author Peter Costello surmised through exhaustive research and reports gathered during research for his comprehensive book, *In Search of Lake Monsters*, that Ireland appears to have more than one type of unidentified aquatic animal.

One of the first clearly documented Connemara monster sightings was from Lough Fadda in the south of the region. A number of reliable eyewitnesses were on hand to verify the terrifying experience in 1954 of Clifden librarian, Georgina Carberry, who retold her chilling tale to monster hunter F.W. Holiday some years later.

Carberry recalled the day that she and three of her closest friends came eye to eye with a fearsome creature of the deep while fishing in a small boat on Lough Fadda.

'Well, it was a very long object. We sighted it rising, coming out from an island on the lake. At first, one of our company thought it was a man swimming in the lake, then she said, "Oh, now look at it!" It wasn't a man swimming, but a very big object, which we watched for a long time coming very leisurely towards us, swimming along slowly. So we kept watching it till eventually it got very near us.

'We began to get a bit worried. I was sitting nearest to it and it came in to within twenty yards of us. I was the first to move and jumped back and the other three who were sitting behind me did likewise.

'As soon as we moved it swung right around a rock, which was near the shore and dived, and we could see these awful big rings in the water as it was sinking.

'The mouth, which was open when it came in quite close to us at the shore, was huge and the eyes, I can't really remember. I distinctly remember that the whole body had movement in it. We could distinctly see two big humps showing behind its head, out of the water. We noticed the tail, when it swung around the rock, was a kind of fork, a V-shaped tail.'

Georgina's testimony of events were readily backed up by her three companions, and in 2001, when American lake monster expert, Nick Sucik, visited the area, he talked to the only surviving witness on that day in 1954 and found that she remains haunted by the experience.

'Ann vividly recalled two bulges emitting from the head, which she said may have been its eyes,' said Sucik. The incident on Lough Fadda – by no means the first sighting of its kind in the area – sparked a global reaction prompting the Loch Ness Investigation Bureau to carry out unsuccessful experiments in the lake.

The monster recorded by Georgina Carberry possesses all the traits associated with the 'conventional lake monster' theory, including a long neck, looping body and narrow head descriptive of the creature or creatures believed to haunt the depths of Scotland's Loch Ness and Ireland's Lough Ree.

However, modern research into Irish lake monster activity has revealed that there appears to be more than one type of unidentified aquatic beast making its presence known to man.

Testimonies from other equally reliable sources on Connemara's many lakes, have thrown up the possibility for the existence of as many as three separate species of monster. Some eight years after Georgina Carberry's infamous fishing trip, another strong witness recounted his

horror at seeing a much different monstrous entity rise out
of another Connemara waterway.

Glinisk national school teacher, Alphonsus Mullaney,
witnessed something he 'had never seen before', while out
fishing with his son on Lough Dubh in March 1962.

'We were working on the bog after school and I had
promised to take young Alphonsus fishing. We carried a
twelve foot rod with a strong line and spoon bait for perch
or pike, of which there are plenty in Lough Dubh. For a
while I let the boy fish with the rod and used a shorter rod
with a worm for bait. I got no answer. After five minutes I
decided that the fish were not there that evening, but I
took the long rod and walked up and down the bank.
Suddenly there was a tugging on the line. I thought it
might have been caught on a root, so I took it gently.

'It did not give. I hauled it slowly ashore and the line
snapped. I was examining the line when the lad screamed.
Then I saw the animal. It was not a seal or anything I had
ever seen. It had, for instance, short thick legs and a hippo's
face. It was as big as a cow or even an ass, square faced with
small ears and a white pointed horn on its snout. It was
dark grey in colour, and covered with bristles or short hair
like a pig,' recalled the Galway teacher.

The school master's story evokes a creature much different
from those monsters previously recorded in Irish lakes. It
is from Mullaney's experience that cryptozoologist, Nick
Sucik, returns to stories of monsters recorded in Celtic
tradition.

According to Sucik's research, the Celts knew of two
separate creatures of the deep, the more familiar Éach
Usiage (meaning water-horse) and lesser mentioned Tarbh
Usiage (water-bull).

'In the *Encyclopedia of the Celts*, the water-bull is described as being smaller than "earthly bulls" with cropped ears, short corky horns, short legs and a long, round supple body, with short, sleek, glittering hair, like an otter. Said to appear most often at night grazing near the banks of rivers.'

These monsters have risen from the murk with such regularity in the Connemara region over the last 50 years, that they allow experts like Sucik to form theories of their own on the physical make up and habits of Irish lake monsters. After many years of compiling eyewitness accounts of the often called Peiste or Horse Eel, Sucik is certain we are addressing 'a creature or creatures as yet uncatalogued by science.'

'Despite their bulk and often bold behaviour in the water, these creatures remain timid and alert outside of their aquatic environments,' said Sucik, who was a member of the International Global Underwater Search Team (GUST), who set out to find the Lough Ree monster in 2001.

'It's interesting that while reports show they display curiosity around farm animals, they should retreat at the presence of men,' he said.

Local farmer Tom Joyce has had three close encounters with the Connemara lake monsters. His first was in June 1963, when he was taking sheep in for shearing and he heard an 'almighty splashing' come from the lake. 'I saw this creature's head sticking up out of the water and the sun glittering off it,' he said.

Tom recalls seeing a large greyish hump seven or eight feet long and two feet high in clear view as the thing swam along through Shanakeever Lough into some reeds.

'When it entered the reed bed the grass parted in a way I had never seen it part before. It was obviously the result of a large body entering there,' he said. Tom's second lake monster experience took place many years later on Shanakeever's neighbouring lake Lough Auna in 1980. Tom was a guest at a dinner party in the holiday home of retired Netherlands Royal Airforce officer, Commodore Kort. The party had just retired indoors, when one of the guests spotted an odd shape gliding through the lake 'at walking pace.'

The group described the creature as being upwards of five feet in length but, unlike any regular lake creature, such as an otter, it left no V-shaped trail in its wake. In June of 1982, Joyce caught sight of the creature once more, this time, as with his first experience, it was on Shanakeever Lough as he drove along the lakeside road with a German visitor. It took Tom a moment to realise that what he was looking at was not part of the normal environment, and by the time he reached his house and grabbed a camera the beast had returned to its watery lair.

It comes as little surprise to monster hunters that these creatures have been spotted in lakes situated many miles apart. There has been a long history of land sightings both here, in Norway, Sweden, and Scotland suggesting that 'horse eels, water bulls' or whatever lurks in Irish lakes, are capable of moving across marshy land and into other waterways.

'Considering the tiny bodies of water they've been reported in, not to mention high altitude lakes as well, it goes without saying that these cryptids (unknown animals) are quite capable of amphibious travel,' said Sucik. 'Due to the vast distribution of lakes stretching for miles across the bog lands of Connemara, it is pointless to label any one lough as a particular monster haunt. Just because a horse eel or a water horse was sighted in one bog pool in no way suggests it remains there within its murky lair. In some cases only 20 feet lies between one lake and another. The majority of these freshwater bodies have some connection, active or passive, to the sea, allowing trout and salmon to migrate to and fro, thus providing a constant food source for any large aquatic creature within.'

Sucik's fellow GUST team member, Espen Samuelsen, also has his theories on the existence and proliferation of these beasts. 'We don't really know a whole lot about these alleged creatures, but my guess is that they are migratory animals, they travel out to sea to spawn, and return to live in lakes, just like eels. They are also able to travel over land if necessary, as many witness accounts tell of. They don't just live in Ireland either.'

According to Samuelsen, these unknown animals have been spotted in Scandinavia, Russia, Iceland, Scotland, Wales, Canada, USA, South America, and Japan, where there are stories of similar looking creatures.

'We can only guess how many thousands of years these animals have carried on their migrations from salt to freshwater, weaving from lake to lake and then for some equally mysterious reason, returning to the sea,' said Sucik.

In 1880, a Cashel blacksmith was asked to make an unusually long barbed spear. The story goes that the spear was to be taken to a bridge over part of Connemara's Ballynahinch Lake to free a 30-foot eel with a body as thick as a horse, which had become lodged under the narrow arch. As plans went ahead for ridding the area of the foul monster beneath the bridge, a great rain came and flooded the lake in the process, freeing the trapped thing.

Another tale from nineteenth century west Galway, recounts a similar sized creature, which got trapped in a culvert connecting Lough Derrylea and Lough Crolan. The beast lay trapped in the oversized drain and according to reports, was allowed to rot away. There has been no such hands-on encounters with horse eels in the last 100 years, yet the creatures have continued to entertain, scare, and bewilder those living by western shores.

'It's so peculiar, but many people in Connemara don't think this is such a big deal and they talk as if the horse eels were a normal part of nature with nothing unusual about them,' said Sucik. This attitude is particularly true in relation to one sighting by the Coyne family from the shore of Connemara's Lough Nahooin. On a clear evening in February 1968, local farmer Stephen Coyne, his wife and their five children watched a strange and oversized creature move about out on the lake for many hours until they became bored and decided to return home.

Coyne was out gathering dried turf at Claddaghduff by Lake Nahooin on the evening in question. He was accompanied by his eight-year-old son and their dog. During the work, Stephen saw what he thought was the dog swimming out in the water, and he whistled to usher him back onto the shore.

It transpired, however, that the dog was safe and dry on land and came running to his master on cue. The dark object continued to glide through the water and the dog began to bark at whatever was out there. On hearing the dog's bark, the creature turned towards the shore with its long, thick 'pole-like' head sticking out above the surface, mouth open as if heading for the family pet.

Coyne told F.W. Holiday that he watched the water beast 'swimming around in various directions and from time to time put its head under water, at which point two humps came into view and occasionally a flat tail was seen above the surface.'

'I thought it was just a giant eel, but then I remembered that eels don't put their heads out of water for any length of time,' said Coyne.

The monster maintained its course towards the barking dog and continued until Stephen went to stand beside the pet. At this stage it turned and headed off around the small Connemara lake. Stephen's son ran to the family home and called his mother, who arrived at the shore with their four other children.

The entire Coyne family watched the beast make turns of the small Lough Nahooin. The Coyne's told monster hunter Holiday that the creature easily measured 12 feet in length. Mrs. Coyne said she noticed two protruding lumps on the top of its head and said it had come within five yards of the shore. They recalled that it had an under-slung jaw in relation to its snout and that the interior of its mouth was 'pale'. They did not report having noticed any teeth. The monster of Lough Nahooin continued to patrol the lake as dusk settled over the west of Ireland and all seven members of the Coyne family bade it goodnight, and headed home across the bog.

CHAPTER THIRTEEN

The Irish Crocodile

Pap Murphy will never forget the creature that came from the ground. It crawled out of the overgrown ring fort on the hill above the small fishing village of Cartron along the Mullet peninsula in Co. Mayo, on a clear March morning in 1968.

This much was known, but nobody knew for certain where such a thing had really come from. The first Pap Murphy knew of it was through a riot of barking dogs.

'I heard what sounded like every dog in the village start up at once, so I went out to see what was going on. There were four or five of them snapping, barking, and dancing around this long, dark creature, which leaped and weaved through the air between their attacks. I remember thinking, "What the hell is that thing?" It was at least six feet long and well able for whatever the dogs threw at it,' said the Co. Mayo carpenter. Murphy was just 17-years-old in 1968.

'I will never forget the sight of that thing,' he said. 'It moved down through the field at the back of the houses and onto the street where it was attacked. It was dark grey or possibly brownie/black in colour, moving on short legs, low to the ground. But when it stood on its hind quarters it was lizard-like, and seemed to drag its tail along behind, it must have made six foot tall and sent the dogs crazy. It didn't squeal or bark when attacked and no dog could manage it,' said Murphy. 'A hump went up on its back every time it jerked to move and when it was back flat on the ground it straightened out to its terrifying full length again,' he said.

Through natural instinct or some supernatural governance the creature from the Cartron cairn was intent on seeking sanctuary either in the sea or in another hole similar to the one it had earlier emerged from, and no dog was going to stop it.

'It made several attempts to go into the houses. It ran through gardens and crashed into front doors, which were all tightly shut now. It was as if it wanted to get back underground,' recalled Murphy. The creature's 'otherworldly' proportions have left an indelible impression on Murphy's memory. 'It had a cat-like head on it, a rounded front jaw with cat-like teeth but less sharp, more like the way human teeth are shaped. It was about three or four foot long with another three foot of very thick, strong tail sticking out the back. It was low to the ground and its back legs were slightly longer and more powerful than its front. There were no ears visible on it at all,' said Murphy.

But what made the sight even more strange for everyone present that day, according to Murphy, 'was that none of the older people in the village, some of them in their late 80s, had ever seen such a thing before. People believed it was a supernatural monster and that it had crawled out from the depths of the earth or from hell itself.'

The 'old cairn' above Cartron, denoted on the ordinance survey map as a rath or ring fort, was long known as a place of refuge for foxes or cats over the years. 'This thing appeared well fed and seemed to have been up in years but nobody had ever spotted it until this day. It must have come out plenty of times in the past but had obviously made more careful retreats than now.

'It came into a garden down at the side of my uncle's house where there were a load of boats pulled up. I remember somebody hitting it over the head with a spade a few times and it just lay there, eyes shut, not moving a muscle after that. Everybody thought it was dead and after a few minutes they went away.

'At that time we had a big strong dog and he sat there for a long time looking at the thing, turning his head from side to side as a confused dog will. I was standing around five foot away from it and as far as I could tell the awful thing was all but dead to the world. I remember I was just about to move over to our dog to take him away when, as if you'd turned on a switch, the thing leapt up and attacked the dog. It jerked itself into a gullet under the road, came out again and made off for the beach, which was fifty yards away. The tide was far out and it had a long way to go to the sea. A couple of more dogs attacked it and it died there on the strand.'

Rumours of the beast's supernatural aspect were further evinced when, according to Murphy, 'the thing wouldn't burn.'

'It was thrown onto a bonfire on the beach but did not burn and it lay on the sand for many months after. It did not rot away either as a fish would, but eventually got washed out in the tide,' he said.

'A lot of sea anglers would come from all over and no one could ever establish what it was. It had very fine short hair and looked to the world like a cat's head on a giant otter's body, however, most said it was too big and powerful to be an otter. It had claws on it so strong it was more like a wildcat,' said Murphy.

'To this day I cannot understand why people back then attacked something like that. Why not let it go to where it wanted to go?'

It was also a pity, as Murphy points out, that nobody had the sense to pick it up and bring it to a taxidermist. Yet, strange as this dark creature appeared to the quiet village of Cartron, it was not the first time an unidentified monster of such unearthly proportion had made itself known in the Mayo area.

During the barbaric land confiscations by Oliver Cromwell's roundhead forces in the mid-seventeenth century, Catholic landowners were forcibly displaced or murdered under the war cry 'To Hell or Connacht'. The far reaches of the western province were given over to the former landowners by the English warlord, as this was the one area of the country with the least natural advantages. It was also thought that there was more to Cromwell's 'To Hell' analogy than initially met the eye. The west of Ireland has long held the highest count of unidentifiable lake monster sightings from anywhere in the country. The region's lakes and waterways are allegedly alive with creatures of monstrous proportion, which were just as active at the time of Cromwell's genocide as they reportedly are today.

Descriptions of creatures known locally as the Water Horse, Horse Eel, Master Otter or Dobhar Chú, the Water Bull and the Irish Crocodile are common across much of counties Mayo, Leitrim and Galway. These unknown monsters make up a hidden zoo of infrequently glimpsed cryptids, or mysterious animals, living in the waterways and bog holes of Connacht and, like the beast of the

Cartron cairn, are thought by many to hold supernatural powers.

In his book *A Description of West Connaught* published in 1684, Roderick O'Flaherty describes a fearsome creature known for its hostile attitude towards passers-by on Lough Mask in Co. Mayo.

'There is one rarity more, which we may term the Irish crocodile, whereof one, as yet living, about ten years ago (1674) had sad experience. The man was passing the shore just by the waterside, and spied far off the head of a beast swimming, which he took to be an otter, and took no more notice of it; but the beast it seems lifted up his head, to discern whereabouts the man was; then diving swam under the water till he struck ground: whereupon he ran out of the water suddenly and took the man by the elbow, whereby the man stooped down, and the beast fastened his teeth in his pate, and dragged him into the water; where the man took hold of a stone by chance in his way, and calling to mind he had a knife in his jacket, took it out and gave a thrust of it to the beast, which thereupon got away from him into the lake.

'The water about him was all bloody, whether from the beast's blood, or his own, or from both he knows not. It was the pitch of an ordinary greyhound, of a black slimey skin, without hair as he imagines. Old men acquainted with the lake do tell there is such a beast in it, and that a stout fellow with a wolf dog along with him met the like there once; which after a long struggling went away in spite of the man and his dog, and was a long time after found rotten in a rocky cave of the lake when the waters decreased. The like, they say, is seen in other lakes in Ireland, they call it doyarchu, i.e. water-dog, or anchu, which is the same.'

The comparisons between O'Flaherty's Dobhar Chú, as it is known today, and the beast slain at Cartron 300 years later are striking. Yet just 38 years after O'Flaherty's publication the dreaded Dobhar Chú was to strike again. This time the master otter, or Irish crocodile, is said to have taken the life of a young woman at a lake in Co. Leitrim.

In the middle of a small, rural cemetery towards the northern end of Leitrim lies the grave of Grace Connolly who, according to local legend, was fatally mauled by the fierce monster on Glenade Lake between Manorhamilton and Bundoran.

The memory of Grace Connolly's terrible death is kept alive, in the main, by an unusual and haunting effigy embossed on her tombstone. Carved on the soft sand stone is an image of an otter-like monster doubled in two from an injury incurred by a hand-held spear sticking through its neck and protruding from its stomach.

Grace Connolly died on 24 September 1722. According to local lore, the Dobhar Chú came out of Glenade lake while she was washing clothes at the shore, and viciously mauled her to death. Connolly's bleeding body was discovered by her husband, Terrence McLoughlin.

To his horror, the Dobhar Chú was still resting on top of his love. McLoughlin is said to have run the monster through with a spear, but the cries of the beast alerted its mate, a second Dobhar Chú, to the scene and McLoughlin was forced to flee on horseback pursued across country by this awesome beast. It is said the monster chased McLoughlin, and a man known as Gilmartin, for over 20 miles across open country. The pair eventually stopped up at an outhouse and barricaded themselves behind their horses to await the pursuant beast.

On reaching his mate's killer, the Dobhar Chú rushed under the horses' legs to attack the men, but as it emerged from beneath them, one of the men stabbed and killed it.

A second gravestone with a similar Dobhar Chú effigy was said to have lain at nearby Kinlough cemetery at the southern end of Glenade Lake up until the beginning of the twentieth century. This stone was said to belong to McLoughlin, and accounts of its effigy describe a horse-like creature from the water. McLoughlin's gravestone, unfortunately, became broken over the years and was used as wall stone.

The gruesome legend of Grace Connolly's death has enthralled both Irish and internationally renowned cryptozoologists, who are certain that there are creatures in the depths of Irish lakes such as the enigmatic Dobhar Chú, yet to be catalogued by science.

'One question, which I believe is fundamental to the entire Glenade Lake mystery from a historic sense is, if this tragic incident did not occur, then why portray the creature, which attacked and killed Grace Connolly on her gravestone in such detail?' said Gary Cunningham, who has investigated the Dobhar Chú for many years.

In his research, Cunningham states that 'we cannot rule out the possibility that the Dobhar Chú or master otter may be a surviving member of a prehistoric mammal lineage.'

Another possible identity for the Dobhar Chú, according to the Newry-based cryptozoologist, includes a giant species or subspecies related to the European otter. 'A genetic bottleneck caused by factors such as inbreeding, geographical barriers such as mountains or islands, or even recessive genes from its evolutionary history could have resulted in a radically different otter,' said Cunningham.

Earlier research carried out by historian, Patrick Tohall, into the enigmatic Dobhar Chú highlights its supernatural aspect. Writing in the Royal Society of Antiquaries of Ireland in 1948, Tohall recorded accounts from witnesses who said that 'even the slightest portion of its pelt could save a ship from being wrecked, a horse from drowning, or even a man from gun-shot wound or any other serious affliction.' Tohall heard that the Dobhar Chú was the seventh cub of a seventh cub of the common otter, and thus a master or super otter. The master otter's links to the world of the supernatural would also go some way to explain Pap Murphy's version of events where the beast he came across at Cartron could not be burned and did not rot like the carcass of a normal animal.

Less than two months after the encounter at Cartron, the island of Achill off Mayo was to become the focus of attention when an enormous otter-like beast with a greyhound's head and a long thick tail appeared to a number of witnesses. Achill Island is Ireland's largest island running 20 miles from the narrow sound that links it from the mainland to its tip at Achill Head.

Sraheens Lough is a small circular expanse of water, approximately 400 feet in diameter. It is said locally to be bottomless and is likely to be the filled crater of an extinct volcano.

On 1 May 1968 two men, John Cooney and Michael McNulty, came across what they believed to be the legendary monster of Sraheens Lough. The incident occurred on the road from the island village of Keel, heading towards the mainland. The men caught something huge and lumbering crossing the road in the headlights of their van, which seriously unnerved the pair. Shortly after

10 p.m. a strange creature motioned across the road from the lake into some undergrowth on the far side.

'We could see it clearly,' the two men recalled in Peter Costello's book *In Search of Lake Monsters*. 'It was between 8 and 12 feet long, with a long neck like a swan only much bigger. The tail was very thick. It was moving at an angle to us and we couldn't see exactly how long it really was,' they told Costello.

'And it was weaving and curving. It was dark brown in colour and was slimey and scaley. The eyes were glittering. I don't know whether it actually looked at us, but it disappeared in an instant into the thick undergrowth and we didn't stop for further enquiries.'

While initially shocked, the men were not entirely surprised by this encounter as there had always been talk of a monster at Sraheens Lough. Nor did it surprise them when two months later, two hitchhikers reported a monstrous beast while passing the same Achill lake. In an article in the *Evening Herald*, the hitchhikers described the beast as being 20 foot in length. It had a head like a greyhound and a long thick tail. The hitchhikers' sighting followed a similar experience retold by 15-year-old Gay Denver of Achill, who said he heard splashing sounds while cycling home from mass. It was early evening and when Denver parked his bike to investigate the noise, he spotted a large animal near some trees close to the lakeshore. Denver described the beast as being much bigger than a horse and said it moved along in a 'jumpy way'. He said its head looked like a sheep with a long neck and a thick tail behind.

The teenager said the beast's back legs were larger and more powerful looking than its front and was about 12 foot in length. According to cryptozoologist, Gary

Cunningham, the beasts seen at Sraheens Lough bear striking resemblance to the Dobhar Chú of Glenade Lake legend. They also hold true to the unknown animal from the cairn at Cartron some months earlier.

'It would seem that the creature of legend – the Dobhar Chú or Master Otter – is very much alive and had been residing at a small lough on one of the most isolated regions of Europe as recently as 1968,' said Cunningham.

Far south of Mayo, but also on the rugged western coastline is the equally beautiful and isolated route known as the ring of Kerry. Lough Brin, 10 miles north of the town of Kenmare, has been the location of numerous lake monster sightings between 1893 and 1954. The monster of this mountain lake has been nicknamed Bran after the hound of Fionn Machumhail who, according to legend, drowned at that spot while hunting a stag and whose ghost is said to come back to the spot as a water hound. The Lough Brin monster was reportedly seen up until the mid 1960s, and by all accounts is said to be about 14 foot long with two big eyes on its forehead, and at times resembling a horse and not overly dissimilar to other Horse Eel descriptions.

Lough Brin is cited in W.R. Le Fanu's book *Seventy years of Irish Life*, published in 1893, as being the dwelling place of a 'dreadful beast'.

On a visit to the area in 1999, monster hunter Nick Sucik turned up one witness who, although reluctant to talk of his encounter, did admit to having seen the monster. 'I didn't know what it was, I thought it could have been a seal,' said the 70-year-old witness. But as Sucik points out, 'a seal that was capable of scaling mountains a good 25 miles from the ocean, I think not.'

On Christmas Eve in 1954, a local farmer, Timothy O'Sullivan, was by the lake herding cattle. He saw what he thought was a line of ducks on the water. The 'ducks', however, began to rise higher off the surface until O'Sullivan could make out a row of fins 'standing each, two feet tall'. Costello's *In Search of Lake Monsters* also tells of a 12-year-old boy who, in 1940, saw 'some strange animal lying on the shore of Lough Brin, basking in the sun. It was black, with four short legs.' Other reports tell of huge waves rising from the small mountain lake and 'strange splashing noises', which were often heard by passers-by.

CHAPTER FOURTEEN

Claws Out

The puma, the lynx and the Scottish wildcat are not native to the Irish countryside, yet recent Alien Big Cat (ABC) sightings have shown that such beasts, or crossbred variations, are living and breeding in woodlands across the country.

On a clear spring morning in April 2002, Sandra Garvey and her 17-year-old daughter, Ciara, encountered a 'very large and very wild looking' feline running through the woods near their North Tipperary home. Strange as this creature seemed at first glance that fresh Saturday morning, its appearance only convinced the pair of the existence of the big cat they had picked up in the headlights of their car two months earlier.

'There's a very large wildcat in the woods around here; we've seen it twice now in as many months,' said Garvey, a psychologist and lecturer living at Knockfune, Co. Tipperary, on the edge of the remote mountain forests near Rear Cross.

'It's not your average moggie, or even a large feral cat. It's much bigger and stronger than that, in fact, it's almost as big as a medium sized dog,' she said. 'It's a definite hunter, you can tell that because it has that kind of look about it, strong muscle tone and powerful claws,' she said.

This north Tipperary ABC was first spotted by Garvey in February 2002 from her car at night. 'I picked it up in full beam and nearly drove off the road I was so shocked. I'd seen plenty of foxes, feral cats and pine martens in the woods around here before but nothing like this.'

Garvey said she watched the cat cross in front of her on the road, before she pulled over and watched it disappear into the woods.

'I didn't get to see its face the first time, but its bulk and its tail were very distinctive.' The tail, according to the witness, was particularly striking in that it was not as long as the tail of a domestic cat and was much thicker. 'This animal's tail was short and bushy and had rings on it like that of an American raccoon,' said Garvey. 'The second time we saw it was when we were out walking in the morning, and it ran in front of us at a clearing before scrambling up a steep verge and into the forest.'

Garvey's testimony flies in the face of orthodox zoology, which states that there's no evidence, nor has there ever been any evidence, to suggest that Ireland supports a wildcat population, indigenous or imported. However, her sightings are in no way isolated incidents. There has been a spate of reported ABC encounters from independent witnesses walking and working in the woods of East Limerick and North Tipperary stretching back over ten years prior to Garvey's 2002 experiences.

On recounting her run in with the 'wildcat' at school the following week, Garvey's daughter, Ciara, discovered that her teacher, Jeff Griffin, Vice Principal at Villiers Secondary School in Limerick, had also seen such a beast three years beforehand at the adjoining Keeper Hill woodland. A keen walker, Griffin, and his wife said they came face to face with what he initially described as 'a fine

looking animal by any standard. It would have been about
two foot long and 18 inches tall, greyish in colour with sort
of bushy ears. It walked more like you'd imagine a lion to
walk than a regular cat. It had a certain strut to it, and it
wasn't in the slightest bit put out by us being so close,' he
said.

Like Garvey, the Griffins also caught sight of the North
Tipperary big cat from the safety of their car as they
approached an entrance to their local woods. 'This thing
literally walked down the side of the road towards our car.
I pulled in and he walked straight past the door of the car.
He carried on up the road and when we turned our heads
to see what he'd do next, we saw him look over his shoulder
to eye us up one more time, and then jump through a
hedge and into the forest,' said Griffin.

According to the Limerick teacher, the most interesting
feature about the Keeper Woods ABC was its short tail,
ringed and black around the end, clearly matching the
description of Garvey's later sighting. After further
research, both Griffin and Garvey firmly believe that the
cats they saw were an exact match for the elusive Scottish
wildcat, a catalogued species, sighted occasionally
throughout Scotland, but never documented by zoologists
in Ireland.

Controversy has long raged over the possible existence
of a native Irish wildcat like the Scottish variety, and
similar to those found in many mainland European
countries such as France and Spain. Wildcats were
distributed across the whole of Europe from Africa
towards the end of the last ice age. These creatures would
have found easy passage into Britain on the then existing
land bridge, but Ireland was cut off from this mass long
before Britain itself became severed from the rest of

Europe. Zoologists and natural historians say that the wildcat never made it over to Ireland.

The argument for and against the existence of an Irish wildcat is fuelled on one side by the wealth of anecdotal evidence and reliable eyewitness account and on the other by the sheer lack of hard and fast scientific proof.

In his incisive book *Mystery Cats of the World* author and cryptozoologist, Dr. Karl Shuker, examines the case for and against the Irish wildcat with testimony dating back to the early nineteenth century.

Sceptics today are quick to put down the notion of an indigenous Irish wildcat and alleged sighting of such a beast as little more than the observed activity of the pine marten, a member of the weasel family.

Shuker also found this argument raging during the course of his research into testimony by experts in previous centuries. However, the Dutch doctor was also to discover that the inhabitants of 'the remote glens of western Kerry' in the mid 1800s 'knew of the pine marten and of a genuine wildcat form.'

According to Shuker, they even had separate names for the two creatures – calling the marten a 'tree cat' and the wildcat a 'hunting cat'. Shuker also found that in 1904 a Dr. R.F. Scharff wrote, in a report for the Irish Cave Committee, that he had discovered the fossil remains of one very large feline form alongside that of a smaller cat in the Edendale and Newhall caves near Ennis, Co. Clare. The larger cat fossil he described as the remains of a wildcat and most likely of African descent.

Scharff also contended that this creature might not yet be extinct and that many such creatures may live today in the more remote mountainous regions of south-western Ireland.

Scharff's evidence proved inconclusive for the science community, however, who later said that the bones he had catalogued were most likely the remains of a large feral specimen.

After years of argument on both sides of the Irish wildcat debate, it would appear that what is truly needed is a live sample or some irrefutable photographic evidence of such a creature.

After lengthy examination of zoologically documented description and photographic evidence of the European and Scottish wildcat, both Griffin and Garvey are adamant that what they saw in North Tipperary was of similar breed.

According to British wildcat experts, wildcats spotted in Scotland have much bushier tails than their domestic tabby relations. These tails have three to five distinct black bands or rings running to their end. They also appear to be twice the size of a normal feral cat.

'After we saw this thing at Keeper, we carried out our own research and if I was to go for it, I'd say what we witnessed was the Scottish wildcat. I went through books and magazines, and although at first, we thought it was a lynx, we're certain now it matches the Scottish cat's description.'

Experts explain that wildcats are shy creatures. They live around the borders of woods, staying well hidden during the day and come out to hunt at dusk and at night. 'I'm off a farm originally, so I wouldn't be given to fanciful leanings where it comes to animals. I know this cat exists and I know others who have seen it,' said Griffin.

Some years before Jeff Griffin's ABC sighting at Keeper woods, an equally credible witness had his own encounter with a similar looking beast in a forest just two miles away.

Seán Breen, a conservation ranger with the Government's National Parks and Wildlife Division, was quite literally shaken, when he spotted a 'very sizeable cat' in Dundrum woods in 1993. Breen drove into the remote forest at night to do a head count on fallow deer as part of his ranger duties.

Dundrum woods is a large area of mostly coniferous forest with some oak stretching over thousands of acres close to the Tipperary/Limerick border. During the course of his night's work, Breen caught sight of a creature in his torchlight, which he said, 'was not one bit afraid of me.'

'I shone the light through a bunch of trees and it caught onto this thing, which was unlike anything I'd ever come across in all my years as a wildlife ranger,' said Breen. 'It was a very large cat and if I were standing in Scotland when I saw it, I would have said, "that's a Scottish Wildcat".

'It wasn't a massive thing like a jaguar, but it was about twice the size of a normal cat and it wasn't afraid of me. It was sitting quite still on the stump of a tree looking towards me. As I went towards it, it made no sign of moving away, so I left it where it was and cleared off myself. Usually when you come across a creature in the middle of the woods, they'd flee as you approached them. This thing was going to wait, I presume, until I got nearer and then I suppose it would have moved off, but courage wasn't my strong point in the middle of the night looking at this fellah,' said Breen.

'I wouldn't want to scare people from going into the woods at Dundrum and the chances of seeing that cat again, in a couple of thousand of acres of forestry, would be tiny. These cats are apparently quite nocturnal. The chances of seeing them during the day would be very slim and they wouldn't be tied to any one set of woods either,' explained Breen.

The Tipperary ranger has not seen the mysterious Dundrum big cat since this initial encounter and said that to the best of his knowledge, there is no substantial evidence that wildcats live in the forests of North Tipperary. However, the later and similar sighting by Garvey in 2002, prompted a great deal of interest and speculation from wildlife experts around the country and from the Irish media.

RTE radio presenter, Derek Mooney, visited Rear Cross and gave over his entire *Mooney Goes Wild* Sunday morning radio show to the probability of there being an Irish wildcat.

In an interview with local newspaper, the *Nenagh Guardian*, Mooney said that 'the chances of it being a genuine wildcat are very slight from what I've been told by scientists. However, there is the possibility that someone could have brought a wildcat into the country.'

The paper also quoted Jimmy Greene, a wildlife ranger, who believes that wildcats do exist in Ireland. Greene once witnessed a wildcat and its kitten while patrolling in the early hours in the Slieve Bloom mountain range in Co. Offaly some years ago, the *Nenagh Guardian* reported.

'I knew straight away it was not an ordinary cat. It was a pure wildcat. You have to be up early in the morning or out at night to see them. I didn't think we had them in Ireland before that, but there are also reports of them from Co. Wicklow,' said Greene, who now works as a ranger in counties Laois and Offaly.

The most popular theory to support the existence of wildcats in North Tipperary, and Ireland as a whole, is that those sighted are the hybrid result of many years of interbreeding between imported, or escaped, Scottish specimens and the local feral population.

In Co. Sligo, a well-known ABC, referred to locally as the Temple House Cat, is said to make regular and unnerving appearances in and around the grounds of a guesthouse by the same name.

'They're as big as collie dogs and are completely wild. Lots of people around here have seen them,' said Sandy Perceval, proprietor and host at Temple House. According to Perceval, the Cooper family of Markree Castle, a neighbouring estate, imported a number of Scottish Wildcats in the 1880s.

'We've been seeing them for 30 years now, and I know they were seen before that. At the moment we have two blacks, a smoky grey, and a tabby, which turn up every now and then. They seem to have survived by crossing with the feral cats in the vicinity.'

Perceval's description of the wildcats compliments those of the North Tipperary ABCs. 'They're not afraid of you. They're so sleek and self-assured, and they just look you straight in the face and walk calmly away into the bushes. When you see them you get more than just a dash across the road, you really get a good look at it,' he said.

Temple House runs shooting holidays for their mainly European clientele and, according to Perceval, many guests from France have told him that they witness similar wildcats in the Arden region, where such cats are also known to exist.

'We wouldn't shoot them,' he said. 'They don't seem to impinge on the stock here at all, in fact, I think they're more likely to be keen hunters and part-time scavengers picking up already dead birds and rabbits from the forest floor,' claimed Perceval.

According to British wildcat expert, Mark Fraser, 'Wildcats are shy and wary animals active at night, mainly around dawn and dusk. Rabbits, hares and small mammals are their principal prey, but quite large birds and animals freshly killed on the roads, may also be taken. They sometimes store, or cache, uneaten prey by hiding it under vegetation.'

Perceval said that despite the likelihood of many years interbreeding with the local feral, the Temple House cat is still the same size and stature as its Scottish ancestors. 'I worked in Scotland for two years and saw these cats frequently. Those on our estate are very similar except for colouring, due to the cross-breeding. I'd say the cats we have here today weigh about 20lbs and would be around half a metre in height.'

The Co. Sligo host dismisses the theory that wildcat sightings are just the confused result of pine marten encounters. 'We have pine martens on the land here, and they have a very distinctive face like a weasel's. A large male pine marten would only be half the size of these wildcats,' he said. The controversy over the existence of an Irish wildcat will, no doubt, rage on until hard evidence is laid on the zoological slab.

But Ireland has also played host to other ABCs over the years, which are most definitely not native to this island. A series of large feline paw prints discovered on open ground along the north Antrim coast during the summer of 2003 prompted fears that a member of the mountain lion family was prowling this scenic tourist spot.

Following numerous sightings of a 'very large cat' in the area and a after a bloody spate of mysterious livestock killings, police in Northern Ireland conceded that they were likely dealing with 'at least one' big cat on the loose in a 150 square mile zone of North Antrim.

Fears were first heightened when a farmer found one of his 70kg pedigree rams dead on his farm in what bore all the traits of a big cat attack. The attacker had bitten into the ram's side, and over a kilo of meat had been taken from the animal.

Bushmills, Co. Antrim farmer Robert Calvin knew it was not the work of dogs and accepted the attack was linked to reports of a female puma spotted in the area earlier in the week. However, by the time Farmer Calvin's stock had been hit, a full-scale investigation into big cats on the loose in the Portrush/Bushmills area was underway between the PSNI (Police Service Northern Ireland) and the USPCA (Ulster Society for the Prevention of Cruelty to Animals).

Early in the investigation USPCA chief executive Stephen Philpott said, 'We're a bit concerned by sightings with descriptions of a big cat the size of an Alsatian but twice as broad, powerfully built and dark tan in colour. To the best of our ability and as far as we can say it is a member of the mountain lion family, most likely a puma,' he said.

The authorities in Northern Ireland believed the offending cat or cats roaming the northern coast were escapees from a private and illegally held collection of exotic animals.

While the big cat continued to make his presence known by taking out stock in farming communities Philpott moved to assure the public there was no immediate danger, but that the creature might never be captured.

'I can't say it will never pose a threat to anyone, but they're more afraid of people and only come out at night. I don't think we'll ever get it. It's very unlikely.'

The North Antrim big cat was seen again though and caused further alarm when a mauled sheep was reported on another farm in the area.

The farmer in this instance described the injuries to the sheep 'like nothing he had never seen in 60 years of sheep farming.'

USPCA boss Philpot said the injuries were consistent with those found on other sheep and a ram killed recently in the area. Their wounds suggested they had been attacked by a large animal.

By the end of September 2003 the search for the Antrim big cat had narrowed to a 150 square mile wooded area near the village of Ballybogey outside Portrush.

But as the net tightened, differing reports of big cats sighted in the area brought USPCA chief Philpot to the conclusion that they were not only tracing a brown coloured puma but also that there was a black panther roaming the hills near Ballycastle.

As livestock continued to be attacked residents gave the creature or creatures the ominous nickname of The Beast of Ballybogey.

A helicopter and police air support unit was now dispatched as part of an operation to try and catch or kill the animals.

But the search proved fruitless. As Philpot predicted early into the investigation, 'It (the big cat) will pick a spot it's comfortable with, feels safe in and then we'll never see it again.'

It wasn't long 'till police resources were also being stretched as the search dragged into winter and PSNI Chief Inspector and wildlife officer Mark Mason likened the hunt to 'trying to find a needle in a haystack – except this needle has four legs and it's not afraid to use them.'

'Quite obviously that sort of operation can't be justified on a daily basis – the resources just aren't there,' Mason announced amid growing concern amongst farmers as lambing season approached.

'But I would point out that police are routinely armed in the area and can certainly bring in suitable firearms to deal with big cats,' he concluded.

To date the North Antrim big cats have not been uncovered and experts can only conjecture as to their fates. It is felt that as the animals most likely came from captivity (from a private collection) and were never truly wild they would most likely starve to death in the hills and forests of this rural coast line but there are also camps who believe they could easily survive for years foraging and running regular sorties into the abundant livestock in the region.

Also in Northern Ireland during the winter of 1996 and 1997, the former Royal Ulster Constabulary (RUC), received numerous reports of sightings of what people described as a young lion, 'probably dangerous', stalking through woods and rural back gardens around the town of Omagh in Co. Tyrone.

A crack squad of RUC marksmen were dispatched to the region after one particularly convincing sighting, and on 17 February 1997 a big cat was cornered and shot dead at Fintona, Co. Tyrone. The animal, however, proved not to be a lion but a rare African caracal lynx known to breed in certain mountainous areas of southern Europe, and a rare and endangered species. The dead lynx, however, had a collar on its neck and was later found to be the property of an amateur exotic animal collector from Omagh.

'We've had a number of sightings of big cats in the Tyrone, Armagh and Down areas over the last number of years,' said Chief Inspector Mark Mason, wildlife officer with the Police Service Northern Ireland (PSNI).

The PSNI were investigating up to five reports of big cat sightings in the Dungannon, Aughnacloy area of Co. Tyrone during May of 2002. Amongst the reports filtering into Mason's office was the discovery of a five-inch wide footprint denoting a cat the size of a puma.

'Although people keep mentioning pumas and so on, some of the sightings were of large black cats, which could be more accurately described as being of the smaller panther variety. But, some of the reports certainly would appear to be of puma size, which we would colloquially term as medium sized cats,' said Mason.

One such report from Aughnacloy, on the border of Tyrone and Monaghan, reported hearing 'something going on like a fight between cats' and when they went out in the morning, they found these footprints five inches across. Others claimed to have actually seen the animals.

'The usual descriptions were of something big and shaggy like a dog,' said Mason. On New Years day 1999 a '5ft long, 3ft wide, green-eyed feline, brown and beige, dirty and unkempt' was seen by several witnesses in the Aughnacloy area before appearing at nearby Sixmilecross.

The animal was never traced by then RUC marksmen and the local *Belfast Telegraph* newspaper rubbished the claim that it was a puma, stating that the beast was more likely to be a large St. Bernard dog, which had been reported missing from its home in nearby Beragh some weeks earlier. In this particular case, however, neither dog nor ABC were found, and so the mystery continues.

CHAPTER FIFTEEN

Aiming for the Stars

For over seventy years, during much of the nineteenth and twentieth centuries, Ireland held in her possession the largest telescope in the world, facing skywards at Birr Castle, Co. Offaly.

It was from this location, deep in the Irish midlands, that the first galaxy was discovered in the course of a series of experiments carried out by the third Earl of Rosse in the 1840s with the aid of newly designed, telescopic lenses.

The giant wooden framed spyglass still stands at Birr Castle today. It is in perfect working order and is now a popular tourist attraction on beautifully maintained lands. As the race to reach outer space took off towards the middle of the twentieth century, Ireland's astronomical endeavours got somewhat left behind.

For a short time during the 1970s, however, one Dublin based amateur astronomer did lay claim to having developed the largest working telescope in the country and, in the process, achieved a lifelong ambition with the discovery of a new star.

Eamonn Ansbro's celestial catch of 1976, known today as Nova Vulpecula, was quickly verified by observatories worldwide, including Greenwich in London and Massachusetts in the United States.

With a background in meteorology, Ansbro soon established a career in 'optical engineering.' He developed telescopes for amateur astronomers around the country, and established his own industrial optics manufacturing plant in Cork. His continued fascination with overhead illuminations have led him to become an authority on all things identifiable and, more recently, unidentifiable in our skies.

In the summer of 2002, Ansbro put the final touches to his own purpose built observatory at Kingsland, Co. Roscommon. Part of this multi-faceted, high-tech development has been specifically constructed to trace and record the activity of Unidentified Flying Objects (UFOs) or, as Ansbro prefers to call them, AOPs (Anomalous Observational Phenomena), which enter the earth's atmosphere.

Coming from a scientific background, and at constant pains to impress and educate the science community through his work, Ansbro has had to doctor his terminology considerably in relation to ufology and his conviction that Extraterrestrial Intelligence (ETI) is out there.

'For my own research purposes I call them AOPs. The reason for this is that I know that UFOs do not equate to aliens. There are an awful lot of people out there in the so-called UFO community who, when they perceive an unidentified flying object automatically think, "Alien Life Form." In scientific circles, if you mention the term UFO you're quite literally finished, it's like a bad mantra in those circles. What I am trying to do is build a bridgehead between ufology and science,' he said. And Ansbro has every good reason to be cautious as to how he carries out his work at Kingsland.

The self-taught astronomer travelled to San José in the United States in 2001, where he delivered three papers to the NASA run SETI (Search of Extraterrestrial Intelligence) project in a bid to raise funds to further his research at Kingsland.

SETI was initiated by the United States Government during the 1950s. The purpose of SETI was to find some sort of conclusive evidence that intelligent life existed beyond the confines of our planet.

SETI scans the skies for proof of extraterrestrial life. This is done with the use of radio telescopes and other detection equipment, largely in the form of deep space radiation transmission.

Scientist Dr. Bernard Oliver, working on the SETI programme, has long stated his belief in the possibility that an 'interconnecting galactic community of advanced cultures already exists'. However, the work carried out by SETI does not ally itself to the populist approach or theories on UFOs as operational spacecraft.

On the other side of this planet, from his skywatch retreat in the north west of Ireland, Ansbro's plan is to lock onto UFO or AOP activity with his own specially designed camera equipment.

'The development of the instrumentation for this type of research is geared for observing objects that may have a natural cause or might be of an extraterrestrial nature,' he said.

Ansbro chose Roscommon as a site to further his studies of outer space for good reason. According to his own research and experience, UFO activity is common over the greater Boyle/Co. Roscommon region.

'This happens to be an active area, there have been frequent sightings here for many years,' he said.

The instrumentation at Kingsland Observatory has been described by Astronomy Ireland member, Mike Foylan, as 'one of the most advanced robotic observatories in private hands anywhere in the world.'

Astronomers from universities in Britain and from noted observatories in the Czech Republic, Italy, and Armagh have expressed interest in visiting Ansbro's labs. Kingsland Observatory is situated on an acre of land in the remote out-back of the northwest. It consists of three, high-powered telescopes in separate silos, used by the astronomer for his own astral endeavours, which during 2002 included a masters degree in astronomy.

Attached to the roof of his house is the equipment used for tracking UFOs. There are 11 high-powered cameras running at equal distance around a disused chimney breast and pointing to all areas of the open sky.

'Each camera takes a sector of the sky and each is capable of picking up an object either stationary or moving, which will then trigger two other tracking cameras situated elsewhere in the garden. These extra cameras are in sync with each other, and they can track that object until it disappears,' he explained.

Ansbro's initiation into the world of UFO experience began in 1991, by accident, when he was asked to investigate a number of sightings of strange objects reported over the southern coastal area of Bantry in Co. Cork.

Ansbro had been working in Bantry producing industrial optics at his own plant at the time of the call. He had made contact with the local astronomy community including astrophysicist Hermann Van Belligen, director of the nearby Schull Planetarium, which at that time was the first port of call for people who had experienced close encounters with unusual lights in the sky.

Van Belligen approached Ansbro with a list of names and addresses of the individuals in the southwest who had contacted his place of work with witness accounts of alleged UFO sightings. According to Ansbro's 1999 book, *Extraterrestrial Intelligence: A Reality*, he 'compiled over 120 investigations into separate UFO reports, including 35, which were particularly extensive.'

'I realised that what was going on in Cork and Kerry was very real and could not be passed off as meteorological phenomena, aircraft activity or figments of people's imaginations,' he said.

His interviews were with a cross section of local society including farmers, factory workers, and people who ran local businesses. 'They were ordinary people who had no previous background with UFO experience and, with few exceptions, they seemed to be reliable, stable, sound individuals,' he said.

One typical report centred on the appearance of six small, illuminated objects, which could only be identified by the witness as 'spacecraft'. These six objects of light were then followed in the sky by the appearance of a huge craft coming in over the water from Bantry Bay.

'Initially it moved from a location about three miles distant into the vicinity of the witness in a split second, then it hovered nearby for about 10 minutes,' according to Ansbro's reports.

'They described it as being about the size of an aircraft carrier and only 500 feet above a nearby river. When it was only 200 metres away from them, they described it as looking like a big city turned upside down with thousands of lights,' he recalled. This was a particular striking account, as it was verified by more than one witness, always a plus in adding credence to the virtually unexplainable.

A total of 120 close encounters were related to Ansbro in strictest confidence. 'Witnesses told me they were willing to speak of their experiences as long as they could remain anonymous,' he said.

'They were ordinary people with families; they didn't want any intrusion from the media and they didn't want to risk exposing themselves, their family or friends to ridicule.'

These initial UFO revelations were to be the ground-stone on which the former meteorologist would later build his theories on how to identify, and eventually predict the appearance of these earth-visiting UFOs.

After setting down the details of over 120 UFO sightings in Ireland, Ansbro went about educating himself on the global UFO phenomenon.

From his garden shed headquarters in Clontarf on the north side of Dublin city, he compared the Cork experiences with thousands of similar reports from the United States and other locations around the world.

'My independent research showed that what was happening in Ireland in relation to UFOs was consistent with what was happening in countries all over the planet. It seemed that cultural influence did not distort the descriptions of UFO sightings, whether they occurred in Africa or Ireland,' he said in his 1999 work.

Between 1991 and 1994, Ansbro continued to collect real life experience and anecdotal evidence of Irish UFO encounter.

In September 1993, the years of cataloguing all seemed to fall into place. He suddenly heard from several individual witnesses, all at different locations in the south west, who claimed to have seen a UFO at the very same time that another individual from Cork reported an experience of being aboard a 'space craft' and 'engaging with its occupants.'

'It seemed impossible that so many individuals could have independently fabricated the numerous details involved in this event,' he said.

From here, the former Gatwick Airport meteorologist began to set down a number of theories of his own and publish papers in astronomy journals on the topic of UFO activity.

After plotting the locations of UFO sightings in the Cork/Kerry region, Ansbro discovered a huge concentration of activity crossing one area in particular, known locally as Coomhola, Co. Cork.

The small Cork townland became a hub for UFO activity, and presented an important landmark for Ansbro. There also appeared to be a large amount of witness reports coming from the north west of the country near Sligo, and further east at Monaghan, and also from the Dublin area, which were also set down as landmarks for his studies.

It was at this point that Ansbro set about developing an early prototype for his unique, spacecraft-tracking camera, which was to capture the movements of the UFO as never seen before.

The camera's function, according to a newspaper interview with its inventor in 1998, was to lock onto the UFO and 'see what kind of elements are emitted from the space craft by zoning in on their propulsion emissions.'

Although he has now distanced himself to a large extent from these earlier theories, Ansbro's 1999 findings on the

UFO phenomenon over Ireland make for interesting reading.

Drawing on his knowledge of astronomy, he tried to imagine the most likely routes a visitor would take in getting to our solar system via spacecraft from 'any of the 300 stars within 60 light years.'

'Extraterrestrial visitors to our planet would approach from a certain star, planet or lunar related orientations.' This, according to Ansbro, presented the hypothesis that it might be feasible to predict when a UFO is most likely to appear.

This theory means that UFO visitations are not just random occurrences, but highly organised passings, 'whether or not we humans understood the logic involved,' he said.

Ansbro's prediction theories coincided with his coming into contact with Roy Dutton, an English-based aeronautical engineer. Dutton, like his Irish counterpart, had also been compiling UFO sightings, and was of the opinion that 'there was a methodical observation of the planet by intelligence of non-terrestrial origin.'

So, now the ETs were watching us and, according to both Ansbro's and Dutton's research, possibly had been for many thousands of years. In more recent times, however, Dutton had built up a database of 1,300 'good quality' UFO sightings from around the world going back as far as the 1800s.

The two astronomers combined their findings and verified their joint theory that the earth was being circumnavigated by extraterrestrial craft on what Dutton coined 'orbital tracks'.

'When we entered the data from my Irish investigations, he [Dutton] found that 80 per cent of them matched the most likely times suggested by his own time graphs for the Bantry area,' said Ansbro.

Now, the Irish Ufologist had found a like-minded individual and so began to reason out the idiosyncrasies of our luminous visitors.

'There are at least 660 known orbital tracts used by enormous extraterrestrial craft, which can circumnavigate the earth in 64.3 minutes,' Ansbro reported to a national newspaper in 1998, figured out by means of Dutton's findings.

'It is conceivable that a mothership, travelling along any one of these tracks, releases smaller interstellar robotic probes, which in turn orbit our planet on surveillance missions and are seen by humans as UFOs,' he said.

How Ansbro pinpoints the time and place for the appearance of these 'smaller craft', exiting ships travelling at speeds of up to '25,000 miles per hour' remains a mathematical mystery. His predictions are solely based on the study of Dutton's 'orbital tracks', which apparently circle our earth like an American Airlines' traffic control map.

It wasn't long until Ansbro put his money where his mouth was. In December 1998, hundreds of UFO hunters headed out to the hills and vantage points of Ireland to await the outcome of a number of Ansbro's UFO predictions.

The prediction site areas included Dromod in Leitrim, Ballinasloe in Galway, Rathmore in Kerry, Mallow in Cork, Urlingford in Kilkenny, and Coole in Westmeath.

Ansbro himself headed to Bull Island in Dublin Bay, an alleged UFO hotspot on a par with Bantry in Cork and Boyle in Roscommon, which were also on his prediction list.

As it turned out, Dublin Bay did receive a unidentified visitor on the prescribed night, as did a number of the other sites, according to Ansbro.

The occasion was captured, not on Ansbro's hyper-sensitive camera, but by an individual 'who could feel something', so he left his camera shutter open for a few moments at the predicted time. When the film was developed, a UFO was visible.

At the time this was happening in Dublin Bay, a local radio station switchboard was jammed by excited callers reporting a 'strange star-like light hanging directly over the bay, which seemed to be flickering in different colours.'

The Dublin Bay photograph is one of particular importance to Ansbro, and his then colleagues at PEIR (Programme for Extraterrestrial Intelligence Research).

Ansbro's ongoing search for extraterrestrial intelligence and a vantage point to observe outerspace brought him to Boyle, Co. Roscommon, where he now lives with his wife Catherine. He describes Boyle as an 'excellent location'.

'There are many orbital tracks criss-crossing Ireland and it is easier to have clear predictions in areas where the number of tracks intersecting is low,' he said.

Boyle is one such spot and according to findings by its recently arrived resident, 'there are just three intersecting tracks at Boyle, which makes it easier to develop a time graph for the area' and so track any potential, unidentifiable visitors.

However, Ansbro's current negotiations with SETI and the scientific community have led him to keep his feet firmly on the ground in this regard, and to deal with any possible UFO phenomena in purely theoretical terms.

Ansbro is now seeking recognition from organisations such as SETI for his own line of exploratory research entitled, 'Search for Extraterrestrial Visitation (SETV)'. This is a big undertaking for Ansbro, as it would be for SETI if they were to fund him.

Since it was established in the 1950s, most SETI researchers have, according to Ansbro, focused mainly on distant stars. 'The bulk of their work is based on the hypothesis that extraterrestrial intelligence exists and is technology based.' He concurs that, 'if this were the case, it is possible that extraterrestrial probes may have already reached our solar system and might be detected using existing terrestrial technologies,' most of which Ansbro has in his own back yard.

SETI research is based on the premise that there may be extraterrestrial civilisations, with an understanding of physics and technology that is beyond ours.

This premise, according to Ansbro, has long been deemed reasonable within the scientific community.

'It seems reasonable to consider that extraterrestrial intelligence may already have successfully applied theories and technologies that our scientists have only begun to explore,' he said.

This is the rationale for a SETV (Search for Extra-terrestrial Visitation) research strategy. This UFO tracking equipment was still being tested during the summer of 2002.

'Each of the 11 cameras used to obtain the target information have been designed to obtain high-quality images in extremely low light conditions. Increased funding levels would allow the use of multiple infrared cameras on these platforms, so that a target could be acquired while not in the visible range,' said the inventor.

'I need to find the spectrum and composition of a number of these AOPs, and with current instrumentation

I believe I've cracked it. Not only can I now track the object, but there is a very small scanner at the end of a complex system of lenses, which will scan to memory the particular square of sky, where an object appears, so the chances are very high that it will record a spectrograph of the objects.

'This scanning wide-field spectrograph is a very important piece of equipment in order to find out the composition of AOPs. It has never been done before, but I believe it is highly workable.'

Ansbro cites two European projects, one in Italy and one in Norway, he believes he can work with from Kingsland to further the search for extraterrestrial intelligence. His bid for international funding might yet bear fruit, as the US government has invested millions every year into SETI related projects since its inception.

'Most of my life has been mission impossible. I've pulled it off in a lot of areas, particularly in regard to optics, and I'm certainly going to do it on this one. There has to be more than this out there,' he said.

CHAPTER SIXTEEN

UFOs come to Boyle

On a cold wet night in October 1997, a group of people gathered in the back bar of a small public house in the quiet town of Boyle, Co. Roscommon. The group had never met before and although all were residents of the northwestern town, they only knew each other's faces through passing on the street. The company now jostled together anxiously waiting over cups of tea, and the odd alcoholic drink, in anticipation of strange news.

The group had assembled to hear about an incident, which allegedly occurred in the hills outside the town a number of weeks earlier. The incident had attracted a lot of attention from the national media and other departments, which had no direct bearing on every day life in this relatively rural area.

A Sunday newspaper report from 21 September 1997 talked of a mysterious crash in the Curlew Mountains, just two miles from Boyle and described as 'phenomenal' the interest in the occurrence from both the gardai and army. The report sparked intrigue amongst townspeople. It wasn't long before reports filtered into Boyle of isolated country roads, normally used only by farmers and their livestock, being blocked off by uniformed men, and of army helicopters and foreign accents heard patrolling the area.

Such covert activity soon attracted the attention of members of the Irish Centre for UFO Studies (ICUFOS), and their sister group PEIR (Programme for Extra-terrestrial Intelligence Research), who smelt the dealings of a possible *Men-in-Black* scenario right under their noses.

The area around Boyle, taking in parts of Co. Sligo, Roscommon, and Leitrim, had long been a sighting ground for UFO activity.

Stories of inexplicable lights flashing across the sky and appearing in clusters out of nowhere before disappearing just as quick, have been frequently reported in the northwest over the last 100 years.

Ireland's great poet and dramatist, William Butler Yeats, who lived and wrote in the area for much of his life, was himself witness to such unaccountable illuminations.

'We could see a small light low down on Knocknarea, seven miles off and it began to move upward over the mountain slope,' wrote Yeats.

'I timed it on my watch and within five minutes it had reached the mountain summit and I, who had often climbed the mountain, knew that no human footstep was so speedy,' wrote Yeats.

In his excellent television documentary, *Tell Me Captain Strange*, Colum Stapleton talked to local garda, Eugene McHale from Grange in Sligo, who had a very peculiar encounter with a UFO during the 1990s.

'We were on patrol duty and our attentions were drawn to a rather large light shining out from the Mullaghamore direction along the beach. Our first instinct was that it was a helicopter and it was engaged in some search or other, so we decided to travel down to Mullaghamore.

'On our way down we noticed that the light had moved towards Classybawn estate where it landed. We saw it rest there fully illuminated for a minute, and as we came to the end of the road it disappeared as if we had turned off a switch,' said McHale.

Excited as they were about the 1997 Curlew mountain incident, ICUFOS members, Eamonn Ansbro and Alan Sewell found themselves stumped after they visited the alleged crash site and found inconclusive evidence linking the spot to any form of alien landing. This, however, did nothing to perturb the investigation team. They gave the assembled crowd at the Boyle pub a presentation on worldwide UFO phenomena in which they said Boyle played a focal role. Over the next few years Boyle became synonymous with Irish UFO encounters.

Shortly after the October 1997 meeting, a group of locals set up their own UFO society in which they encouraged people with common interest to air and share their views and experiences.

The Western UFO Society was set up by Boyle resident and former hotelier, Betty Meyler, who reported her own close encounter with UFOs not long after.

One of the society's first outings was a Sky Watch at the picturesque holiday resort of Lough Kee Forest Park on the outskirts of the town. The group acquired the key to the 130ft high Moylurg Tower on the grounds of Lough Kee, from where they were in command of a magnificent vista of both sky and horizon.

On 14 December 1997, the newly formed Western UFO society witnessed six lights skimming across the water of the Roscommon lake. One of the members who held a video camera, managed to freeze-frame a still in which, according to Meyler, 'the shape of the UFO is clearly visible'. Not all of the group saw the UFOs that night, and it was some months later when Meyler had her own debut close encounter.

'I was looking out from the porch window of my house when I saw what looked like a huge red star appear out of nowhere before it simply disappeared after a couple of seconds,' she said. 'It reappeared lower in the sky and repeated this vanishing act at least seven times in different positions – always moving from west to east,' she said.

A few weeks later on 8 November 1999, while looking out her bedroom window at six in the morning, Meyler reported seeing a bright cigar shaped object, 'like the fuselage of a plane, all lit up but without the wings', streak across the sky four times in succession.

'I rang Sligo airport and confirmed with the manager that there were no aircraft in the vicinity at the time,' she said. This second experience copperfastened Meyler's belief in the existence of UFOs, and the possibility of extraterrestrial life visiting earth. 'I think it would be very arrogant for any human to believe they are the only intelligent beings in the galaxy,' said Meyler.

Within months of getting started, the Boyle based group had grown in number and were receiving regular calls from around the country regarding sightings and extraterrestrial experience.

'Suddenly all sorts of people were coming out of the closet to tell of their experiences and relate their sightings of UFOs, some dating back 30 or 40 years,' said Meyler.

After some publicity in the media, the organisation changed its name to the all-encompassing UFO Society of Ireland. On the first anniversary of capturing the UFO video still, the society returned to Moylurg tower. This time the group were more overwhelmed. Members now saw 'a huge white light, which flashed yellow, green, and red and then just disappeared.'

'We later saw over 20 lights appearing and disappearing and finally a huge white bright light, which streaked across the sky and then also disappeared,' said Meyler. 'We were told later that what we had actually seen were meteorites, but I don't think so,' she said.

Meyler has been working on the idea of establishing a UFO visitor education centre in Boyle to collect information, display models, and present theories on extraterrestrial life. 'Boyle is obviously on a vortex for UFO traffic, so people visiting the area who hope to witness UFOs could contribute to and learn from such a centre. The town has really embraced the whole UFO phenomenon, and it would also act as a signal to the alien craft that we are ready to receive them on earth,' she said.

This is the crucial point at which Meyler's views on what a UFO actually is, contrast starkly with the views of many other parties with an interest in ufology.

Meyler is of the opinion that we are in the presence of benevolent aliens who 'will help us overcome our modern evils and wicked ways'.

'We have entered a new age of enlightenment drawing on the energies of our ancient ancestors, and I believe extraterrestrial visitors can sense this good feeling and will visit us very soon,' she said.

One self-proclaimed 'paranormal provocateur' and host of the Irish-based web magazine, Blather.net, Dave Walsh does not see eye to eye with Meyler's benevolent alien theories.

'There would appear to be two main strains of UFO related religious belief,' said Walsh. 'The first comprises those who believe in the 'nasty greys'. These are generally alleged sufferers of nasty abduction experiences or conspiracy theorists. The second are those who believe in benevolent aliens who will allegedly save us.

'Both are inherent belief systems, which suppose that life as we know it has, or is about to, come to an end due to the interference of extraterrestrials,' he said.

According to Walsh, groups like ICUFOs and the UFO Society of Ireland fall into the second category mentioned above. 'They don't necessarily believe in the "nuts and bolts" of alien craft as such, but identify the UFOs themselves as Merkabahs or divine chariots of light, which surround the traveller, aura-like and have come to earth on peaceful terms.'

Walsh concludes, however, that he does not dismiss their beliefs. 'I'm interested in them, as much as I'm interested in people's beliefs in lake monsters or God,' he said.

Many members of the UFO Society of Ireland, of which Meyler is president, are reluctant to reveal their names due to what she describes as the 'unwarranted cynicism surrounding the area.' She remains confident and outspoken on the issue, however, as do many of her co-members.

'I've had three sightings, which all looked quite similar,' revealed one member of the society.

'A bright coloured star shape appeared high in the sky; it travelled slightly from one side to the other, flashed off and reappeared elsewhere above the horizon. I can't say where they come from for certain, but I reckon they're travelling through time from a parallel dimension, and interfering with our reality, unbeknownst to themselves even,' said the society member.

Meyler remains adamant that whatever unidentified objects are coming into our atmosphere mean well and should be treated peaceably. Following her own experience on 8 November 1999, when she saw 'cigar-shaped objects, which made no sound whatsoever hurtling across the sky over Boyle', Meyler contacted a friend of hers who she claims is very psychic.

'The message my friend received was, "Tell Betty that the UFOs she saw were there to assist the passage of time, to ensure the correct sequence of events in the new millennium",' recalled Meyler.

'I could not understand what this meant at the time, but upon reflection, later in the New Year, I realised that this must be referring to the fact that there was absolutely no trouble at the time of the millennium changeover as had been forecast, such as computers crashing and airplanes falling out of the sky. What an amazing message to get!'

From her home, Meyler produces a monthly newsletter, which is sent out to more than 50 members of the UFO Society of Ireland, in which 'recent sightings' are outlined. From these witness accounts, Meyler has drawn her own conclusions as to why UFOs appear in one place more often than another.

She believes that the bulk of UFO activity over Ireland travels along ancient 'lines of magnetic energy, which circle the earth' known as Ley lines.

She states that most of the great ancient monuments around the world, including the Pyramids, Stonehenge, and New Grange, and many lesser megalithic sites are built on these Ley lines, and that extraterrestrial craft travel along these natural 'energies or vortexes'.

'There are a lot of megalithic tombs around the Boyle area, such as the fantastic Carrowkeel passage tombs. Boyle is also positioned on a Ley line.'

However, it is this suggestion that UFOs are attracted to lines of alleged magnetic energy running around the world, which most unsettle researchers like Walsh.

'There are certainly possible connections between ancient sites around the world and UFO sightings through history,' said Walsh. 'These locations became important in early times due to environmental and anomalous phenomena, such as lights appearing in the sky. However, linking UFOs to Ley lines sounds like a case of putting the ufological cart before the megalithic horse.'

Walsh is quick to debunk the theory that these lines could possibly work as a magnetic conduit or any other form of energy for extraterrestrial intelligence to lock onto.

'Referring to Ley lines as "invisible magnetic lines that circle the earth" is nothing less, at this point in time, than new-age waffle,' stated Walsh.

According to the Blather author, an English man by the name of Alfred Watkins coined the term 'Ley line' back in 1921, to describe the apparent alignments of ancient sites in Britain and other countries.

This apparent alignment had already been claimed by nineteenth century antiquarians. 'However, more recent aerial photography has since shown that much of the earlier Ley research was inaccurate, calling much of the original faith in exact alignments into question,' he said.

'During the 1960s the concept of Ley lines got somehow dragged into collusion with the vague concept of "earth energies", which fuels much of the off-the-rack "magnetic energy line" bunkum we are stuck with today,' he said. 'The subject area is a total mess as far as popular conception goes. Many people, who would otherwise take a real interest in the subject will dismiss it all as rubbish because of all the wild conjecture, which has been thrown into the pot,' said Walsh.

Despite her detractors, Meyler stands by her theories. In the society's February 2001 newsletter, she reports on a husband and wife driving on the N16 from Strokestown to Boyle who saw an 'enormous saucer-shaped, white light about 500 feet off the ground with brilliant rays shining down from it close to Boyle Golf course' and near a noted megalithic landmark.

According to the newsletter, the couple saw the lightshow and turned to each other to ask if one could see what the other was looking at. They told Meyler the experience was so scary they did not stop for another look.

Meyler has drawn her own conclusion on this particular close encounter. She said that 'the place this craft was spotted in, is over an ancient mound called Knockadoobrunsna. It is a very ancient megalithic site, which has been carbon dated to 2500 BC and is believed to be the burial place of Caesar who, according to the book, *Invasion of Ireland*, was the first goddess to come to Ireland. She is reputed to be the granddaughter of Noah, who for some reason or another, put her out of the ark. She obviously got herself another boat and eventually landed in Ireland,' said Meyler.

Drawing further on the energies of the earth and of the mind, Meyler recently included a calendar of predictions in her newsletter. In these she gives the locations and times she claims UFOs will appear throughout the country. The predictions are garnered by means of 'crystal dowsing'.

'It's a purely psychic exercise,' explained Meyler. The process is simple enough. The dowser clears her mind and focuses her attentions down the length of a slim chain, to which a crystal pendant is attached.

From the reaction of the pendant to a series of questions, she can ascertain whether or not we should expect to see any UFO activity over the skies in the coming month.

The process runs as follows. 'Will there be a UFO sighting over Kilkenny on 6 June 2002?' asks Meyler. If the pendulum swings one way it will mean an affirmative – the opposite direction would mean a negative. She then figures out what time it will arrive at by a series of similarly placed 'yes' or 'no' questions.

'The pendulum works for me. I find out all sorts of things with the crystal. If you came to me with very bad headaches, I would find out what caused your headaches by use of the pendulum. I do this by a technique pulling on bio-energies from the earth. You could be allergic to beef, pork, or butter and I would find out through dowsing. I'm psychic and it works for me,' she said.

CHAPTER SEVENTEEN

Sweeps

Jim Flora, an ex-American soldier and Gulf War veteran, wasn't looking for UFOs when he moved to Ireland in 1996, but three years later, they found him. Flora had experienced various sightings of 'extraterrestrial craft', as far back as 1975 when he worked as a nurse in a hospital outside Albuquerque, New Mexico, but his recent move to Glaslough, Co. Monaghan, escalated these encounters tenfold.

'I wasn't looking for it (UFO activity) in Ireland, it was inadvertent,' said Flora, who set up the Irish Ufology Forum Outreach & Paranormal Studies organisation after a 'flap' of UFO activity over the skies of Monaghan in 1999.

The former combat nurse's new address sets off alarm bells when mentioned in proximity to 'strange lights in the skies' and visitations by alien life forms.

Flora lives just three miles from the village of Glaslough, the home of late Irish UFO pioneer, Desmond Leslie, who recorded many sightings of 'alien craft' over his family seat at Castle Leslie, near the Co. Monaghan town.

Leslie and Flora were to become good friends before the former's death at the age of 79 in 2001. The two shared an avid interest and conviction in the theory that, not only are we frequently visited and monitored by alien beings, but that aliens have been amongst us for thousands of years and that the governments of many of the top economic powers have liaisons with these beings.

Members of Flora's Irish Ufology Forum receive newsletters and literature every month from his home HQ at Corbeg outside Glaslough.

'Our members report back to us with their sightings and we cross reference all encounters from Donegal to Rosslare,' he said.

The group also receives up to three new calls from people who claim they've been abducted by aliens or UFOs in Ireland every month, according to Flora.

He has developed a screening questionnaire for these callers, and said he can only follow up on so many depending on how legitimate they sound, or how much time and/or experience he feels he has to offer.

Regardless of the legitimacy of Irish abductee claimants, Flora has been kept busy around the clock since he set up in 1999 with calls from around the country reporting sightings, and asking advice on how best to view UFOs.

'In 1999 there was a serious flap of UFOs over Monaghan. Almost every night we would get them over Glaslough, and the whole family became enthralled,' said Flora who also goes under his former military code name Sweeps roi-den Fox.

'We soon started signalling them and I gradually managed to establish telepathic contacts with these entities,' he said.

Flora's ability to make contact with what he knows 'are alien life forms' is founded on experiences he had more than 20 years ago in the United States.

'I went to work for the Navaho Indians as a nurse with the Navaho Tribal Council back in 1975 on their reservation in New Mexico,' he said. 'I worked as an in-service director for their all-new Navaho financed, Navaho built and Navaho staffed hospital. I remember being picked up at the train station in Albuquerque by several members of the council and what we witnessed as we travelled up through the mountains towards their capital reservation site blew me away.

'It was approaching dusk and there was this one huge cloud in the vast sky, which drew my attention. As I was looking at this cloud, a silvery object suddenly came from the left of it. It was a giant disk-like shape moving very fast out of the cloud cover and then it slowed a while and went behind the cloud again as fast.

'I'd been watching it with great fascination and I turned to my new Indian friends and said, "did anybody see that thing?" and they just looked at each other and said, "Oh yeah, we saw that, we see a lot of that kind of thing around here." It was no big surprise to these people,' said Flora.

The new director nurse was later to find out that he was 'smack in the middle of the Utah, Colorado, New Mexico, Arizona field – known as the four corners area', which has been allegedly rife with UFO activity and 'US government cover ups' for almost 60 years.

'Talking more to the Navaho I found out that UFOs go way back in native American history, over thousands of years back. They talked about such things as being ancient but these are things, which western cultures have only recently picked up on.'

After many years working in the Middle East as a combat nurse during the Gulf War, Flora returned to Ireland where he'd previously built a family home near Glaslough, for his Irish wife's parents in 1982. He moved back to

Ireland full time in 1996, and not long after, made contact with aristocrat ufologist, Desmond Leslie.

'As an aristocrat I suppose Desmond could afford to be a little eccentric and there was a feeling that he was allowed for by the people of the area. I've found that in Ireland, people really worry about what others think about them but I don't think Desmond gave too much of a damn about what anyone thought,' said Flora, who is highly outspoken on his conviction that alien life-forms populate Irish skies.

On 3 February 2001, Flora appeared in the *Belfast Telegraph* beside a picture of what appeared to be a 'snowball type' spacecraft captured over Glaslough the previous month. 'I was telepathically contacted and told to go outside in two minutes. It was 12.40 a.m. and exactly two minutes later, I saw a giant hairy snowball stretched across the sky. It came from the south east and arched to the south west. It actually crossed from horizon to horizon in four to five seconds. In the tail of the UFO I could see several smaller globes similar to craft that has been spotted in Mexico,' he said.

Flora claims that through meditation he can open himself up as a contactee for visiting extraterrestrials.

'I meditate daily and on several occasions here, at home, I have made contact with aliens through meditation,' he said. 'It's like a word in your ear or in your mind, you can hear it, it's a very audible thing, well not to anyone else but to me at that time.

'They'll say something in whatever voice they're using. Sometimes it's a very feminine voice and other times a masculine voice. The first one I heard was "go out now" and you don't hesitate when you hear a voice like that,' he said.

'I don't go around hearing voices, but when something like that comes through very strong on your consciousness, you're just impelled to follow it and to go at its direction, especially if you're sitting there with your camera.

'They might say go out now or in three minutes, and if you go out at the time they say, they'll be right there. When they say go outside, they'll even tell you the sector of the sky to look in,' he said.

Since 1999 Flora has been working on enhancing his telepathic abilities and said that sometimes now, he can act more on hunch that the craft are there than by placing himself into a meditative state.

'There was one time I didn't have a telepathic link going on, but I just got this hunch without words. People today have been taught to think in words, most people have never entertained the ability to think without words, but I try to go on hunches sometimes,' he said.

It was late on a bright July evening in 2000 that Flora's first major 'hunch' came true.

'I'd never usually go outside just on a whim when it starts to get late, because at that time I'm usually busy indoors, but this time I just got a feeling I had to go outside and I brought my video camera and placed it on the car because it felt like the right thing to do at the time,' he said.

'I walked outside on the little gravel path surrounding the house wondering to myself, "what the hell am I doing out here at this hour?"

'For some reason I haphazardly cast my eyes straight above me and about 100 feet above me or about the length of a football field overhead was this plasma disc, solitary in a clear blue sky, no clouds, no interference or anything.

'It was a beautiful glowing orange plasma disc pictured many times in central America. It was huge and it was shaped like a rugby ball.'

According to Flora, 'these plasma entities are very highly evolved, but as soon as I got my camera ready it disappeared.'

Flora has captured a wide range of UFO visitations on video footage over his Monaghan home and compiled these in a three hour video – *UFOs over Ireland* – available to members of his organisation. He has also written a book entitled *Trying to light the match – Kicking the one reality habit*.

According to Flora, 'we have entered a consciousness era swing' and that 'our whole idea of what reality is, is changing. There are so many different things flying in and out of our realities today, such as psychic ability and other paranormal phenomena, which are being accepted by people formerly trapped in more conventional realities.

'People are paying attention to the little synchronicities, which happen in their day-to-day lives. Simple things like when you get a letter or a phone call from somebody you haven't seen in ages, but who you had just thought about a couple of days previously.

'These things are important and shouldn't be blocked out. There are some people who are on the ascendant and are willing to explore the possibilities of alternative realities, but there are still a lot of people who put themselves in the one reality box and shut themselves up. It's disquieting and uncomfortable to shed an old value system,' said Flora on the theme of his book.

'My whole idea is to get the message out and give people choices of realities, let them explore for themselves what might be out there.'

In regard to UFO acceptance and denial, he points the finger at governments, who he claims 'champion the one reality because they are comfortable agents of control.'

'There has long been an international cover up of extraterrestrial encounter and UFO activity on and near earth by successive governments.

'If news was allowed to get out that there was something better and faster and more intelligent than any systems we have now, or something more powerful than our own scientists could manage, how would people believe that control of the country could be maintained,' he said.

The Irish Ufology Forum Outreach and Paranormal Studies newsletters are full of cuttings from celebrated authors, such as Timothy Good, who supports the claim that governments are at present studying alien spacecraft, which may have crashed or was captured in the last 50 years.

'Governments of Britain, America, Canada, Australia, and other countries believe that UFOs exist,' stated Good.

'The United States is researching an unspecified number of alien spacecraft and alien bodies. They are currently test-flying some of these craft at Dreamland, the super secret military base in the Nevada Desert,' Good said in his book *Alien Liaison*.

However, when Jim Flora isn't mulling over one conspiracy theory or another, he is out practising what he preaches by indulging in contact with alien life forms. 'Some are very nuts and bolts type craft,' he said. 'We don't need a mass landing to prove extraterrestrial life exists; they have bases here on earth now. They've been here for thousands of years, some of them look like you and me, some are very humanoid, some aren't. Some take up more ephemeral forms than others.

'They've been behind the scenes of human development and evolution for centuries, going back hundreds and thousands of years more notably in the last 25,000 years,' he said.

'NASA have made a lot of sightings on the moon and it is believed there are a lot of bases on the far side of the moon. I know from personal contacts that the US army has catalogued 34 different alien species and that they have eleven different alien craft under wraps. As a former US army security agent, there comes a time when you're allowed to talk about these things, but they don't like it.

'Hardly surprising,' he says, 'as many of the major governments have liaisons with these entities.'

And these are the same entities, which Jim Flora himself claims to have seen and communicated with in and around the fields of his house at Corbeg near Glaslough.

'The ones that I've seen I think are a holographic type of projection. I've seen them in the field over there when the craft was flying over, usually after telepathic contact,' said Flora pointing to a nearby field. 'They were very humanoid and were clad in green coveralls, from the head area right down to their base.

'It's difficult to comprehend this phenomenon if you haven't seen it before, but there is a definite difference between UFOs in the conventional alien craft sense to other paranormal experience such as ghosts or fairies,' he said.

'If they were spectres they wouldn't be way up in the sky as these things are, they'd be down to earth within another frame of reference.'

Although he claims he has 'never been abducted', Flora has attended abduction support group sessions in the US, and is surprised there is not the same level of help sought here in Ireland.

'These people are pillars of the community; they're not neurotic or psychotic. You become so immersed in their stories and the plainness of their character,' he said.

'There is no routine stereotyped person who is more likely to be abducted than another,' said Flora, who said he gets two or three calls a month from people believing they've been abducted.

'We have to prequalify these claims, however, and we have a questionnaire that we designed especially, so we can get a better judge as to whether they are delusional or if they perhaps have had an experience beyond their comprehension. Some of them you feel like you want to follow up and investigate with hypnotic therapy or to just catalogue, listen and recommend on to support groups.

'There are hundreds of support groups all over the world and there are more and more people being abducted all the time; this is a global phenomenon,' he said.

The most common form of alien interference or abduction according to the Glaslough ufologist, is 'car stopping on roads and lost time from anywhere between a few hours and five days.

'There might be two individuals who have parallel things happen to them during their lost time, which comes out later in separate testimony. Physically they were gone and no one can account for their disappearance. It can be a very difficult thing for people to come to terms with,' he said.

According to Flora, 'we're just realising the possibility of all possibilities and that is that all possibilities exist. There isn't one reality.'

CHAPTER EIGHTEEN

At home to the Other Side

Castle Leslie, seated outside the small village of Glaslough, Co. Monaghan, has been a hive of supernatural activity and paranormal daring-do down many generations of its colourful inhabitants.

Literary works and first hand experiences of ghosts, UFOs and lake monsters have long been associated with the picturesque, nineteenth century Leslie family seat.

Situated six miles north of Monaghan town and just three miles south of the border, the wonderfully maintained castle, dating from 1878, stands on 1,000 acres of lush Irish pasture.

The castle's most recent and colourful exponent of the paranormal, was celebrated author and ufologist Desmond Leslie. Famed as the eccentric Irish aristocrat who wrote extensively on UFO encounters, and of alleged contacts with extraterrestrial life, Leslie's conviction that we are not alone in the universe remained with him up to the time of his death in the South of France in 2001 at the age of 79.

Leslie grew up at the Co. Monaghan family seat, and after numerous early inexplicable experiences at Glaslough and while attending prep school in England, his fascination with UFOs was firmly planted.

He recalled that one night while at prep school his 'dormitory was suddenly lit by a brilliant green glare as an immense green fireball moved slowly across the sky and disappeared behind the Sussex Downs.'

Born in 1921, Leslie's early encounters stayed with him into his twenties, when he began to research the influence, which 'flying saucers and UFOs' had on ancient civilisations across the world.

He took out the ancient 18 volume Hindu epic, *Mahabharata* and found it 'was just packed with flying saucers, H-bombs and laser beams.'

According to Leslie, every civilisation he studied, including the Irish, had its UFOs and its gods, who came down in 'beams of lights and fiery chariots.'

'My hair stood on end when I read of weapons like "Kapilla's Eye", a ray focused through a great ruby that could shatter distant mountain tops,' Leslie said of the ancient *Mahabharata*. There was also the Brahma Weapon, which 'contained all the energy of the universe and must never be used. When it was eventually used, terrible clouds roared up into the upper atmosphere, there was a flash ten times brighter than the sun. The army was so burned that only the outline of their bodies could be seen on the ground,' reported Leslie.

'The survivors threw off their armour and washed in the nearest river but even so, after a few days their skin turned red, their hair and finger nails fell out and they died of a mysterious sickness,' said Leslie of his readings.

But Desmond Leslie also kept his studies close to home in Glaslough, and particularly around the estate of the castle, where he claimed to have observed unidentified flying objects on many occasions.

It was here in 1976 that his daughter Samantha, who now runs Castle Leslie, had a terrifying experience with mysterious lights in the Monaghan sky.

She told a journalist at the time that 'a ball of light came crackling through the basement window, pulsating and changing colour from red to yellow to orange.' At 15-years of age, young Samantha reported she was 'petrified' and 'ran upstairs screaming.'

Leslie's name as an outspoken authority on all things extraterrestrial had already been made at this time, and he said he was not surprised at his daughter's encounter.

He believed that the experience was prompted by his involvement in an RTE programme by telephone earlier that day. 'They were curious,' he later explained. 'They traced me through the telephone system, and then sent something to investigate,' he claimed.

Desmond Leslie came to international prominence through his collaboration with American George Adamski, an ice-cream trader-turned-mystic-turned-lecturer who caught the public's attention in 1950 with claims that he had made contact with, and travelled in the space ships of, a race of amiable Venusians.

On hearing these claims, Leslie wrote to Adamski from Glaslough. In time he was to combine his own research with the American's experiences and they co-authored the book, *The Flying Saucers Have Landed*.

The work captured the emerging cold war spirit of the time, and the public's appetite for postwar technologies. It became a bestseller, which was translated into 50 languages.

The Flying Saucers Have Landed contained fantastic photographs, produced by Adamski of these golden haired Venusians.

Leslie remained great friends with Adamski up to the American's death in 1969, and visited him often in California, where he reported many UFO sightings. In

1954 he wrote home to his wife, and told her of 'a beautiful golden ship in the sunset, but brighter than the sunset.'

Adamski and Leslie's book was soon denounced by the scientific community, including such respected commentators on the unexplained as Arthur C. Clarke. However, the pair stood by the veracity of their experiences. Adamski spoke enthusiastically about his travels through space with benevolent aliens and of cities on the dark side of the moon.

To his credit, Adamski was proved correct in his predictions of the existence of the Van Allen radiation belts, which blanket the earth, and the firefly phenomenon of space flight, confirmed by Uri Gagarin more than a decade later.

'It's all too easy to dismiss a mere handful of men when we have "science" to back us up, but that is the lazy way out. The claims that the world was round, that wax could record sound, that the ether could carry radio waves, that rays could penetrate and see inside matter, and that a heavier than air machine could fly were all dismissed in their day as impossible and contrary to scientific knowledge,' said Leslie.

According to the Monaghan aristocrat, we have been offered an alternative to taking the scientific approach and to sending missions into space to look for extraterrestrial life. That alternative is to accept that beings from 'these strange worlds come to visit us first.'

'That they reveal to us a little of their art, their life, their lore, their science, their religion and philosophy from which we may benefit a little.'

There are some people who swear on their lives, like Adamski, that they have 'spent hours in the company of men from more a highly evolved world and managed to recapture some of the spiritual beauty of their knowledge and philosophy.'

In the foreword to Adamski's next book, *Inside the Space Ships*, Leslie said that the author 'finds himself in that same awkward position as the native of Brazil who was given a ride in a helicopter. He's had his ride. The helicopter has gone away. He tries to tell his tribe what happened but there are no words in his language to describe it adequately.'

The book's many claims, however, were often too fantastic for any person, lay or scientist, to digest. In *The Flying Saucers Have Landed*, Leslie stated that earth's first visitors from Venus had arrived in 18,617,841 BC. He accounted for the precision of this calculation by attesting it was derived from 'ancient Brahmin tables' and cited the Brahmins as 'exceedingly accurate people.'

'Why should they risk a public landing? Their ship would be impounded for evasion of custom duties and their clothes would be torn off and sold as souvenirs,' he said.

Closer to home, Desmond Leslie began cataloguing stories of UFO sightings around Ireland, and joined forces with some high profile, mostly Anglo-Irish characters like himself, who shared the same penchant for extraterrestrial life forms.

Leslie worked closely with fellow Anglo-Irish aristocrat, Brinsley le Poer Trench, the 8th Earl of Clancarty, who prompted a debate on UFOs in the British House of Lords and became the chairman of the Lords UFO study group. Drawing on his own Irish experiences, Lord Clancarty claimed that, 'a landing, in which beings reveal themselves, must come very soon. I believe that with our nuclear problems and those of pollution, there is concern for us coming from outerspace.

'There have to be civilisations out there that have existed for thousands of years and that watch us. They must be worried as we are going wrong with all this nuclear stuff so these beings are becoming bolder and bolder.

'When they appear I just hope governments get together, cease building nuclear weaponry and go for open contact,' said the 8th Earl of Clancarty. He also kept close watch on the Co. Sligo estate of Lord Mountbatten, where UFO sightings were reported from as far back as 1965.

One of Mountbatten's hired hands at his Broadlands estate, an odd-jobs man by the name of Briggs, claimed to have witnessed the landing of an alien craft on the grounds. In an interview, carried out by Leslie with Briggs, the worker told how he had been 'approached' by 'beautiful golden haired' beings, who invited him aboard their ship.

In one of Desmond Leslie's last interviews before his death in Antibes, he told Irish film maker, Colum Stapleton, of his lifelong mission regarding UFOs and earth visitations.

'My role was to show that they [UFOs] have always been around and probably invented us by cross breeding,' said Leslie.

'In the last 50 years, more and more sightings have come to light, and eventually when it does come to a big landing people will say, "oh good, at last", particularly the children who grew up on it and they'll say, "where have you been all this time?"'

Leslie, a former World War II spitfire pilot, died wholly convinced that earth is a quarantine planet and an experimental greenhouse for superior alien races.

'Some people just can't bear the thought that we're not the most intelligent creatures in space and that we are probably one of the least intelligent – otherwise we wouldn't be here,' he told Stapleton.

'This is a quarantine planet and an experimental laboratory. It is one of the most exciting planets in the universe and I don't think they [extraterrestrials] are going to let us destroy it,' he said.

Desmond Leslie's interest in the supernatural was, more than likely, sparked at home by his father's musings and experiences with the paranormal. Sir Shane Leslie, third baronet of Glaslough, was born at the castle in 1885.

Originally named John Randolf, he renamed himself Shane, and became heavily involved in Irish nationalism, which saw him fight on the side of Irish freedom against Britain during the Easter rising of 1916. Shane Leslie was a colourful man, both of letters and dress; he was often spotted sporting a saffron kilt.

After graduating from King's College, Cambridge, where he became a Roman Catholic and where he took his new name, Leslie travelled to Russia, where he met Tolstoy and became influenced by his social theories.

However, Shane regularly extended his interests from politics into the field of the paranormal, and particularly that of ghosts. In 1955 he brought out *Shane Leslie's Ghost Book*. The book was the culmination of a lifelong interest of collecting ghost stories of all calibre, from poltergeists to death warnings from around Britain and Ireland.

Castle Leslie's 14 bedrooms are lavish in their layout and decor and more than one of its fine rooms boast a haunting from the Leslie lineage. Today the castle remains in the Leslie name and is open to the public as a luxury guest house. The famous red room is a favourite for those wishing to spend a night within the walls of a haunted castle.

It is said that the ghost of Norman Leslie, who died fighting during World War One, appears in this room frantically searching for something or other. The family talk of Lady Marjorie, Norman's mother, who awoke there one night to see what appeared to be her dead son, enveloped by 'a cloud of light' towards the end of her bed.

The apparition of the young soldier was beside a chest of drawers and was flicking through a pile of papers, and seemed quite intent on finding one letter in particular.

The spirit's search was cut short, however, when Lady Marjorie came to her senses and addressed the ghost of Norman Leslie. The elderly woman broke the silence of the eerie scene and asked him, 'Why, Norman, what are you doing here?'

The ghost turned to his mother, smiled and faded away. But the author Shane was to have his own haunting experience at his family castle, which he wrote about as follows.

'Curiously enough, Uncle Moreton, who died in 1925, was one of the few of the dead whose apparition I have seen. There is a type of apparition, which is visible to a sleeper in the first moments succeeding sleep. It has nothing to do with the previous dreaming nor has it any particular reason for appearance.

'It has occurred to me three times and each time so vividly, as to be overwhelming. For several hours after each appearance, I could not collect myself sufficiently to continue with ordinary life. My sense told me I had seen figures from the other world. This has only occurred to me after waking and while feeling perfectly assured that I was awake.

'I awoke at Glaslough two years after Uncle Moreton's death and to my surprise I saw him standing in the room. I was completely in possession of my senses and could see every object.

'Uncle Moreton said very deliberately to me, "I don't mind what you have written about me, but Uncle Stee will mind very much."

'I had recently written a sketch of his career, which I had classed under "Sublime Failures". This message was apparently correct, for Colonel Stephen Frewen, Lord Carson's father-in-law, was much annoyed, which I learned later. It was all so vivid that I could not think of anything else for several hours,' wrote Leslie.

There have been numerous reports of mysterious noises, and bells tolling of their own accord in the castle. Guests have also reported shadowy figures in the corridors and hallways of the old home.

The third member of the Leslie family to play a part in paranormal outings in Ireland and abroad, was Desmond's uncle and Shane's brother, the explorer, author, and monster hunter, Captain Lionel Leslie.

Lionel Leslie is most noted for his underwater expeditions in Scotland's Loch Ness as a revered monster hunter, but he was to become a regular visitor to the lakes of Connemara and a number of waterways in midland Ireland as well.

It was a sighting in 1954 of a 'creepy' monster on Connemara's Lough Fadda, by a number of friends out on a fishing trip in a small boat that prompted the captain's first Irish expedition.

The west coast of Ireland has a similar habitat to that of western Scotland, with which he was well acquainted.

Lionel Leslie believed a variant of the Scottish monster could easily exist on these shores.

In October 1965, Lionel was granted permission to explode a quantity of gelignite in the centre of the small western lake. The aim of the task, according to the monster hunter, was to send shockwaves through Lough Fadda and disturb the monster into surfacing. The team set two kilograms of the explosive against a rock near to where the 1954 sighting had occurred and let it blow.

Amongst the wild confusion and high splashings that followed, the team reported seeing a 'large, blackish object violently breaking the surface' about 45 metres away.

There was no tangible evidence after the explosion experiment, but the team and the captain went away convinced that the object they saw rise was indeed an unidentified animal, and in their eyes, a lake monster.

He was quoted later in the *Irish Independent* as saying, 'I am satisfied beyond any doubt that there is a monster in Lough Fadda.'

Two years later, Leslie was back on the Connemara lake, this time with a net measuring 50 feet with a breaking strain of 350lb. The net was set on a channel across a narrow stretch of lake for over two weeks but poor weather halted the expedition in its tracks.

Captain Lionel Leslie was to carry out net dragging operations on three more Connemara lakes. One of these was with celebrated monster hunter and author of *Dragon on the Disc*, F.W. Holiday, who had also worked exhaustively on Loch Ness.

The three searches turned up no result, however, as chains repeatedly caught in water lily roots and the expeditions ended disappointingly in spite of numerous previous sightings on all waterways searched.

In October 1982, a survey of Lough Derg led by Leslie, with the assistance of the Academy of Applied Science in Boston, reported a contact with a large underwater object, which was described by the captain as an 'unidentified aquatic creature.'

'During the first week the roller chart registered a solid moving object, not less than five feet in thickness, from top surface to underneath,' Leslie wrote in a letter to the *Irish Times* after compiling the results of his survey.

'It can be described as an unidentified aquatic creature and could possibly be the same as the one described by three Dublin priests on Lough Ree in May 1960. Its origin may have been the sea, but it is now land locked by the hydro electric dam,' said Leslie.

– CHAPTER NINETEEN –

The Roswell Connection

The world was rocked during the summer of 1947 by the greatest story ever told. Earth had been visited by alien life forms and a 'spaceship' had crash-landed in the deserts of New Mexico.

From the South China seas to the small town of Cahersiveen in Co. Kerry, an intense wave of UFO activity was reported during the first half of July of that year. Accounts of giant flying objects surrounded by 'halos of light' were documented across three continents as the world embraced the possibility of a visitation by beings from outer space.

In fact, the latter half of the 1940s was a peak time for UFO encounter worldwide. Science fiction, it seemed, had taken on a whole new slant in the devastating aftermath of the first atomic bomb, dropped by the Americans on Japan two years previously. In post war and pre cold war cultures, people were on the lookout for new threats, new technologies and new enemies. The race for space was barely in its infancy, but talk of Martians and flying saucers had wholly captured the public's imagination.

It had been less than ten years since Orson Wells terrified American radio listeners with his dramatisation of H.G. Wells *War of the Worlds*, which induced panic with its real-time news casts of invading Martians. The world of

1947 seemed quite prepared to accept such a scenario, albeit on a more passive front.

Cahersiveen on the northwestern edge of Kerry's Iveragh peninsula was a much darker place in 1947 than it is today. The government's rural electrification scheme had yet to illuminate the far reaches of the emerging republic, so peculiar lights in the sky were certainly an oddity worth noting.

In the early evening of 10 July 1947, Cahersiveen butcher, Michael O'Sullivan, and four other individuals reported seeing a series of strange, unidentified flying objects, described by one witness as being 'like a glittering bracelet', circling the small southern fishing village.

According to O'Sullivan, what they saw in the sky that evening was an object 'edged with a brilliant white halo of light; a flying saucer about 15 feet in diameter.' The thing 'swooped down noiselessly' over the town and flew off at terrific speed in a northwesterly direction.

The Cahersiveen UFO sighting appeared in that Saturday's *Irish Press* under the questioning headline 'A Flying Saucer?' The report read:

'Mr. Michael O'Sullivan, victualler, Quay Street, Cahersiveen, told our correspondent that he saw a circular object in the sky last evening coming from the north west and travelling noiselessly at high speed. It was about 15 feet in diameter and was flying at about 1,000 feet. Four other people were reported to have seen the object.'

The following week the provincial newspaper, *The Kerryman*, caught up with more witnesses of the Cahersiveen flying saucer.

'Round-Shaped Flying Object Seen Over Cahersiveen' ran the large headline in the next Saturday's *Kerryman*.

'Mr. James Devine, Provisions Merchant Church St. said the object seemed to reflect the rays of the sun and described it as "like a glittering bracelet". Our Cahersiveen correspondent says that enquiries made at the meteorological station at Valentia, revealed that no parachute balloons, which it was thought had been observed, were released that day.'

Gardai are reported to have taken statements from a number of people who claimed to have seen the object. As isolated as this encounter in south west Ireland may have seemed, it was, in fact, only one of a series of sightings around the globe during the first two weeks of July 1947. The Cahersiveen encounter occurred within days of the world's most celebrated UFO incident.

The so-called Roswell incident of July 1947 is without doubt the most enduring UFO legend to ever circulate this planet. It is a compelling series of events, heavily laced with alleged government cover-up and fantastic eyewitness accounts. It has as many detractors as it has ardent defenders, and has been as willfully elaborated upon as it has been vehemently denied by United States intelligence agencies.

The events that led up to the Roswell incident began on 2 July when there were numerous reports of unidentified flashing lights over the New Mexico desert. One week later, local farmer William 'Mac' Brazel stumbled upon the wreckage of an alien aircraft, seemingly crashed on part of his ranch. Brazel's find resulted in the first ever admission by the US military that there was such a thing as 'flying discs', as UFOs were then called.

On examination of the wreckage, which was said to have been made from a metal which would not break, dent or burn and was said to have been inscribed with peculiar hieroglyphic symbols, a US military agent told Brazel that the object 'was not of this earth'.

Despite the military's open statements on first receiving the wreckage, the weeks, months and years that followed Brazel's discovery were steadily shrouded by government backpeddling on what they had initially said.

From Roswell in New Mexico to Kerry in the south of Ireland and on to China, where a large flying saucer bearing the same description of a 'halo of light' was also reported by hundreds of witnesses in the first week of July 1947.

In west Kerry, Michael O'Sullivan's son, Séamus, recalls the stories his father told him of that evening when Cahersiveen was visited by at least one UFO in the same week as the Roswell and Chinese incidents.

'My father was walking down the street where he had grown up, and just as he was taking the corner, he saw a great light,' said the witnesses son.

'It looked to him what he thought a space ship would look like, with a lot of lights on it, hovering far above his head, before it swooped down and flew away without a sound, higher up into the sky and away towards the sea,' said Séamus O'Sullivan.

Michael O'Sullivan used the popular expression 'flying saucer' in his description of the strange lights, as the term UFO had yet to be coined.

'It would have been completely out of the ordinary for him to have come out with something like that if it wasn't true. He wasn't a man to exaggerate anything like that,' said Séamus. 'In 1947 there weren't too many lights around here so anything bright, which caught the eye overhead was reported.

'What he saw scooped down right over him, moved on for a couple of seconds and disappeared again. Thankfully he wasn't alone and there were a few witnesses there that evening,' said Séamus.

With the passing of more than half of a century, it is doubtful the origin of the crashed New Mexico craft, or that of the Cahersiveen incident, will ever be known.

Up to 160 witnesses, all locals from the Roswell area gave evidence and made statements about the incident, which they claim were never examined or followed up on by the military. After loading the two kilos of wreckage into the back of his trailer, Brazel took it to the local sheriff's office, who immediately informed Roswell Army Air Field.

From here a Colonel Marcel took over from the sheriff, and made a statement to the press saying that 'The Roswell Army Air Field has gained possession of a flying disc on a ranch in the Roswell region.'

In the ensuing clamour of media attention, Marcel's statement was withdrawn by higher brass, and Brazel was held incommunicado for over a week as the CIA took over affairs in the New Mexico region. In the weeks that followed, a new statement from the air base was drawn up which stated that it was, in fact, a 'weather balloon', which was found by William 'Mac' Brazel.

The weather balloon story was never accepted by the townspeople and was eventually recanted as untrue by authorities in 1994 amidst new evidence and a new investigation.

The 160 witness accounts from Roswell (pop. 49,000) continued to tell a different story as the alleged cover-up continued. Many of those who initially testified would also change their stories, and later said they were forced into silence by threats from visiting government agents and by the military police.

In one incident, a radio transmission from a station in the neighbouring city of Albuquerque, talking about the find of a 'flying disc' at Roswell, was halted in mid transmission and the station was warned not to continue with similar items or their licence would be revoked.

Another young woman, who claimed to have found parts of a flying saucer in her garden, said she was threatened by the police and told that 'it was a very big desert out there where no one would find her bones.'

In 1994 under pressure from a Republican congressman from Roswell, the US congress admitted that a cover up had been initiated to mystify the Roswell incident, and that the weather balloon story had not been entirely accurate.

And yet, that is as far as the intelligence agency was prepared to go regarding fresh information on the issue. On the other side of the fence, however, there has been no shortage of voices to support the possibility of an alien craft crash landing at Roswell in the summer of 1947, which was covertly seized by the authorities.

Monaghan based ufologist, and founder of the Irish Ufology Forum Outreach and Paranormal Studies organisation, Jim Flora, is one such voice.

'There have been a string of UFO incidents throughout the mid-twentieth century, which were just blanketed over by the powers that be,' said Flora.

'The American Government was afraid at the time of the Roswell incident. Their fears were manifold, but fell primarily at the fact that they had just entered a cold war situation with the Russians, and couldn't let other nations know they possessed crashed alien technology,' said Flora, who believes the United States Government has seized eleven extraterrestrial crafts.

'They were also still very worried about the effect on the American psyche so soon after World War II. If this news got out that there was something better and faster and more intelligent than any systems they possessed themselves, or that their own scientists could manage to produce, how would people ever believe they could control the country?

'Then there is the fear that they would enter a *War of the Worlds* scenario, sending the nation into hysterics over potential invasion,' Flora said.

No amount of conspiracy theory, however, can take from the probability that what Mac Brazel discovered on his land was perhaps just the latest prototype of military hardware, crashed or jettisoned from the nearby air base.

Roswell Army Air Base was, in fact, home to the elite 509th Bomb Group, which dropped the first atomic bombs on Hiroshima and Nagasaki two years previously. It was also considered the most secret and important base in the US air forces. Also of interest is the fact that the New Mexico desert, which surrounds Roswell, was used for many years as a testing ground for this atomic weaponry.

What has emerged concerning the weather balloon yarn of 1947 is that a very real cover up was put into play, but it was likely to be one blanketing a secret government programme under development for spying on the Russians.

The details of Project Mogul were only to come out in the early 1990s in a post cold war era. According to US military sources, Roswell Army Air Base was the site of development for a new 'long-range nuclear detection facility'. In 1947 the Russians had yet to detonate any atomic or nuclear weapons, but the US were placing sophisticated probes, in the shape of weather balloons, in the upper atmosphere, which would pick up acoustic waves when and if an atomic or nuclear device was tested. According the United States government, this is what was discovered at Roswell.

CHAPTER TWENTY

The IUFOPRA Files

'As the man looked out to sea, he observed two large bright orange objects flying north-westwards towards Wicklow. Both objects were the colour of the setting sun, and cast reflections across the water. It was a clear night, and the witness kept the objects in view for a minute or more as they glided silently inland. He was not frightened by what he saw, just curious, though he was reluctant to speak to anyone about his experience until some months later, for fear of ridicule.'

This anonymous account is just a tiny part of a growing database of UFO related encounters over Ireland, compiled by the Irish UFO and Paranormal Research Association (IUFOPRA).

According to the group, this particular case occurred just across the Wexford border, around 1980, at Clones Strand, about six miles south of Arklow town in Co. Wicklow, when a local resident was returning to his home at approximately 2 a.m. after a late stroll to the nearby village of Castletown.

One year later the same individual, who is described in the report as a 'non drinker', was to meet with another 'bizarre' display of anomalous lights, but this time he was not on his own.

'The following summer the same man was giving a lift to some friends from Dublin, who were staying at a local caravan site. Their jokes to the (former mentioned) witness about "seeing little green men" were very quickly forgotten when, on a pitch dark road, orange and white lights appeared behind their car. In a scene reminiscent of the *Close Encounters of the Third Kind* movie, they slowed down.

'As they manoeuvred the car to the side of the road, the "car" behind overtook them – by lifting off and flying over their roof. The craft veered off to the right, again towards the Wicklow border a couple of miles away, and disappeared into the night sky,' ran the report.

IUFOPRA was set up in 1987 under an ambitious mission statement: to 'conduct, promote and encourage unbiased scientific research of UFOs and related phenomena throughout Ireland and the whole world.'

The organisation was founded by members of the British UFO interest group (BUFORA), who now act as the governing body and mothership for the Irish operation. IUFOPRA divide their time and resources between research into UFO encounter, and other more earthly paranormal experiences including ghosts, poltergeists, and classic hauntings.

Kathy Crinion has had a life long interest in the paranormal, and one that stretches back many generations of her family. She became a member of IUFOPRA in 1991.

With a background in psychology, Crinion's main area of interest is not so much in UFOs, or the potential for alien life forms visiting earth, but in those unexplainable phenomena occurring in our own homes and sometimes in our minds.

'People get in touch with us who think their house is haunted so we go out and, with their permission, document their experiences and run a number of tests on the building in question,' said Crinion.

According to the Co. Meath psychotherapist, IUFOPRA's main tool in detecting ghostly energies is an Electro Magnetic Frequency (EMF) reader. 'It picks up different levels of magnetic frequency, which tend to be higher in areas that are known to be haunted,' she said.

While numerous theories and modern technology can help rationalise many of the weird goings on in houses and homes, sensitivity is the first rule of thumb for the IUFOPRA operative.

'These people don't come to us for nothing; they're looking for reassurances both mentally and physically with the hope that whatever is happening in their homes can be stopped. At the very least they are also looking for an explanation as to why these things should happen in the first place.

'Some people are just happy to tell their story, and get reassurance from people who believe them. They often become very disturbed by what they've seen in their own homes.

'It's not quite the same as the UFO phenomena, which has been very much out in the open over the last 50 years. The ghosts and haunting side of the paranormal is a more personal thing, and people in Ireland are very closed about such issues,' said Crinion.

She cites one particular instance, where a Dublin family had been pushed to the very edge by a recurring apparition in their home. 'We were called out to a house on Griffith Avenue in Dublin, where the residents regularly saw a woman standing at the top of their stairs. What was odd about this woman was that the family actually recognised her apparition as a distant member of their family. Of course, when we went out we didn't see anything, but the EMF readings were particularly high at the spot where she was said to manifest, and our investigators found the same location much more chilled than the rest of the house,' said Crinion.

IUFOPRA's main aim is to document paranormal phenomena reported around the country, but their expertise in the area has allowed them, on occasion, to get more involved.

'Most often we act as a middleman who can put people in touch with a psychic, priest or some relevant form of help who can deal with their particular area of the paranormal.'

In some instances, the IUFOPRA investigator has been able to rule out the classic haunting scenario through evidence, which would suggest the presence of 'poltergeist activity', which she believes is brought about solely by the energies of the people in the house.

A poltergeist is a 'noise ghost', as opposed to the classic visual apparition more commonly associated with ghosts, and it generally manifests itself in the form of objects smashing against walls or to the floor, doors locking or slamming suddenly by themselves, and sounds or voices eerily resounding around a building.

'Poltergeists usually stem from people's energies, mostly from the energies of young people or those going through intense hormonal change, such as prepubescent teenagers, pregnant women or newly born babies and their mothers,' said Crinion.

'The mind is a very strong thing, and because we don't use more than half of it we don't know exactly what the other half is capable of. Where there are bad feelings in a house, where there is fighting, and where there is tension or pent up anger and emotion it can very easily manifest itself as an outside energy form and bring about polterkinetic energies. Energy is an amazing thing because it won't die,' she said.

According to Crinion, most classic cases of things-that-go-bump-in-the-night, or even during the day, are not caused by a ghost or spirit activity at all 'but by pure energy.'

'Whenever we're notified of a poltergeist, there's usually a teenager involved with the house. There tends to be some form of untapped hormonal energy at play there. The same has been documented in houses where there are disabled or autistic children. They are using different parts of their brains, and so are pulling on different energies. For the most part, people have become so robotised in their actions that the mind knows exactly what it has to do in advance of an action. This has reached such a stage that our energies have become focused. Teenagers or disabled individuals are constantly tapping into different areas of the brain and producing different mental energies,' she said.

As far as the phenomenon of apparitional ghosts are concerned Crinion is less sure. 'The visual side of a haunting could, I suppose, be energy absorbed into that building over many years. However, people who claim to see ghosts in fields, would kind of take from the building theory.

'I'm not quite sure about ghosts returning from the "other side", although I'd like to believe in the other side. But then, I'm not sure I'd like to think that you'd have to come back in order to take care of unfinished business either. I'd like to believe the other side would have something better to offer, and that you wouldn't want to come back. However, I'm not disputing the fact that spirits do come back because of unfinished business, or that they become trapped somehow between this world and another.'

'We've found that these things tend to happen more at night, maybe because your mind is more attuned to what's going on, on a psychic level,' she said. And some strange happenings are not necessarily paranormal either.

'It has been proven that you can go to sleep and wake up in the middle of the night and see a figure or people at the foot of your bed, which is actually being projected from your mind into the room. It has nothing to do with spooks or hauntings but is a purely psychological phenomenon.'

The same cannot be said, however, when the testimony comes from a group of people who claim to have witnessed a ghostly encounter or UFOs and the IUFOPRA researcher has come up against this on numerous occasions.

Crinion lives near Trim, Co. Meath, home to the largest Anglo Norman Castle ever built in Ireland by the banks of the River Boyne. Trim Castle was built in 1173 by Norman knight Hugh de Lacy, three years after the Normans invaded Ireland. Two-thirds of the castle's imposing curtain walls still stand at Trim, making it an intriguing site to visit for thousands of tourists every year.

'I was told by a friend who worked at the information centre at Trim Castle that a group of German visitors saw the ghost of a monk at an altar at the side of one of the ruined buildings there,' said Crinion.

Impressed, the German visitors told the guide that they had seen 'the great special effect', thinking it was part of the tour. But the guide knew nothing about it and told them that they never staged re-enactments, so the visitors were left with no explanation for their vision.

'The guides at Trim Castle say that none of them will go into the keep above where the dungeon used to be on their own first thing in the morning, or stay around at night because it's just too scary in there,' said Crinion.

However, according to the Meath psychologist, some people are quite happy to live with ghosts. 'I know of one woman, also in Co. Meath, who has lived with a ghost all her life and now she wouldn't have it any other way. She sees it as part of the house. It's the ghost of a woman who comes to make tea every morning in her kitchen. Younger people are more scared of these things while older people tend to accept them more readily,' she said.

Crinion's penchant for the paranormal stems from a childhood spent listening to such stories from people, who she said 'would have no business telling lies about such matters.'

'My Dad heard the banshee's cries at the time of his sister's death, and he remembers that the priest in attendance pretended not to hear it. His father actually saw the banshee on a wall outside a hospital crying and combing her hair. These people are not likely to lie about this sort of thing. I grew up with these stories. It was just part of everyday life in our house,' she said.

She remembers hearing of a relation on her mother's side of the family, who fell foul to a supernatural phenomenon known as the 'stray sod'.

'This is said to happen to people while walking through a field when all of a sudden, they wouldn't know where they were anymore. There'd be hedges all around and you couldn't find your way home. Some people think it was that you'd stepped on the ground where an unbaptised child was buried.

'The story I heard was of a woman in Rathfarnham in south Dublin who, while coming home on a bike, saw a dog by the ditch and got off the bike to pet the animal. Her hand was said to have gone right through the dog and when she looked around her, she couldn't figure out where she was.

'She was suddenly in a field with hedges blocking all view. She went down on her knees and prayed and when she opened her eyes again everything was back to normal,' recalled Crinion.

The instance of the 'stray sod' resembles another very Irish phenomenon of supernatural cursed earth, the *Fear Gortagh* or *Hungry Grass*. This is a potentially fatal phenomenon for anyone unfortunate enough to walk upon such land. Those who fall victim to the *Fear Gortagh* are sent into paroxysms of great hunger and will expire within a matter of hours if they don't eat copious amounts of food. It is said that the hungry grass occurs on the patch of land where victims of the Great Irish famine of the 1840s fell down and eventually died from the hunger inflicted upon them. Many instances of the *Fear Gortagh* have been documented on farmlands around the country from the early part of the twentieth century.

Crinion's work with the paranormal isn't merely tied down to this earth, however. Much of IUFOPRA's investigations centre on the phenomena of Unidentified Flying Objects (UFOs). 'Like the hauntings, people send us their UFO sighting reports and we catalogue and cross-reference each one.'

As a relatively darkened outpost on the northern edge of the Atlantic Ocean, Ireland provides an enviable sighting ground for all manner of UFOs. Yet, despite our year-round, inky night-skies and low levels of urban light pollution, very little research had been published on Irish UFO encounter until IUFOPRA compiled their *UFOs Over Ireland: Status Report* in the early 1990s.

'When we get a UFO report, we check with the meteorological stations and other astrological charts to make sure that what was witnessed was not a natural phenomenon such as a meteorite or a weather balloon.'

From the outset IUFOPRA delivered an open-minded mission statement with regard to the possibility of a genuine sighting. 'While we recognise that at least 90 per cent of the reports of UFO sightings can be identified or classified as astronomical, it is the remaining 10 per cent that we are concerned about.'

And while they view 'the modern study of UFOs as one of the most important phenomena of our time', they remain ambiguous in their classification of the origin and nature of these phenomena.

'Many theories abound as to the origins of UFOs, mainly as natural phenomena or possibly advanced (alien?) technology,' they said. 'IUFOPRA recognises that there are a number of explanatory hypotheses and does not advocate to any particular theory.'

'We just want to document Irish cases. We're not a group who are going out saying that we are seeking the truth,' said Crinion.

The group's first port of call (and most fecund source in compiling their *UFOs over Ireland: Status Report*) was the Irish tabloid press. On 13 April 1996, *The Star* newspaper ran a story on a driver travelling along the Armagh/Monaghan border who 'spotted – in broad daylight – a bright light behind his car. The object pulled up alongside his left-hand side and then darted in and out of the trees at considerable speed.'

Other sightings were reported from Armagh City and across South Armagh at the same time.

IUFOPRA's report on this sighting highlighted that 'local people, used to military activity in the area, insisted that the objects they saw were not British Army helicopters, or signal activity, and some people have associated the objects with a cattle mutilation some time earlier in the Camlough area.'

While drawing on the wealth of 'sensational' information emanating from the red-top press, IUFOPRA are quick to point out, that 'the majority of these newspapers do not, and never will, in our opinion take the UFO phenomenon seriously enough to warrant it the respect it deserves, and many sensationalise these stories for entertainment purposes only and, of course, to sell their newspapers.'

Over the years, however, there have been numerous reports of UFO encounter from the more reliable source of members of the Garda Síochana. A front page article from *The Irish Press* on New Year's Day 1979, told how 'Gardaí and an Army helicopter crew took part in a search for a UFO sighted over counties Roscommon and Sligo on New Year's Eve.'

The article quotes a garda stationed at Boyle in Co. Roscommon, who said he saw it for about two minutes and called members of his family to view it with him.

'It was the strangest thing I ever saw in my life. It was moving very fast in a northeasterly direction. It was like a big flame in the sky – very bright with a tail of light. It definitely was not an aircraft. We watched it for a few minutes until it disappeared out of view. It did not appear to fall to earth,' said the garda.

Many years later, the *Evening Herald* reported on two garda patrolmen who witnessed low-flying lights travelling above power lines from their car near Limerick. The gardaí said they observed a 'large object in the sky with two lights, one at the front and the other at the back', near Askeaton, Co. Limerick. The article quoted other witnesses in Limerick city who reported 'a silent craft like a Jumbo jet gliding over rooftops, that looked like it was about to touch electricity pylons.'

On a more officious tone, the Irish Government was addressed in 1981 by former Taoiseach [Prime Minister], and then Minister for Transport, Albert Reynolds about the number of investigations that had been launched into UFO sightings.

'A Dáil Mystery of the missing UFOs' ran the headline in the *Irish Independent* on 11 March 1981.

'Mr. Reynolds told Mr. Michael Keating in the Dáil [the Irish parliament] yesterday that a total of eight sightings of Unidentified Flying Objects had been reported and investigated by the authorities in the last ten years,' said the report.

'Mr. Reynolds listed sightings at north-east Alihies, Co. Cork; Enniscorthy, Co. Wexford; Ballymacouda, Co. Cork; Sligo; Limerick and the Killiney, Whitehall and Naul areas of Dublin. All had been investigated but there were no positive findings,' he said.

– CHAPTER TWENTY-ONE –

The Psychic Squad

Not since the heyday of the Victorian parlour game has the fortune teller been in such high demand. Twenty-first century Ireland is awash with round-the-clock 'online psychics,' standing by to take your call and reveal your future.'

This huge demand, on what is largely seen as an entertainment industry, reflects our cash rich culture, as it did for the upper classes of the late 1800s, who amused themselves no end with séances, tarot cards, and crystal ball readings, bringing such occult dabblings into vogue.

While today's 'online psychics' offer a quick fix to a curious public unsure of their career or romantic prospects, we still know very little about this supernatural ability to access hidden information.

Ever since the first scientific experiments into psychic ability were carried out during the early nineteenth century, the phenomenon has remained an area heavily shrouded in academic psychobabble.

What we do know is that psychics and clairvoyants appear to have the capacity to acquire information by paranormal means, that is, beyond the natural range of the senses. Precognition, commonly referred to as fortune telling, is another common psychic trait, which allows the practitioner visions relating to some future event.

These phenomena tend to be harnessed by the psychic through the use of props including tarot cards (decorated with esoteric and occult symbols), palm reading, astrology, crystal dowsing, and deep meditation.

While anecdotal evidence from all cultures and all corners of the globe outweighs any hard-and-fast scientific proof or theory on psychic phenomenon, it is an area which the world's major political powers have long been keen to utilise.

Over the last 50 years, various international governments have initiated top-secret programmes to investigate how they might harness the power of psychic ability to their best advantage.

During the 1970s, the CIA employed a team of psychics at the government funded Stanford Research Institute, ostensibly to pinpoint Russian nuclear submarines and nuclear bases from a distance through a system they coined 'remote viewing'.

The institute was intrigued by New York artist Ingo Swann who, in 1973, showed how he could vividly describe a place, down to fine environmental detail, when given only the precise latitude and longitude.

This system of remote viewing was soon picked up on by families of missing people, who contacted psychics to assist in the search for their loved ones.

In Ireland, many respected psychics have involved themselves in this area of psychic detection. Waterford clairvoyant, Stan Phillips, has been successful in locating bodies and helping to ease the distress of relatives.

Phillips has been involved in a number of high profile missing person cases on request of the families and has insisted that their names be removed for reasons of confidentiality.

'I was approached by the family of a man who had been missing for over two years. The man had been involved in the drugs trade, and was believed to have been murdered. The family wanted information and, at worst, a body in order to get some sort of closure on what had become of him,' explained Phillips.

'This man's mother came to me and I asked her to tell me all about him, and what she knew of his last known actions. From this information I named a place some way out in the country, and asked her would that be a particular destination where he would go. It turned out that he had a son in a village nearby, but what I could visualise at the time was a wooded area with mountains in the background. Three weeks later, a decayed body was discovered in those woods. It took three months to identify it as the corpse of the man in question.'

Although Phillips has involved himself in these cases, it is far from his favourite area of psychic practice.

'It's the more difficult end of the psychic spectrum, simply because you are working with so little. But I reckon I can get at least a 50 per cent success rate on every case taken,' he said.

'All I need is a bit of background on the individual or place. I ask who the person is, where they were last seen and then somehow, I get a picture of them going somewhere or doing something until a place will crop up in my mind. Sometimes a map might help me visualise an exact area.'

Psychic and pagan priestess, Sandra Ramdhanie, uses tarot cards to help her mind focus when approaching what she calls the fairly 'draining process' of remote viewing.

Ramdhanie agrees with Phillips that this practice takes a lot out of the person involved. She has been involved in a number of successful remote viewing cases, but her first experience with this form of psychic ability stands out the most for her.

'I was out in the United States in 1991, and met with a famous psychic named Judith Farina, from Chester in Connecticut. We did various tarot readings for each other and generally got on well. She then contacted me on my return to Ireland,' said Ramdhanie.

'She wanted to know if I could help her in a missing person's case she was working on. I was tired but I agreed, and got my tarot cards, which act for me as a short cut to my subconscious because I've worked with them for so long.'

According to Ramdhanie, tarot cards are comprised of primary colours and occult geometric designs, which act as a catalyst in opening the gateway to your subconscious.

'She told me that a young girl of about 18 years had gone missing in the New Jersey area. As she was thinking of the person I put a card out and said, "she's got long dark hair and I can see a river."

'She told me, "that's right, she disappeared while doing water sports."

'I find that your psychic talents flow best when you're very tired; particularly as your conscious mind prepares to fall asleep. It's a time when inspiration can flood your brain. I remember I was like that in this particular instance.

'One minute I'm reading from the cards, the next minute I'm looking down, fixed above a scene of a girl's body lying faced downward on the dry shore of a river. When I saw her first, I thought she was on a beach with the tide out. I then saw what appeared to be an overgrown, hexagonal pipe leading into a river. I told her I could see a mark on the neck of the body, and a pattern on her back like a 3D effect flashing as if there were symbols on her body.

'I remember then I went in closer, and that was when the reality struck that it was a real person I was seeing. For a while I felt I was looking at a cartoon or dream-like image, but when I moved in closer, the reality set in and that's when it cut off for me. I remember saying, "Oh no! I'm seeing blood, I'm feeling sick".'

After the phone call from Farina, Ramdhanie rang another friend in New Jersey where the girl was reported missing and asked her to look out for the case in the papers. 'Three days later my friend rang me up and read out a newspaper article saying that the body of a missing 18-year-old girl had been found lying face down on a half dried creek bed. She'd been stabbed to death and the word "shit" was carved into her back.'

According to Ramdhanie, remote viewing can be as simple as dreaming or as she calls it, 'astral travelling'. 'People can often spontaneously remote view in dream time,' she said. 'It is only stressful when you bring it on yourself.'

Working in an area so alien to conventional thinking, Ramdhanie explains her psychic ability in simplistic terms. 'I think being psychic is just being able to see the bigger picture and the very small pictures all at the same time.'

Phillips also underplays his skills in clairvoyance. 'I have absolutely no idea how it works; you just go down a road of trust with your senses. It's about knowing when to pick up on the right connection and tapping into that connection.

'For example, I had a woman with me and I took down her date of birth, which I do sometimes to work out numerology that can reveal a lot about a person. As it turned out she shared a birthday with my daughter. So I looked for a connection and as our daughter was adopted many years ago, I decided to use that and said "what's this about adoption?" Well, she turned to me and told me that herself and her husband had just set out to adopt a child and were going to ask me about their chances of success.'

Other psychics are more graphic when describing their 'gift'. In her book, *Time Travels of an Irish Psychic*, Sheila Lindsay described her 'gift of seeing and hearing on a higher level of consciousness' as a journey though time.

'To me time is not a straight line. I feel it all around me,' wrote Lindsay. 'I can float forwards or backwards or sideways in time; I can see the past or the future or the present in another place.

'The ocean of time is all around us; as with the ocean at the seaside, some of us are better swimmers than others. People who have the gift of perception can move easily through time,' she said.

Dublin-based Catholic priest, Fr. Pat Collins, who lectures in psychology would agree with Lindsay that some people are more attuned to the subconscious than others.

'There are certain combinations of personality types where you have people with high intuition, good access to the unconscious, and considerable confidence about information, which comes in on the non rational channels,' said Collins, who has had his own precognitions come true and believes he has inherited some psychic ability through his mother's side of his family.

'It's like a short wave radio; you might have confidence on some of the wavelengths that other people would have no confidence on. I think it's a purely natural gift and some are more receptive to these gifts than others.'

Phillips and Ramdhanie both operate as tarot card readers and claim to have the ability to divine future events.

'I get different kinds of communication,' said Ramdhanie. 'Sometimes telepathic images come up in my mind, other times I see the future, present, or past as pictures like the image on a television screen. It can come in a series of images and often I'll be left to piece the story together. Over the years I have come to learn how to decipher my normal train of thought from the telepathic information coming in,' she said.

There are countless stories from those who visit reputable fortune-tellers and come away in awe of how a complete stranger could reveal their most guarded secrets. Over the years, various journalists have had their sceptical natures rocked by the perceptiveness of psychics they have interviewed.

Writing for *Ireland on Sunday,* reporter Patrice Harrington met British psychic Helen Parry-Jones, and was rendered speechless by her powers of perception.

In her report, Harrington describes Parry-Jones as a medium who claims to have contacted John Lennon, John F. Kennedy, George Bernard Shaw and Adolf Hitler.

It all happened half-way through the interview as follows:

'Parry-Jones: "I know that your grandfather suffered with his heart and lungs and when he died he went very quickly. He's here now."

'P.H.: "Can you see him?"

'Parry-Jones: "Yeah, he's quite a big, well-made man. He loves his food. He's got a lot of farming situations around him and he's very much an outdoor worker. He says you're 23 – how old are you?"

'P.H.: "I'm 23. My grandad died of a heart attack and he was a farmer."

'Parry-Jones: "Now I've got a women called Mary in the spirit world asking for you. She's with your grandad and she's very close to him. They're together all the time. She died around the time of someone's birthday, because everyone's writing cards."

'P.H.: "My nanny's name was Mary and she died at Christmas time."

'Parry-Jones: "That explains the cards. Your nanny tells me she died on the 26th of December."

'P.H.: Speechless.'

From her home in Cobh, Co. Cork, White Witch of the Isles Helen Barrett, puts her psychic abilities to the ultimate test by hooking herself up to a polygraph, or lie detector.

'The polygraph works at the speed of thought and reacts promptly to shifts in emotion. It allows me to be more comfortable with my feelings on certain predictions that I make.'

And Barrett makes no small claims either. Amongst her CV of precognition are such illustrious events as the death of Princess Diana, and the September 11th attack on New York's Twin Towers.

Fortunately for Barrett and for a largely sceptical public, she makes many of these predictions on Cork radio station 96FM, where she has become a familiar voice.

In January 2001 Barrett told 96FM presenter Neil Prenderville that, 'An iron bird would sweep across America. A steel fountain pen would descend into a cloud of fumes. A five pointed building would be involved in some way and the stock market would crash on the day.'

Barrett claims that her own birth was predicted as far back as the eighteenth century and that she was destined to lead Ireland's 3,500 witches and wizards.

'In 1775 my ancestor Michelle D'Bharoid actually said I would be born in the cove of Cork and that I would have a ladder in my hand,' said Barrett. The ladder is a particular feature on the white witch's palm, which she says is a mark of ascendancy. Barrett claims she was trained in the art of psychic ability by 'the council of elders at sacred and secret sites in Kerry and Cork.'

The white witch finished, 'when you focus on something your mind will provide an answer. It's like if you meet somebody and you can't remember their name, but in the course of the evening that name will come back to you because you have asked the question in the back of your brain. It's the same with clairvoyance. The future is very much like a record in that the sound has already been left in the grooves.'

APPENDIX

CO. ANTRIM

The ruin of Dunluce Castle, near the Giant's Causeway on the Antrim coast, is haunted by the plaintive singing and unrelenting floor sweeping of a woman known as Maeve, who drowned with her lover while attempting to elope in a small boat across the rough northern sea.

— *Dunluce Castle, Portrush, Co. Antrim. Tours of castle ruins organised from April to September. Contact the Northern Ireland Tourist Board, ph. 028 90246609.*

The ancient ramparts and hallways of Ballygally Castle is said to be haunted by a noble woman reputed to be in constant search for her lost children.

— *Ballygally Castle, Ballygally, Co. Antrim. A three star hotel open to guests year round, ph. 028 28583212.*

The ghost of Elizabeth Dobbin is believed to aimlessly wander the corridors of Dobbins Inn Hotel at Carrickfergus. This lady of the house was murdered by her husband, a former mayor of Carrickfergus, who caught her in an act of infidelity with a man he is also said to have butchered.

— *Dobbins Inn Hotel, High Street, Carrickfergus, Co. Antrim. Two star hotel open to guests year round, ph. 028 93351905.*

A number of walkers in woodland at Downhill, near Benone caught sight of an Alien Big Cat (ABC) at least 20 inches tall. The matter was highlighted in the *Belfast Telegraph* on 16 August 1997 but no specimen was ever found.

A wild fur-covered beast, nicknamed 'The Beast of Ballymena' is said to roam the woodlands in the town's immediate area. The animal could not be catagorised by witnesses as a large cat or dog as it was allegedly seen standing on its hindquarters.

Co. ARMAGH
The heritage city of Armagh is reputedly haunted by the ghost of vicious murderer Bellena Prior who was tried and hanged for the crime of boiling her neighbour's child alive in 1888. Her desperate apparitional figure has been seen in many of the city's old quarters.

– *Information on city tours available from Armagh City and District Council, ph. 028 37529600.*

Reports of cattle mutilations in Co. Armagh during 1997 mystified local farmers, as they could not be ascribed to any known dog or wild beast. The incident featured in the *Fortean Times* magazine at the time. Cattle mutilations in the US have long been linked to UFO activity.

Co. CARLOW
The canal lock at Bestfield, north of Carlow town, is said to be haunted by the ghost of a drowned haulier. Since the end of the nineteenth century boat owners who moor at night or pass through Bestfield Lock, have heard strange knockings on the hulls of their craft.

– *Bestfield lock, Bestfield, Carlow, Co. Carlow. Further information from Waterways Ireland, ph. 01 8680148.*

Six large, darkened grass circles appeared on the surface of three football pitches in Clonegal during the summer of 2002. The circles, measuring 30 feet in diameter, each contained a smaller inner circle. Local folklore tells of a 'fairy carriage', which travelled along the town's river.

Huntingdon Castle, built in 1625 in the picturesque village of Clonegal in south Carlow has amongst its ghosts a troupe of Franciscan Friars who patrol the ground's 800-year-old Yew Tree Walk. The castle is also haunted by Lady Esmonde often seen with her spectral white cat. The ghost of eighteenth century Bishop of Limerick James Lesley has also been encountered at Huntingdon.

– Huntingdon Castle, Clonegal, Co. Carlow. Tours of gardens and house available on request, ph. 054 77552.

Co. Cavan
A field on the estate of Ross Castle known locally as 'hangman's hollow' is believed to be haunted by the ghost of Richard Nugent, lord of the castle in the mid-sixteenth century. Nugent was famed and feared under the name of the 'Black Baron' and was infamous for hanging men and women alike.

– Ross Castle, Mount Nugent, Co. Cavan. For holiday rental year round, ph. 049 8540237.

The small village of Killeshandra has its own death warning, like the banshee, but in the form of a Black Coach, which has often been seen down the ages racing through the town and back roads. The area is said to have been a sacred site for druidic ritual 3,000 years before the advent of Christianity.

Co. Clare
The phantom village of Kilstiveen, said to have been swallowed by the sea in ancient times, comes into view

beneath the surface of the Atlantic in a bay south of Lahinch as a forewarning of death and disaster.

The ground at Rineen Hill near Lahinch is said to produce haunting experiences for those who camp upon it. Tents are mysteriously uprooted in calm weather and belongings are scattered. Rineen Hill was a spot where many dead British soldiers were laid out after fighting in 1916.

Co. Cork

The townland of Coomhola, three miles north of the seaside town of Bantry, is regularly used by UFO interest groups as a sighting ground for UFOs. There was a 'flap' of UFO sightings in the area in the early 1990s.

The spectre of a White Lady haunts the ramparts of Charles Fort near Kinsale. Her form is that of Mrs. Wilful Warrender, the daughter of the first colonel of the fort, from the late seventeenth century. She threw herself off the battlements after her new groom, Sir Trevor Ashurst, was accidentally killed by Colonel Warrender who then killed himself in despair.

– *Charles Fort, Kinsale, Co. Cork. Tours of fort available daily between 9 a.m. and 5 p.m. Contact Cork and Kerry Tourism, ph. 021 4255100.*

Fishermen on Lough Attariff witnessed a 'long, dark brown monster with large glittering eyes' in the summer of 1966. They said the creature was over 100 yards away and they could tell by its size that it was no ordinary aquatic animal.

The Medieval ruin of Ballynacarriga Castle near Dunmanway is the home of a fearsome and devilish

'Pooka' believed to dwell in the darkened depths of a chute, known as 'Moll the Pooka's Hole'.

– Ballynacarriga Castle, Dunmanway, Co. Cork. Further information available on castle ruins from Cork and Kerry Tourism, ph. 021 4255100.

The seaside town of Cobh boasts a number of haunted buildings including the Pillars Bar, a former Methodist Church and now a public house, which has regular occurrences of poltergeist activity experienced by both staff and customers.

– Pillars Bar, Westbourne Place, Cobh, Co. Cork. Open year round, ph. 021 4815211.

In the summer of 1985, people visiting the grotto at Ballinspittle said they saw the statue of the Virgin Mary move. The phenomenon was reported many more times that year at various grottos throughout the country.

Co. Derry

In the early half of the twentieth century a funeral carriage was seen travelling through the night sky over Magherafelt. The phantom hearse was seen by many onlookers just days before many members of a well-known family with strong Celtic roots died suddenly.

Springhill House near Moneymore is haunted by the caring ghost of Olivia Lenox-Conyngham whose family lived at Springhill for over 300 years and whose husband ended his own life with a pistol in his 64th year. Her ghostly image has been seen overlooking the cots of children at the house. The building is now held in fantastic repair under National Trust.

– Springhill House, 20 Springhill Road, Moneymore, Magherafelt, BT457NQ. Tours available daily from March to September, ph. 028 86748210.

A number of UFOs were sighted over the Galliagh area in June 1998 by various independent witnesses. The UFOs were described as 'round objects seen spinning high in the sky'. The three reported objects were described as 'reflective, but noiseless'. They moved across the sky, and two shot vertically upwards 'straight up into the atmosphere'. The other continued flying across the sky and vanished.

A phantom 'black coach' was reported travelling though Derry city in the early 1980s by two people en route to visit a sick friend. The coach had no driver, nor did it make any noise while moving down the road. When the people arrived at the home where their sick friend was staying, they were informed that he had just died.

– *Information on tours of Derry city from the Northern Ireland Tourist Board, ph. 028 90246609.*

·CO. DONEGAL
The Pullan caves near the village of Ballintra are said to resound with the echoes of low pipe playing on moonlit nights as the often-witnessed phantom piper of Pullan sets about his ghostly music.

– *Pullan Caves, Ballintra, Co. Donegal. Further information from North West Tourism, ph. 071 61201.*

In the space of 18 months, between 1983 and 1984, 10 villages in west Donegal were struck by freak, bolts of lightning causing untold damage to houses and communications.

A two-humped monster was reported in the relatively small lake of Lough Muck in the latter part of the nine-

teenth century. The monster reportedly swam aggress-
ively after a woman working at the lakeshore in 1885.

Co. Down

A ghost ship belonging to Lord Blaney, which sank in 1833,
appears on the waters of Carlingford Lough as a
forewarning of imminent death or disaster.

Gillhall estate near Dromore was one of the most
celebrated haunted houses in the country until it burnt
down in 1970. The site is still said to be haunted by a
young woman and a phantom coach, which will still arrive
as if at the door of a great house.

*– Gillhall Estate, Dromore, Co. Down. Further information on the ruin from the
Northern Ireland Tourist Board, ph. 028 90246609.*

The ghostly figure of a lady has been seen drifting silently
through the main hall of Killyleagh Castle on Strangford
Lough. It is thought that the ghost is that of Anne, first
Countess of Clanbrassil, who bravely defended the fortress
from Cromwell's marauding forces.

*– Killyleagh Castle, Killyleagh, Co. Down. Self-catering apartments available in
castle towers year round, ph. 028 44828261.*

Co. Dublin

The bridge at Portobello Harbour in Rathmines is said to
be haunted by the ghost of a lock-keeper, who drowned
himself at the spot after being sacked for drunkenness. The
man was blamed for the deaths of a number of passengers
on a horse-drawn bus which toppled into the canal on 6
April 1861.

A giant black cat, with fire red eyes has made many
appearances at Killakee House, now a popular restaurant,

at the foothills of the Dublin mountains. The apparitional cat is thought to be the spirit of an animal burnt alive by members of the eighteenth century Hell Fire Club, situated close to the house, during satanic ritual where it was worshipped in place of the devil.

– Killakee House, Killakee Road, Rathfarnham, Dublin 16. Restaurant open year round, ph. 01 4932645.

Ghostly voices and a chilling presence are said to permeate the vaults of Saint Michan's Church in Dublin's north inner city where dry conditions have wonderfully preserved a macabre array of corpses dating back over 800 years. The vaults are now closed due to an act of vandalism in the early 1990s

– St Michan's Church, Church Street, Dublin 7. Further information from Dublin Tourism, ph. 1550 112206.

The desperate ghost of a woman is said to haunt the environs of Gammon's Hill in Monkstown. The apparition is thought to be that of a widow who betrayed a group of religious refugees during the bloodthirsty crusade of Oliver Cromwell.

Heavy footfalls, unexplainable surges in temperature and forceful gusts of wind are all part of the ghostly experiences regularly felt at Old Kilmainham Gaol in the southwest of the city. The jail was opened in 1796 and closed in 1924 and saw many executions during that time including the shooting dead of 16 Irish soldiers for their part in the rising of 1916.

– Kilmainham Gaol, Dublin 8. Tours daily between 9 a.m. and 5 p.m., ph. 01 4535984.

Co. Fermanagh

A stable-lad from Tempo Manor, who was brutally murdered by his master in the sixteenth century and buried under a flagstone, is said to cause disturbances at the old house ever since his skull was dug up in the early half of the twentieth century.

– Tempo Manor, Tempo, Co. Fermanagh. Further information from the Northern Ireland Tourist Board, ph. 028 90246609

The ghost of a man, dressed in clothes from the early nineteenth century, and a large dog made themselves apparent at Castle Archdale during the 1970s. The original castle which dates back to 1610 is all but gone and is today the site of a popular leisure centre.

– Castle Archdale, Irvinestown, Co. Fermanagh. Hostel accommodation available year round, ph. 028 68628118.

The ancient seat of the Earl of Erne on Fermanagh's Lough Erne is also home to a peculiar manifestation known as the 'White light of Crom'. The phenomenon of a mysterious rolling white light is said appear over the lake by the Earl's home of Crom Castle.

– Crom Castle, Newtownbutler, BT928AP. Tours available daily from April to September, ph. 028 67738118.

Co. Galway

The former castle home of W.B. Yeats at Thoor Ballylee near Gort is said to have a ghostly presence on its twisting stairwells, which Yeats often wrote about. Staff at the refurbished tower have spoken of ghostly feelings while in the building and a ghostly photograph was taken in Yeats's sitting room in 1989.

– Thoor Ballylee, Gort, Co. Galway. Tours available daily from June to September, ph. 091 31436.

The family home of Jackie Fahey in Corrib Park, Galway city, was the location of a high profile haunting in 1996/97. The home was plagued by poltergeist activity after the Fahey's grandchild Sarah Louise was brought home to live there.

Numerous lakes around Connemara have been the sighting grounds for independent lake monster encounters. Lough Auna, Fadda, Nahooin, Dubh, Shana-keever Lough and Derrylea Lough have all produced varying accounts of long necked or bull headed fearsome monsters both swimming in and crawling out of the lakes.

Renvyle House to the west of Galway city was home to man of words and friend of W.B. Yeats, Oliver St. John Gogarty during the early half of the twentieth century. Now a luxury guesthouse there have been many reports of ghostly apparitions of a tall man stalking the corridors of Renvyle house.

– *Renvyle House, Connemara, Co. Galway. Hotel accommodation available year round, ph. 095 43511.*

CO. KERRY
The ghost of a Victorian gentleman with a particular interest in the female guests who check in at Dromquinna Manor Hotel in Kenmare often makes his presence felt. Known as 'the randy spook' to hotel staff, the ghost is reputed to come into very close contact with some of the guests.

– *Dromquinna Manor Hotel, Kenmare, Co. Kerry. Hotel accommodation available year round, ph. 064 41657.*

The Spanish-built fort of Dún an Oir on the Dingle Peninsula is believed to reverberate with the eerie cries of agony from the ghosts of a surrendering Spanish garrison trapped and butchered by English soldiers in November 1580.

– Further information available from Cork and Kerry Tourism, ph. 021 4255100.

The mountain lake of Lough Brin near Kenmare is reputed to be home to a monster up to 12 metres in length and has been described as a cross between a giant seal and a mythical dragon. Witnesses said they saw the creature on land and it had four short legs.

Co. Kildare

An often encountered ghost in room 222 at Kilkea Castle, Castledermot, is said to be that of the infamous Wizard Earl, Garrett Óg Fitzgerald, who practised 'black arts' on the site. Guests at the castle, in particular those staying in room 222, have reported sheets being pulled off their bed and objects moved around the room.

– Kilkea Castle, Castledermot, Co. Kildare. Hotel accommodation available year round, ph. 0503 45156.

A spate of UFO activity was reported in a field behind the Catholic Church in the village of Clane in 1969. Ufologists claim the field has a high electro magnetic reading which could account for any number of paranormal phenomena taking place there.

The ghost of a bleeding soldier with a phantom black dog haunts the college grounds at Clongowes Wood. The soldier is thought to be the ghost of Marshal Wogan Browne whose family built the first castle there in 1667.

– Clongowes Wood College, Naas, Co. Kildare. Further information and tours on request, ph. 045 861042.

Room two in the House of Rhetoric in Maynooth College was converted into a shrine to St. Joseph after tragic events took place there. Two young students took their own lives in the room on separate occasions while a third suicide attemptee spoke of a presence in the room, which compelled him to end his life.

– St. Patrick's College, Maynooth, Co. Kildare. For further information and daily tour times ph. 01 7083576.

Co. KILKENNY

In Kilkenny city the ghost of a tall thin woman with long flowing hair has been seen hobbling on crutches near St. John's Parochial Hall. She has been reported by a local priest and a couple leaving a dance in May 1969 and is believed to be clad in a long, dark coat.

The upper floor of Foulksrath Castle on the Kilkenny to Ballyragget road resounds with the heavy thud of ghostly footsteps every year in early November.

– Foulksrath Castle, Jenkinstown, Co. Kilkenny. Hostel accommodation available year round, ph. 01 8304555.

In Ireland's only recorded 'witch trials', Dame Alice Kyteler was tried in March 1324 for witchcraft and for poisoning her four husbands. She was sentenced to be whipped through the streets of Kilkenny naked and burnt at the stake. Kyteler was imprisoned in a room at Kilkenny Castle from which she escaped.

– Further information from Kilkenny Tourism Council, ph. 056 51510.

The spectral image of a blue lady is known to appear and has put the heart across a number of staff at Kilkenny Castle in Kilkenny city. The phantom is said to appear at various spots around the beautifully maintained castle grounds, particularly in the main courtyard.

– Kilkenny Castle, Kilkenny city, Co. Kilkenny. Tours daily year round, ph. 056 21450.

Co. Laois

A helpful troupe of ghosts at Ballymoy Castle near Portlaoise are said to busy themselves with cleaning and sweeping various rooms and corridors every Saturday morning.

Private residence

Ballaghmore Castle near Borris-in-Ossory is thought to be haunted by the sorrowful ghosts of the parents of Barnaby MacGiolla Phadraig who imprisoned his forbearers on command of Henry VIII because they wouldn't renounce their Irish ways. Workers at the castle and Prince Michael of Greece who stayed there in the early 1990s sensed their presence in one particular room.

– Ballaghmore Castle, Dublin Road, Borris-in-Ossory. Guest accommodation year round and daily tours available, ph. 0505 21453.

Co. Leitrim

A family curse is blamed for the phenomenon of a 'Weeping Wall' in a house on O'Connor Island on Lough Allen. The wall is said to ooze liquid slime and cry aloud when tragedy is about to befall the family. The wall last wept in the 1940s.

Private residence

Glenade Lake, between Bundoran and Manorhamilton, was reportedly home to a fearsome monster known as the 'master otter' or Dobhar Chú measuring up to eight feet in length. The creature reportedly killed a woman on the lakeshore in the eighteenth century and an effigy of the Dobhar Chú can be seen on her tombstone in the nearby Congbheil cemetery.

– Further information from North West Tourism, ph. 071 61201.

CO. LIMERICK

Banging doors and startling apparitions are part of the hauntings at PJ's Pub on Catherine Street rumoured to have more spirit in it than comes out of the bottle.

– PJ's Pub, Catherine Street, Limerick. Open year round.

The twelfth-century tower of Castle Garde at Pallas Green is haunted by a ghost in silken robes who swishes up and down the narrow stair wells of the former seat of the O'Grady clan. There are numerous tales of bloodshed attached to the ancient fortification.

Private residence

Schoolboy John Keely reported seeing a fairy man at a crossroads between Ballingarry and Kilfinney near Rathkeale in 1938. He returned to the spot the next day and a number of local men allegedly witnessed the youngster converse with two fairies from a hiding place in a nearby bush. The fairies are said to have fled when the men came out from behind the bush.

Workers at Glin Castle, Glin, home to the Fitzgerald family for 800 years, reported poltergeist activity in the form of slamming doors, flickering lights and inexplicable footsteps on bare boards while working on the now luxury hotel.

– Glin Castle, Glin, Co. Limerick. Hotel accommodation available between March and November, ph. 068 34173.

Co. Longford

The Gate lodge in front of new guard's barracks on Battery Road in Longford town is said to be haunted by the wailings of the sick and dying. It was built on the grounds of the old county hospital.

– Further information from Longford Tourism, ph. 043 42577.

The headless ghost of murdered British Army officer Captain Blundell has been seen at various points around the village of Granard. Blundell's headless body was discovered in his quarters with the door locked from the inside in the early eighteenth century. A verdict of suicide was passed but it is thought that the father of a local girl murdered the captain because of his advances on his daughter.

Co. Louth

A rectory on Carlingford Lough known as Mount Trevor House is known to be haunted by a girl in a red dress and by noisy ghosts whose footsteps resound around the upstairs of the building.

Private residence

A remote, water-filled quarry in Faughart is said to be haunted by the ghost of a murder victim whose body was dumped there in the early twentieth century.

Clothing said to belong to the fairy folk were discovered in Carlingford after local publican PJ O'Hare and school teacher Brendan McKevitt followed 'dancing lights' in the nearby mountains. Mr. O'Hare is the current custodian of these tiny threads.

A couple driving close to Termonfeckin in 1966 reported the horrible apparition of a beast with a 'horses body, a man's head and huge bulging eyes', which loomed up before them on the dark road. The couple were known locally as reasonable minded people and the issue was reported on in the press at the time.

CO. MAYO

Pap Murphy of Cartron on the Mullet Peninsula recalls a six-foot long monster, with a cat's head and an otter's body that came out of an ancient cairn in the village in 1968. The creature fought with local dogs until it made its way to the sea. Many in the village thought the creature to possess supernatural qualities.

Glendarry Lake near Achill Sound is said to harbour a monster of fishlike appearance, dark brown in colour, between eight and 40 feet long, with four legs and a thick tail.

Numerous witnesses encountered a monster by Sraheens Lough on Achill Island during the 1960s. The creature, said to be up to 10 feet long and to move in a lumbering fashion on land, was seen by two men on the road by the lake. It was also seen in the lake by a 14-year-old boy passing on a bike.

CO. MEATH

The ghost of Lilith Palmerston, who was strangled to

death at her home in Skryne Castle, is said to haunt the ancient stronghold today. Lilith Palmerston was murdered by a psychotic courtier who forced his way into her chamber after his advances were ignored. As well as screams in the night a white lady has also been seen running through Skryne Castle clutching her throat.

– *Skryne Castle, Tara, Co. Meath. Further information available from Meath Tourism 041 9880305.*

The Franciscan College at Gormanston, formerly owned by the Preston family from 1326, has provided an eerie death warning for the family through the centuries. All foxes on the lands would gather on the lawn at Gormanston and whine in the days preceding and following the death of a family member. They are known today as the 'Gormanston Foxes'.

– *Private golf club, ph. 01 8412203.*

Co. Monaghan

The haunted Red Room at the fabulously furnished Castle Leslie near the village of Glaslough is a favourite lodging for the rich and famous who choose to stay at this luxury guesthouse. Ghostly figures have also been spotted traversing the corridors of the nineteenth century Leslie family seat.

– *Castle Leslie, Glaslough, Co. Monaghan. Hotel accommodation available year round, ph. 047 88109.*

The ghost of a tall, gaunt man dressed in a dark cloak with a light under his left arm is believed to haunt the road from Clones to Scarva. Many independent accounts have testified to the same apparition. He is believed to be a man

who was murdered on that road in the early twentieth
century.

Co. OFFALY

The grounds of Mount St. Joseph's Cistercian Monastery
across the border from Roscrea in Co. Tipperary is said to
be haunted by the spirit of Lord Mountnugent who
formerly resided on the castle grounds and is said to have
done battle with the devil which eventually killed him.
Floating lights are seen leaving the adjoining graveyard
where he was buried.
Private

The privately owned Leap Castle in Coolderry near
Roscrea has a ghastly history of bloodshed dating back
to the fifteenth century. It is haunted by the screams
and laughter of a young girl who fell from its eastern tower
and the chanting of monks from its adjoining ruined
church.

The gothic splendour of Charleville Castle on the
outskirts of Tullamore is complemented by the ghosts of
its past. The old nursery room is haunted by children's
voices while the presence of a ghost of a disabled boy, who
was thought locked away for many years, has also been felt.
– *Charleville Castle, Tullamore, Co. Offaly. Tours available daily, ph. 0506
29908.*

Co. ROSCOMMON

Three Dublin priests reported seeing a long necked
monster on Lough Ree while on a fishing holiday in the
area. The three priests agreed that the creature was not a
normal aquatic animal.

The former residence of the King family from Boyle is said to be haunted by a 'Green Lady'. The ill-coloured ghost is said to have been a servant who locked herself into her room eating nothing but raw vegetables until she went 'green like a cabbage' and died.

An encumbered ghost is said to walk the quiet back roads of Rossaun, near Strokestown. He is thought to be the spirit of a famine stricken man attempting to walk to a place of passage where he could emigrate to America during the great famine of the 1840s.

Co. Sligo

There have been numerous sightings of large wildcats on the grounds around Temple House close to Lough Gill. The Temple House cat is thought to be 0.5 metre high and a descendent of Scottish wild cats which were brought into the area in the 1880s.

– Temple House, Ballymote, Co. Sligo. Guest house accommodation available year round, ph. 071 83329.

The Lighthouse on Oyster Island off Rosses point is said to have a number of ghosts in residence.

– Further information from North West Tourism, ph. 071 61201.

The grounds of Lissadel House near Drumcliff are thought to be haunted by two female ghosts walking in conversation through the lush gardens. The two have been seen carrying flowers and painting equipment and were recognised from photographsas daughters of former house owner Robert Gore Booth.

– Lissadell House, Ballinafull, Co. Sligo. Guided tours available from June to September, ph. 071 63150.

CO. TIPPERARY

The story of 'Petticoat Loose', has hung over the shoresof Bay Lough near Cahir for over 150 years. The mountain lake is said to be inhabited by a monster in the shapeof a woman with a horse's head who is known to have made various terrifying appearances down the years.

A married couple, Mr. and Mrs. Shelley from Mulinahone, reported a UFO which came down close to earth as if to land in their locality in 1970. The UFO made no sound as it swung down out of the sky in a bright orange glow, turning to red as it came lower before rising again.

A series of poltergeist activity was reported in a house near Templemore where all holy statues and pictures in the house began to bleed. The poltergeist centred on a boy of 16-years-old in August 1920.

A cursed riding whip is thought to hold supernatural sway over a house known as Shallardstown near Clogheen. The whip belonged to a widow who gave instruction not to let her sister know of her death so she could remain at the house. She died and with the aid of a loyal butler her corpse remained at Shallardstown for many years and her ghost has been seen there on many occasions.
Private residence

CO. TYRONE

The ghost of Crevenagh House is believed to be that of the first owner of the home whose apparition is said to manifest throughout the building as a forewarning of the death of the master of the house.
Private residence

A farmhouse, formerly owned by the Wilson family in Cavankirk, in the Clogher Valley is believed to be haunted by the ghost of an errant sibling of the brother and sister who ran the farm there in the early twentieth century. The poltergeist activity and apparitional figures began to manifest after they heard their troublesome brother had died abroad.

Co. Waterford

The Coachouse restaurant and guesthouse at Butlerstown near Waterford city is said to be haunted by a gunman who fell from a window after being shot dead by British troops in 1921.

– *The Coachouse, Butlerstown, Waterford. Open daily for accommodation and dining, ph. 051 384656.*

The austere building of Waterford City's Presentation Convent is said to be haunted by the regular patrolling of a 'White Nun' who has been seen both inside and wandering the road to the back of the convent.

Private

Co. Westmeath

Farragh House Hostel in Bunbrosna is believed to be haunted by a chivalrous ghost who helped a one time owner unpack when she moved into the building on her wedding night.

– *Farragh House Hostel, Mullingar, Co. Westmeath. Hostel accommodation available year round, ph. 044 71446.*

A white, spectral image has been spotted on numerous occasions wandering amongst the ivy clad ruins of Killua Castle, deserted after the break-up of the unhappy marriage of its last inhabitants in the late nineteenth century.

– Killua Castle, Clonmellon, Co. Westmeath. Further information from East Coast Midland Tourism, ph. 044 48761.

Residents at Emo House have long been troubled by a noisy ghost. Persistent door knockings with nobody around and doors mysteriously opening and closing by themselves have all been encountered at the house.

CO. WEXFORD

The ghost of Ann Hamilton is said to haunt Loftus Hall. She was a young noble woman who fell in love with a visitor at the house. She died of a broken heart and has been regularly seen by visitors to the hall. There is also a story of the devil appearing at a party at Loftus hall and vanishing in a ball of fire during a thunderstorm.

– Loftus Hall, Hook Head, Co. Wexford. Tour information available from Wexford Tourism, ph. 053 52900.

Fishermen and locals witnessed a long-necked monster in the sea off Cahore Point in January 1976. The creature was described as looking and moving like a 'big worm'. A similar creature was spotted, 30 miles south off Hook Head when fishermen described seeing a 'huge lizard-like monster with a long neck'.

CO. WICKLOW

The gateway of Aughavanagh Hostel, in the Wicklow Mountains, is known to be haunted by the seven foot tall ghost of a man named Hempenstall, also known as the 'walking hangman' because he hung Irish rebels over his shoulder until they died. Hempenstall was killed in revenge by survivors of the 1798 rebellion at the gates of Aughavanagh.

Glendalough, one of the most often visited tourist spots in Ireland, is reputedly haunted by the ghost of a beautiful maiden in red named Kathleen, who fell in love with the handsome, young St. Kevin, and tried to seduce him.

A humped back monster with a long neck and skinny head was reported on Lough Bray, close to the Dublin border, in June 1963. The creature was described as dark grey in colour and at least 12 feet in circumference.

The Dominican Convent in Wicklow town is thought to be haunted by a former nun.

Reports of a banshee wailing from the old graveyard in Rathnew village have been made on a number of occasions. There are also reports of banshee sightings in and around Rathnew.

BIBLIOGRAPHY

Ansbro, Eamonn & Catherine (1999)
Extraterrestrial Intelligence a Reality

Adamski, George & Leslie, Desmond (1953)
Flying Saucers have Landed. *Werner Laurie*

Bernstein, Morey (1965)
The Search for Bridey Murphy. *Doubleday*

Bord, Janet & Colin (1984)
Alien Animals. *Stackpole Books*

Bord, Janet & Colin (1984)
Modern Mysteries of the World. *Grafton*

Bord, Janet & Colin (1984)
The Unexplained Creatures from Elsewhere. *Orbis Publications*

Byrne, Patrick F (1980)
The Bedside Book of Irish Ghost Stories. *Mercier*

Cockell, Jenny (1993)
Yesterday's Children. *Piatkus*

Costello, Peter (1975)
In Search of Lake Monsters. *Berkley Publishing Group*

Dunne, John J (1999)
Irish Ghosts. *Appletree*

Fahey Family & Faherty, Padhraic (2000)
The Reawakening *Published by the Fahey Family*

Good, Timothy (1992)
Alien Liaison. *Arrow*

Holiday, F W (1973)
The Dragon and the Disc. *Sidgwick and Jackson*

Jackson, Pauline (2001)
  Ghosts of Cork. *Irish Millennium Publications*

Jones, Richard (2002)
  Haunted Britain and Ireland. *New Holland*

Le Poer Trench, Brinsley (1974)
  Operation Earth. *Tandem*

Lysaght, Patricia (1998)
  A Pocket Book of the Banshee. (The Pocket History Series)
  Irish American Book Company

Martin, Michael (2000)
  Titanic Trail

Seymour, John & Neligan, Harry (1994)
  True Irish Ghost Stories. *Senate*

Ramdhanie, Sandra (1996)
  Trapped Between Two Worlds: Experience of a 'Ghost Buster'. *O'Brien Press*

Ritchie, Jean (1992)
  Inside the Supernatural. *Fontana*

St. Clair, Sheila (1994)
  Mysterious Ireland. *Hale*